Transdisciplinary Perspectives on Childhood in Contemporary Britain

In light of the complex demographic shifts associated with late modernity and the impetus of neo-liberal politics, childhood increasingly continues to operate as a repository for the articulation of diverse social and cultural anxieties. Since the Thatcher years, juvenile delinquency, child poverty and protection have been persistent issues in public discourse. Simultaneously, childhood has advanced as a popular subject in the arts, as the wealth of current films and novels in this field indicates. Focusing on the late twentieth and the early twenty-first centuries, this collection assembles contributions concerned with current political, social and cultural dimensions of childhood in the UK. The individual chapters, written by internationally renowned experts from the social sciences and the humanities, address a broad spectrum of contemporary childhood issues, including debates on child protection, school dress codes, the media, the representation and construction of children in audiovisual media and literary awards for children's fiction. Appealing to a wide scholarly audience by joining perspectives from various disciplines, including art history, education, law, film and TV studies, sociology and literary studies, this volume endorses a transdisciplinary and meta-theoretical approach to the study of childhood. It seeks to both illustrate and dismantle the various ways in which childhood has been implicitly and explicitly conceived in different disciplines in the wake of the constructivist paradigm shift in childhood studies.

Sandra Dinter is a Lecturer and postdoctoral researcher in British Literature and Culture at Johannes Gutenberg University Mainz, Germany.

Ralf Schneider is Professor of British Literature and Culture at Bielefeld University, Germany.

Studies in Childhood, 1700 to the Present

This series recognizes and supports innovative work on the child and on literature for children and adolescents that informs teaching and engages with current and emerging debates in the field. Proposals are welcome for interdisciplinary and comparative studies by humanities scholars working in a variety of fields, including literature; book history, periodicals history and print culture and the sociology of texts; theater, film, musicology and performance studies; history, including the history of education; gender studies; art history and visual culture; cultural studies and religion.

Recent titles in this series:

Space and Place in Children's Literature, 1789 to the Present
Maria Sachiko Cecire, Hannah Field, Malini Roy

Ethics and Children's Literature
Claudia Mills

The Child Savage, 1890–2010: From Comics to Games
Edited by Elisabeth Wesseling

British Hymn Books for Children, 1800–1900
Alisa Clapp-Itnyre

Nordic Childhoods 1700–1960
From Folk Beliefs to Pippi Longstocking
Edited by Reidar Aasgaard, Marcia Bunge, and Merethe Roos

Nineteenth-Century Fictions of Childhood and the Politics of Play
Michelle Beissel Heath

Aesthetics of Children's Poetry
Katherine Wakely-Mulroney and Louise Joy

Transdisciplinary Perspectives on Childhood in Contemporary Britain
Edited by Sandra Dinter and Ralf Schneider

Transdisciplinary Perspectives on Childhood in Contemporary Britain
Literature, Media and Society

Edited by
Sandra Dinter and Ralf Schneider

LONDON AND NEW YORK

First published 2018 by Routledge

2 Park Square, Milton Park, Abingdon, Oxfordshire OX14 4RN

52 Vanderbilt Avenue, New York, NY 10017

Routledge is an imprint of the Taylor & Francis Group, an informa business

First issued in paperback 2019

Copyright © 2018 Taylor & Francis

The right of Sandra Dinter and Ralf Schneider to be identified as authors of this work has been asserted by them in accordance with sections 77 and 78 of the Copyright, Designs and Patents Act 1988.

The right of the editor to be identified as the author of the editorial material, and of the authors for their individual chapters, has been asserted in accordance with sections 77 and 78 of the Copyright, Designs and Patents Act 1988.

All rights reserved. No part of this book may be reprinted or reproduced or utilised in any form or by any electronic, mechanical, or other means, now known or hereafter invented, including photocopying and recording, or in any information storage or retrieval system, without permission in writing from the publishers.

Notice:
Product or corporate names may be trademarks or registered trademarks, and are used only for identification and explanation without intent to infringe.

Library of Congress Cataloging-in-Publication Data
CIP data has been applied for.

ISBN: 978-1-138-23210-5 (hbk)
ISBN: 978-0-367-88485-7 (pbk)

Typeset in Sabon
by codeMantra

Contents

List of Figures and Tables ix
List of Contributors xi

Approaching Childhood in Contemporary Britain:
Introduction 1
SANDRA DINTER AND RALF SCHNEIDER

SECTION I
Childhood in Contemporary British Literature and
Literary Criticism 17

1 Writing Plural Childhoods – Some Thoughts Concerning
 the Recent Carnegie Medal Shortlists 19
 ANJA MÜLLER

2 The Adult within the Literary Child: Reading Toby Litt's
 deadkidsongs as an Anti-*Bildungsroman* 34
 KATHARINA PIETSCH AND TYLL ZYBURA

3 The Child Narrator in Contemporary British Fiction and
 Literary Criticism: The Case of Stephen Kelman's *Pigeon
 English* 50
 SANDRA DINTER

4 Children's Literature, Cognitivism and Neuroscience 67
 KARÍN LESNIK-OBERSTEIN

SECTION II
Medial and Visual Constructions of Childhood in Contemporary Britain — 85

5 Children's Television and Public Service in Contemporary Britain — 87
   JONATHAN BIGNELL

6 An Inconvenient Growth: Watching Child Actors, Growing Up, Sideways and Backwards in Contemporary British Film and Television — 103
   KAREN LURY

7 Adults Looking at Children: Books, Bodies and Buying in Children's Book Covers — 120
   JESSICA MEDHURST

8 Reflections on British and American Images of and for Children — 137
   ELLEN HANDLER SPITZ

SECTION III
Historical and Social Dimensions of Childhood in Contemporary Britain — 151

9 Childcare for the Under-Fives in Post-1945 England: Contemporary Reflections on Past Childhoods — 153
   ANGELA DAVIS

10 Contingent Connections: Between German and British Childhoods – Marion Daltrop — 170
   ERICA BURMAN

SECTION IV
Contemporary British Childhoods between Rights and Regulations — 191

11 The Politics of Child Protection in Contemporary England: Towards the 'Authoritarian Neoliberal State' — 193
   NIGEL PARTON

12 Dressing up for School: Beyond Rights and Welfare   210
    DANIEL MONK

13 The Recognition and Distribution of Children's Agency
    in the UK   230
    MICHAEL WYNESS

    Index   247

List of Figures and Table

Figures

6.1	Sue (Claire Skinner) and Karen (Ramona Marquez) combing for nits, from *Outnumbered* (BBC, 2007–2014)	109
6.2	Shivers, sunshine and skin – Shaun Kirk in *Everyday* (Michael Winterbottom, 2012)	114
6.3	"Our bodies are not in a straightforward sense, ours" – Robert and Shaun Kirk in *Everyday* (Michael Winterbottom, 2012)	115
7.1	Front and back cover of *Charlie and the Chocolate Factory* (Penguin Classics, 2015 edition). Source: Cover photograph by Sofia Sanchez and Mauro Mongiello/Trunk Archive. Copyright © Penguin Books, 2014. Author photograph © Leonard McCombe/Time & Life Pictures/Getty Images. Text within the Work copyright © Roald Dahl Nominee Ltd, 1964. Introduction copyright © Sam Mendes, 2014. Reproduced by permission of Penguin Books Ltd	121
10.1	One of Marion Daltrop's creative pieces. Source: Reproduced with permission from the Marion Daltrop estate	173
10.2	One of Marion's Daltrop's photographs of the activities of the Greenham Women's Support Group. Source: Reproduced with permission from the Marion Daltrop estate	182
10.3	Two examples of Marion Daltrop's Greenham pictures. Source: Reproduced with permission from the Marion Daltrop estate	183
12.1	Pupils at Bede Academy, Blyth (Part of the Emmanuel Schools Foundation)	214
12.2	BeLonG campaign in partnership with the Equality Authority	216

Table

11.1 Growth in Demand for Statutory Children's Social Care: 2007/2008–2014/2015   200

List of Contributors

Jonathan Bignell is Professor of Television and Film at the University of Reading. His books include three editions of *An Introduction to Television Studies*, two editions of *British Television Drama: Past Present and Future* (edited with Stephen Lacey), *A European Television History* (edited with Andreas Fickers) and the monographs *Beckett on Screen*, *Big Brother: Reality TV in the Twenty-first Century* and *Postmodern Media Culture*. His articles about television include contributions to the journals *Critical Studies in Television*, the *Historical Journal of Film, Radio and Television*, *Media History* and *Screen*. Jonathan's recent work includes research into science fiction TV of the 1960s and the history of transatlantic television drama. For 20 years, Jonathan has managed teams of researchers on a series of large-scale collaborative projects about television drama, most recently a three-year study funded by the Arts and Humanities Research Council about Harold Pinter's work for television, cinema and theatre.

Erica Burman is Professor of Education at the University of Manchester and a United Kingdom Council of Psychotherapists registered Group Analyst. She is author of *Deconstructing Developmental Psychology* (Routledge, 3rd edition, 2017), *Developments: Child, Image, Nation* (Routledge, 2008) and is co-editor (with Dan Cook) of the *SAGE Encyclopaedia of Childhood and Childhood Studies* (forthcoming). Erica co-founded the Discourse Unit (www.discourseunit.com), a transinstitutional, transdisciplinary network researching the reproduction and transformation of language and subjectivity. Erica's research has focused on critical developmental and educational psychology, feminist and postcolonial theory, childhood studies and critical mental health practice (particularly around gender and cultural issues). She currently leads the Knowledge, Power and Identity research strand of Special Educational and Additional Needs at Manchester Institute of Education. She is a past Chair of the Psychology of Women Section of the British Psychological Society, and in 2016

xii *List of Contributors*

she was awarded an Honorary Lifetime Fellowship of the British Psychological Society in recognition of her contribution to psychology.

Angela Davis is an Assistant Professor in the Department of History at the University of Warwick. Her research interests focus on motherhood, parenting and childcare, and she is currently completing a comparative study of Jewish motherhood in England and Israel. Her publications include *Modern Motherhood: Women and Family in England c.1945–2000* (Manchester University Press, 2012) and *Pre-school Childcare in England, 1939–2010: Theory, Practice and Experience* (Manchester University Press, 2015).

Sandra Dinter is a Lecturer in the English Department at Johannes Gutenberg University Mainz, Germany, where she teaches British Literature from the Renaissance to the present. She recently completed her PhD thesis "Childhood in Contemporary English Fiction: Contesting the Last Vestige of Essentialism" at Bielefeld University, Germany. Her research interests include literary constructions of childhood, contemporary fiction, adaptation theory and the spatial turn. Her work has been published in the journals *Neo-Victorian Studies*, *C21 Literature: Journal of 21st-Century Writings* and *Children's Literature Association Quarterly*.

Ellen Handler Spitz is Honors College Professor at the University of Maryland (UMBC), where she has taught for the past 16 years. She is author and/or co-editor of nine books concerning children's aesthetic lives as well as the arts and psychology. Her writing has been published in *The New York Times*, *The New Republic* and the *Chronicle of Higher Education*, as well as in diverse international academic journals. Her work has been translated into Italian, Japanese, Serbian and Chinese. She has lectured and/or taught internationally in Canada, Europe, the Middle East, Asia and throughout her native US. Her honours and fellowships include the Getty Center in Los Angeles, Harvard's Bunting/Radcliffe Institute, the Stanford University Center for Advanced Study, the Clark Art Museum, the Camargo Foundation in France, the Rutgers Center for Children and Childhood Studies, the Erikson Institute and the New York Institute for the Humanities.

Karín Lesnik-Oberstein is a Professor of Critical Theory in the Department of English Literature at the University of Reading where she is Director of the Graduate Centre for International Research in Childhood: Literature, Culture, Media (CIRCL) and its M(Res) in Children's Literature. Her research focuses on transdisciplinary critical theory relating to identity, as in her monographs *Children's Literature: Criticism and the Fictional Child* (1994) and *On Having an Own Child: Reproductive Technologies and the Cultural*

Construction of Childhood (2008), her edited volumes *Children in Culture: Approaches to Childhood* (1998), *Children in Literature* (2002), *Children's Literature: New Approaches* (2004), *The Last Taboo: Women and Body Hair* (2007), *Children in Culture, Revisited: Further Approaches to Childhood* (2011) and *Rethinking Disability Theory and Practice: Challenging Essentialism* (2015) and numerous chapters and articles across a range of disciplines on childhood, gender and sexual identity.

Karen Lury is a Professor of Film and Television Studies in the School of Culture and Creative Arts at the University of Glasgow. She has published widely in film and television, focusing particularly on children's media and the representation of the child in film. Her monographs include *The Child in Film: Tears, Fears and Fairytales* (IB Tauris, 2010). She was the principal investigator on an AHRC funded project, "Children and Amateur Media in Scotland". She is also a long-standing editor of the film and television studies journal *Screen*.

Jessica Medhurst is a postdoctoral researcher working on constructions of childhood and identity in nineteenth- and twentieth-century literature, visual culture and archives. Her previous work has examined Lewis Carroll's photographs of young girls and images of children in British-occupied Germany. She is currently working in two areas: on a monograph project on twentieth-century constructions of British childhood in the UK's literary archives and on a smaller project into one of the UK's first female professors, Edith Morley. She is also the founder of the We the Humanities initiative.

Daniel Monk is a Professor in Law at Birkbeck, University of London. He has published extensively in the field of children, families, sexualities and the law. Examining a wide range of issues, from home-education and non-conventional families to school exclusions, sex education and bullying, his work aims to develop a dialogue between child law and the sociology of childhood. His current research examines legal assumptions and practices about the sibling relationship.

Anja Müller is a Professor of English Literature and Cultural Studies at the University of Siegen where she has been co-chair of her faculty's research group on European Children's Literature (EKJL) since 2012. Her research interests range from eighteenth-century literature and culture to contemporary drama, intertextuality and adaptation, fantasy, (historical) childhood studies and children's literature. Publications in the latter fields include *Fashioning Childhood in Eighteenth-Century England: Age and Identity* (ed., Ashgate, 2006), *Framing Childhood in Eighteenth-Century English Periodicals and Satirical Prints, 1689–1789* (Ashgate, 2009, ChLA Honor Book), *Childhood in the Renaissance* (ed., Wissenschaftlicher Verlag

xiv *List of Contributors*

Trier, 2013), *Adapting Canonical Texts in Children's Literature* (ed., Bloomsbury, 2013) and *Canon Constitution and Canon Change in Children's Literature* (co-ed., with Bettina Kümmerling-Meibauer, Routledge, 2017). Together with Bettina Kümmerling-Meibauer and Astrid Surmatz, she is co-editing the series *Studien zur europäischen Kinder- und Jugendliteratur* (Winter).

Nigel Parton is a Professor of Applied Childhood Studies at the University of Huddersfield, England, where he has worked since 1977. A social worker by background, he has written or edited 25 books and over 100 chapters and articles in the broad fields of social policy, social work, child welfare and child protection. His most recent book is *The Politics of Child Protection: Contemporary Developments and Future Directions* (Palgrave Macmillan, 2014). He has held visiting Professorships at the Universities of Tampere (Finland), La Trobe (Australia) and Edinburgh (Scotland) and is currently a Haruv-Kempe Fellow at the Kempe Centre, University of Colorado, US.

Katharina Pietsch wrote her master's thesis on "The Adult Within: Literary Constructions and Deconstructions of the Adult–Child Binary". She currently holds a PhD position in the English Department at Bielefeld University, Germany, in the project "Children and Childhood in Literature: Theory – Narratology – Criticism" funded by the German Research Foundation. The project's aim is to propose a literary theory that establishes critical perspectives on childhood, adulthood and generation more firmly in literary and cultural studies. Besides literary constructions of children and childhood, Katharina's research interests include narrative theory, narratology and the politics of form, popular culture and gender and queer theory.

Ralf Schneider is a Professor of British Literary and Cultural Studies at Bielefeld University, Germany. Besides childhood, his fields of research include cognitive approaches to narrative, literary theory, Victorian literature, gender and literature and narratives of migration. He is the author of *Grundriß zur kognitiven Theorie der Figurenrezeption am Beispiel des viktorianischen Romans* (2000) and co-author of *Der Erste Weltkrieg und die Mediendiskurse der Erinnerung in Großbritannien: Autobiographie—Roman—Film, 1919–1999* (2005, with Barbara Korte and Claudia Sternberg). He has co-edited collections of essays, including *Characters in Fictional Worlds: Understanding Imaginary Beings in Literature, Film, and Other Media* (2010, with Jens Eder and Fotis Jannidis), *Blending and the Study of Narrative: Approaches and Applications* (2012, with Marcus Hartner). Two handbooks are currently in preparation: *The Handbook of British Literature and Culture of the First World War* (ed. with Jane Potter) and *Fiktionalität* (ed. with Lut Missinne and Beatrix van Dam).

Michael Wyness is an Associate Professor in the Centre for Education Studies at the University of Warwick. He previously worked at the Universities of Edinburgh, Stirling and Northampton. His research interests are in the Sociologies of Childhood and Education. His book *Childhood* (Polity) was published in 2015, and he has another book due out in 2018 with Sage, *Childhood, Culture and Society*. His previous books include *Childhood and Society* (Palgrave, 2006), which went into a second edition in 2012; *Contesting Childhood* (RoutledgeFalmer, 1999) and *Schooling Welfare and Parental Responsibility* (Falmer, 1995). His research interests are in children's participation, childhood and theory, children's transitions and home-school relations. He is currently working on two projects: "child migrants", identity formation and community support, and parental investment in children's transitions.

Tyll Zybura holds an MA in British and American Studies and currently works as a PhD candidate in the project "Children and Childhood in Literature: Theory – Narratology – Criticism" at Bielefeld University, Germany, funded by the German Research Foundation. He teaches writing-intensive courses on literary constructions of childhood, critical theory and narrative theory, film and popular culture and most recently zombie culture and bio-political representation.

Approaching Childhood in Contemporary Britain
Introduction

Sandra Dinter and Ralf Schneider

Over the last few decades, much public commentary has put the current state of childhood into question. Popular buzz words like 'adultification', 'infantilisation', 'adultescence', 'kidulthood' and 'tweenager' suggest that formerly distinct contours of childhood and adulthood have become blurred (Rudd 2014, 120). Neil Postman's time-honoured dictum of a disappearance of childhood (1982) resonates powerfully in recent populist best-sellers, such as Sue Palmer's *Toxic Childhood: How the Modern World Is Damaging Our Children and What We Can Do About It* (2006) and Richard Louv's *Last Child in the Woods: Saving Our Children from Nature-Deficit Disorder* (2010). It is beyond doubt that demographic change in Western Europe has indeed had unprecedented repercussions on childhood. As Mary Jane Kehily notes, in Britain the model of the patriarchal nuclear family has been steadily supplemented by several other recognised family practices, for instance, "single-headed households, same-sex couples, unmarried co-habiting parents and post-divorce couples who may bring children into new relationships" (2013, 19). A historically low birth rate and an increase in life expectancy mean that families are smaller than they used to be, and multiculturalism has made families and childhood more ethnically and culturally diverse (Graham 1999, 5; Fink 2002, 138). Moreover, the digital revolution has successively exposed children to new media and a range of technical devices, most recently the smart phone. Many children regularly watch television and go online; they are considered the first generation of 'digital natives'. As David Buckingham contends, "[i]n most industrialised countries, children spend more time with media of various kinds than they spend in school, or with their family and friends" (2007, 43). These and other new constellations have fostered new anxieties concerning childhood, such as parental neglect, cyber bullying, cyber grooming, obesity, ADHD, juvenile delinquency and unrestricted access to pornographic and violent material.[1] While it is true that such shifts require new ways of looking at childhood and confront society with new options and challenges, it would be a mistake to assume that childhood has vanished from contemporary discourse and institutional activities.

This volume intends to show that the opposite is the case. Parents in Britain are obviously as much concerned with children and childhood as ever, as are educators and childcare workers; the arts continue to imagine childhood and politics keep regulating it. The contributions collected here provide more insights and inquiries into contemporary dimensions of childhood from the angles of different disciplines in the humanities and the social sciences. Some of the most renowned experts in the field approach childhood in the contexts of art history, critical theory, education, film and TV studies, history, law, literary studies, sociology and social policy. All of these disciplines proceed on the basis of different assumptions and theories about children and childhood, using particular methods and special ways of speaking about these issues. These sets of ideas, approaches and ways of speaking are what we regard as 'perspectives' on childhood. While the disciplines whose conceptions of childhood this volume wishes to survey use specialist discourses, there is no doubt that parents, teachers, social workers and everyone else concerned with children think and speak about childhood in everyday life on the ground of such perspectives, too.

Contemporary Britain is our temporal, national and cultural focus of investigation, although we realise that these are all relational and therefore contestable categories. Strictly speaking, examining the 'contemporary' is a paradoxical task: if the 'contemporary' designates that which happens in the immediate present, then the contributions in this volume are all inevitably retrospective. Even as a mode of periodisation, the 'contemporary' does not refer to a clearly defined time-span. As Philip Tew notes in *The Contemporary British Novel*, "All periodizations are tenuous. Clearly, any such chronological demarcation may be argued to be fraught with conceptual and ideological difficulties, but no more so than any other commensurable definitional generic or movement boundary" (2004, 60). Although most people would probably agree that the term 'contemporary' covers the last 30 years, some events, mentalities or political decisions date back much earlier but still have repercussions on the present state of affairs. The contributions in this volume articulate this predicament: while some chapters refer to the 'contemporary' as the period after 1945, others focus on more recent developments in the 2010s or draw entirely different lines.

In any case, we believe that contemporary Britain, understood in this broad sense, is a context where the tensions and paradoxes of childhood are particularly conspicuous. Although public discourses on childhood in Great Britain are representative of those in other Western countries, in several ways Britain currently holds a unique position among its European neighbours, not least since the Brexit referendum. For many centuries, Britain has been associated with a particular interest in children, especially in the arts. William Wordsworth's and William Blake's poetic visions of childhood as well as the childhood novels by Charles Dickens and his fellow Victorian writers were constitutive in the formation of childhood as a popular topic in European literature.[2] Paintings by the British artists Joshua Reynolds and John Edward Millais were equally influential in the visual arts (Higonnet 1998, 23–37). In the present period, Britain's artistic preoccupation with childhood continues to be remarkable. Feature films such as *Billy Elliot – I Will Dance* (2000), adaptations of recent novels about childhood (e.g. *About a Boy*, 2002; *Anita and Me*, 2002; *Boy A*, 2007) as well as of classics such as *Oliver Twist* (for instance in 2007) or *Lord of the Flies* (1990), and of course the *Harry Potter* series, have brought the wide and often contradictory range of experiences and conceptions of childhood to the awareness of the general reading and viewing public. A musical version of *Billy Elliot* was successfully put on stage in London in 2005, as was a stage version of Mark Haddon's best-seller *The Curious Incident of the Dog in the Night-Time* (2003) about a boy with Asperger syndrome in 2012.

British fiction in particular has demonstrated a vibrant interest in the exploration of the thematic and aesthetic potentials of childhood. Ralf Schneider refers to the popularity of childhood as a topic in contemporary novels as an "unparalleled phenomenon" (2006, 148) in British literary history. Similarly, Katherina Dodou notes, "childhood has become established as one of the major themes in the contemporary British novel" (2012, 238). In the last three decades, many of these novels were on the long and short lists of major fiction awards. Prominent recent examples include Ian McEwan's *Atonement* (2001), Kazuo Ishiguro's *Never Let Me Go* (2005), A.S. Byatt's *The Children's Book* (2009) and Stephen Kelman's *Pigeon English* (2011). Novels from other English-speaking countries, such as Emma Donoghue's *Room* (2010), Roddy Doyle's *Paddy Clarke Ha Ha Ha* (1993), Anne Enright's *The Gathering* (2007), Jonathan Safran Foer's *Extremely Loud & Incredibly Close* (2005), Lionel Shriver's *We Need to Talk about Kevin* (2003) and Christos Tsiolkas's *The Slap* (2008), have attracted many readers. Ever since Frank McCourt's *Angela's Ashes* (1996) and Andrea Ashworth's *Once in a House on Fire* (1998), memoirs of miserable childhoods have constituted another genre that has enjoyed tremendous success in Britain. Interestingly, these texts are written not for children or young readers but for adults. Whereas children's literature may be regarded as a literary genre that frequently touches upon issues relating to childhood due to its target audience, the novels for adults listed above can be perceived as contributions to the general social discourses on childhood in Britain and may be taken as an indication of the fact that childhood continues to stimulate people's imagination, concepts and value judgements.

The socio-political conditions for children in the UK currently suggest a rather bleak picture, especially since the Thatcher years witnessed the emergence of the "neo-liberal politics of childhood" (Wagg and Pilcher 2014a, xii). As late as 1995, the United Nations criticised Britain for its poor implementation of the children's rights convention (Scraton 1997, 182–5). England has also been ranked among the most child-unfriendly countries in Europe (Micklewright and Stewart 2000, 23; Ward 2005). As Carey Oppenheim and Ruth Lister demonstrate, between 1979 and 1993, the proportion of children living in poverty in the UK trebled from 1.4 million to 4.3 million, meaning that a third of all children lived in poverty, a much greater increase than for the population as a whole (1996, 126). Today in the light of the politics of austerity, the UK has one of the highest child poverty rates in the EU (Bradshaw 2011). Although New Labour certainly attempted to tackle the problem of child poverty with a number of policy measures, "this was not enough to achieve their poverty targets nor to cement real change" (Dorling 2014, 99). Another major point of concern is the authoritarian direction Britain has pursued in terms of juvenile law since the 1980s. In the 1990s, "statistical evidence [...] showed that Britain locked away more young people, earlier in their lives and for longer periods of time, than any other European Union member state" (Scraton 1997, 169). As Bob Franklin shows, one drastic legislation was the Crime and Disorder Act of 1998, which comprised "anti-social behaviour orders to tackle harassment by children over 10; parenting orders; child safety orders; curfews; the abolition of *Doli Incapax*; final warnings for young offenders with reparations for victims; electronic tagging; fast track punishments" (2002, 38, emphasis in original). As Stephen Ball (2008) and Ken Jones (2015) point out, neoliberal interests also came to play a significant role in policy changes regarding the education system. From the Thatcher years onwards, education has increasingly been viewed as a "producer of labour, of basic and 'high-skills', of values, like enterprise and entrepreneurship, and of commercial 'knowledge', as a response to the requirements of international economic competition" (Ball 2008, 14). This development has led to "an increasing neglect or side-lining (other than in rhetoric) of the social purposes of education" (ibid.).

Since the 1970s, various public scandals of child abuse and murder and their repercussions in the media seem to have confirmed this precarious status of childhood in Britain. The recent trials for child abuse of celebrities such as Gary Glitter, Jimmy Savile and Rolf Harris, which relate to crimes committed between the 1960s and 1980s, received international media coverage. The deaths of Maria Colwell in 1973, of Jasmine Beckford in 1985, of Victoria Climbié in 2000 and of Peter Connelly in 2006 brought the issue of domestic violence and child abuse in families to the public. The high-profile murders of Sarah Payne and Damilola Taylor in 2000 led to debates about children's public safety and surveillance in the UK. These and a number of comparable cases gave rise to some parliamentary review boards and legislative measures. These include the Children Act of 1989, the appointment of a Children's Commissioner for England in the context of the 2004 Children

Act and the early intervention initiative *Every Child Matters*, which was launched in England and Wales in 2003 (Hendrick 1994, 214–88; Parton 2014, 14–67, 89–104; Wyness 2012, 130–51). From the perspective of social policy change, Britain thus also upholds an extraordinary role in Europe. As Nigel Parton observes, particularly in England "the pace and nature of change seems of a different order to elsewhere and is more self-consciously related to attempts to 'modernise' services and practices" (2006, 1–2).

At the same time, discussions of juvenile delinquency in Britain have undermined conceptions of children's innocence inherited from Romanticism and Victorianism. This was most clearly the case when two ten-year-old boys, Jon Venables and Robert Thompson, abducted, abused and killed two-year-old James Bulger in 1992 (James and Jenks 1996; Krause 2011). However, that was by no means the only case in which the victim *and* the perpetrators were children. Youth riots in some British towns in 2011 caused much outrage and David Cameron's subsequent open outcry of 'Broken Britain' hinted at a fair degree of helplessness and moral panic vis-à-vis juvenile delinquency. Erica Burman suggests that in public debates in contemporary Britain, the child appears to alternate between two roles: being at risk and being risky (2008, 88–92). As Burman puts it: "childhoods are not only unstable, but their instability within the national and international imaginary generates considerable anxiety" (89). On the basis of these conflicting developments, we believe that contemporary Britain provides a fascinating context for the study of childhood and as such warrants further scholarly attention.

The above sketch of some dimensions of contemporary British childhood shows once more that childhood is a multifaceted phenomenon that deserves to be spoken of in the plural (James, Jenks, and Prout 1998, 124–45). It comes as no surprise, then, that the study of childhood, or childhoods, is always an interdisciplinary endeavour. As Allison James and Adrian James note, "childhood is a complex phenomenon, which therefore requires complex understandings that cannot be arrived at by looking through a single disciplinary lens [...]" (2012, xi). Childhood has long outgrown the strict observation of pedagogy alone, as it were. In Anglo-American academia, the multidisciplinary research field of Childhood Studies has grown considerably since the late 1990s and now includes a broad variety of approaches that study the phenomena pertaining to childhood and children in their historical, cultural, geographical, legal, social, psychological and pedagogical facets. The present volume links up with interdisciplinary Childhood Studies, and it attempts to remedy the fact that although many disciplines constitute Childhood Studies, actual multidisciplinary cooperation is still the exception rather than the rule.

Childhood is currently a noteworthy and complex phenomenon on a theoretical level, too. For although it has been invested with high symbolical significance in Western societies at least since the Romantic period, the inevitable aim of childhood is its overcoming and the individual's entry into adulthood. Childhood has thus been theorised as a temporary and liminal state (Jenks 2005b, 53), which at the same time carries enormous weight for the adult. To speak about 'childhood' theoretically, however, only rarely means speaking about individual children. The institutional regulations and the representations of childhood in the arts and the media turn it into a notion, or set of notions, created by adults, diminishing it to a state of heteronomy. As Burman explains:

> Whether cast in terms of nostalgia or repugnance, the category of childhood is a repository of social representations that functions only by virtue of the relationship with other age and status categories: the child exists in relation to the category 'adult'.
>
> (2008, 68)

Thus, there seems to be general consensus about the view that childhood exists in a complex web of power structures. Yet notions of children's agency and voice remain contested concepts in scholarship (Lesnik-Oberstein 2011b). Many academics, particularly sociologists, proceed on the premise that children are social actors who, as Allison James and Alan Prout famously proposed, "are and must be seen as active in the construction and determination of their own lives, the lives of those around them and of the societies in which they live" (2006a, 7). Other scholars have problematised this view as a preconceived and politically engaged notion of childhood.

No matter which stance one takes regarding these issues, it is beyond doubt that enquiries into the contexts, constructions or empirical realities of childhood always implicitly or explicitly relate to the fundamental question "what is a child?" (James and Prout 2006b, 1). This contention implies that any approach to childhood is inevitably preconceived because it provides an answer to this question. The most common answer in recent years has been that childhood is not an essence, a 'thing' to be known and studied, but that it is a social and cultural construct. This assumption lies at the root of many contemporary approaches, both in the social sciences and in the humanities. Hence, constructivism can even be regarded as one "basic premise of Childhood Studies" (Woodhead 2009, 21). Nearly all recent publications in the field that was once called 'the *new* sociology of childhood', but that has now "come of age", as Martin Woodhead (17) puts it, make due reference to the paradigm of constructivism. Likewise formerly unquestioned categories, such as 'development', 'socialisation' and 'immaturity', have been questioned, though, admittedly, more so in some disciplines than others.

Nevertheless, it is important to stress the fact that constructivism does not constitute a coherent approach. As Karín Lesnik-Oberstein astutely observes, "understandings of what constructivist approaches to childhood are and do, and what their consequences are, have a tendency to differ between the humanities and the social sciences" (2011b, 4). In other words, some studies take the idea of childhood as a construct further than others do; some even employ it inconsistently or, despite their constructivist objectives, fall back into essentialist notions of childhood. Constructivist approaches range from the notion of childhood as purely discursive construct to socio-constructivist perspectives, which may be referred to as 'weak' constructivism. Lesnik-Oberstein's claim of a diversity of constructivisms of childhood is likely to apply on an interdisciplinary as well as an intradisciplinary level and will thus doubtlessly characterise the present collection, not least because here we assemble works of scholars whom the scientific community will easily recognise as representatives of different approaches to the study of childhood.

This volume addresses what we perceive as two neglected fields in Childhood Studies. The first and most significant gap we mean to tackle is the relative absence of studies about *contemporary* childhoods. Whereas much scholarship has been produced on childhoods in modernity more generally (e.g. Ariès [1960] 1973; Cunningham 1991, 1995; Zelizer 1994), facets of the more immediate period of the late twentieth and early twenty-first centuries remain marginal. This is a gap that appears to be particularly prevalent in the humanities where diachronic approaches are still popular. Many historical studies, some of which have reached the status of classics by now, trace conceptions of childhood over several centuries.[3] Furthermore, it is striking that studies concerned with more recent constructions of childhood only reach up to the 1990s or end even earlier.[4] If more recent developments are mentioned at all, it is often only in passing and on rather global scales (e.g. Fass 2013; Stearns 2011). Apart from children's literature criticism, which has produced a substantial amount of research concerned with the contemporary period (e.g. Butler and Reynolds 2014; Falconer 2009; Mallan and Bradford 2011), in literary studies, research about childhood in the late twentieth and early twenty-first centuries is only emerging.[5] The established periods of Romanticism and Victorianism and their canonical authors still constitute the focus of most studies in this area.

Most research in literary studies, film studies and art history has also tended to adopt a transnational perspective, analysing the huge cultural production representing childhood in terms of a general 'Western idea' rather than focusing on one precise cultural context (e.g. Higonnet 1998; Lebeau 2008; Lury 2010; Pifer 2000). Adrienne E. Gavin's collection, *The Child in British Literature: Literary Constructions of Childhood, Medieval to Contemporary* (2012), remains one of the few recent studies concerned with childhood in a singular cultural context. The volume also contains a chapter that reaches into the 2000s. We would thus like to start where Gavin's collection ends and offer a volume solely dedicated to a period that is, in our opinion, too often overlooked in scholarly discourse.

Whereas the approaches above are of course all valuable in their own right, it cannot be overlooked, as Harry Hendrick has observed, that when it comes to the post-war era in Britain, sociology holds the academic monopoly over childhood (1997, 6). Therefore, it comes as no surprise that sociologists have provided impulses to organise the study of contemporary childhoods into individual phases, often taking into account relevant shifts in the political climate, such as the rise of Thatcherism, New Labour and the coalition government (Durham 1991; Pilcher and Wagg 1996; Wagg and Pilcher 2014b). Moreover, sociologists currently offer at least one approach of theorising the contemporary period of childhood. Nigel Parton (2006) and Michael Wyness (2012), who are represented in this volume, have suggested reading contemporary childhood through the lens of the theory of late modernity, as originally put forward by Ulrich Beck and his colleagues Anthony Giddens, Elisabeth Beck-Gernsheim and others. These scholars conceive of modernity as a phase that is above all characterised by ontological insecurity, detraditionalisation, individualisation, risk anxiety and self-reflexivity. This perspective implies that various structures, which used to organise and determine societies significantly in the early phase of modernity, have lost ground since the second half of the twentieth century. Thereby, various spheres of life, so this theory suggests, have increasingly become subject to choice. Personal relationships, for instance, now tend to be less determined by class, gender and economic factors than at the beginning of the twentieth century. Only very rarely do relationships last an entire lifetime. Instead, relationships are now built upon emotional affection and mutual commitment (Kehily 2013, 15). Because personal choice and preference play such an important role for the late modern subject, "the self becomes a *reflexive project*", as Anthony Giddens argues (1991, 32, emphasis in original). Subjects constantly scrutinise their choices. Similarly, as Ulrich Beck explains, relationships "have to be established, maintained, and constantly renewed by individuals" (1992, 97). The parent–child relationship, however, remains largely unaffected by these transitions. In an often quoted passage, Beck argues that

> [t]he child is the source of the *last remaining, irrevocable, unexchangeable primary relationship*. Partners come and go. The child stays. [...] The child becomes the final alternative to loneliness that can be built up against the vanishing possibilities of love. It is the private type of re-enchantment, which arises with, and derives its meaning from, disenchantment. The number of births is declining, but the importance of the child is *rising*.
>
> (118, emphasis in original)

In Chris Jenks's words, in this period of late modernity the child "has become the site or relocation of discourses concerning stability, integration and the social bond. The child is now envisioned as a form of 'nostalgia', a longing for times past" (2005a, 19). We believe that there is much to gain from the theoretical perspective of late modernity because it takes account of the rigorous persistency with which childhood and children play a constitutive role for individuals and societies at large. Yet we acknowledge that it provides only one possible narrative for the circumstances of contemporary childhood. Thus far, the theory of late modernity has not been complemented by any serious alternative theoretical frameworks for the contemporary period in Childhood Studies. We would like this volume to draw attention to this gap.

The second major gap we intend to address is what we perceive as a limited number of inter- and multi-disciplinary works, in spite of the self-proclaimed multidisciplinary agenda of Childhood Studies. Much still needs to be done, and the present volume aims precisely at furthering the exchange between the various disciplines involved. Many interdisciplinary works are introductory volumes, anthologies or handbooks concerned with more basic questions concerning childhood (e.g. Jenkins 1998; Kehily 2010; Qvortrup, Corsaro, and Honig 2011; Smith and Greene 2014). Few previous collections have been more focused with regard to their temporal and cultural frameworks, such as Jane Pilcher and Stephen Wagg's collection *Thatcher's Children: Politics, Childhood and Society in the 1980s and 1990s* (1996) and its sequel *Thatcher's Grandchildren? Politics and Childhood in the Twenty-First Century* (2014b). The contributions in the first volume are all concerned with the social and political transitions of childhood under the New Right, whereas the follow-up also contains one contribution concerned with children's literature. Similarly, Jens Qvortrup's collection *Studies in Modern Childhood: Society, Agency and Culture* (2005) focuses on contemporary social issues relating to childhood, though again in the manner of a more global perspective. In contrast, Karín Lesnik-Oberstein's collections *Children in Culture: Approaches to Childhood* (1998) and *Children in Culture Revisited: Further Approaches to Childhood* (2011a) integrate more perspectives from the humanities, but again without a common temporal or cultural focus of investigation. The present collection grants the humanities and the social sciences equal presence and aims to unite them through a concise common contextual frame.

The contributions of this volume are divided into four sections. The first one contains four chapters on childhood from the perspectives of literary studies and critical theory. In the opening chapter, "Writing Plural Childhoods – Some Thoughts Concerning the Recent Carnegie Medal Shortlists", Anja Müller looks at the current criteria of selection of one of Britain's most distinguished literary awards for children's literature. She examines which conceptions of childhood are promoted by the award committee and to what extent the shortlists from 2012 to 2014 comply with these ideas. The next chapter, Katharina Pietsch and Tyll Zybura's "The Adult within the Literary Child: Reading Toby Litt's *deadkidsongs* as an Anti-*Bildungsroman*", scrutinises the different ways in which contemporary British fiction for adults responds to the model of development of the traditional *Bildungsroman*. Using Toby Litt's novel *deadkidsongs* (2001) as an example, they show that this deconstruction applies on the thematic level of literary works but that it is similarly implicated in complex and inconsistent narrative structures. In "The Child Narrator in Contemporary British Fiction and Literary Criticism: The Case of Stephen Kelman's *Pigeon English*", Sandra Dinter pursues a similar path: she examines the trend of the first-person child narrator in contemporary British fiction for adults. Dinter suggests that literary criticism often reduces the phenomenon of the child narrator to the normative question of accuracy. In a close reading of Stephen Kelman's debut novel *Pigeon English* (2011), she illustrates how the child narrator can be approached from a constructivist perspective. Karín Lesnik-Oberstein's contribution "Children's Literature, Cognitivism and Neuroscience" offers a critique of the 'neuro-turn', which is currently immensely influential in the British higher education sector and public debates more widely. Problematising the assumption of a direct and unmediated access to reality inherent in cognitivism and neuroscience, Lesnik-Oberstein draws parallels to how literary criticism commonly theorises the child as a representation of a given and stable reality rather than a textual construct.

The four chapters in Section II focus on medial and visual constructions of childhood. Jonathan Bignell's chapter "Children's Television and Public Service in Contemporary Britain" explores how television broadcasting in the UK constructs and aims to regulate the child as a consumer of TV programmes. Questioning the prevalent idea that children must be protected from watching television, Bignell points to the various potentials TV holds for young viewers. In the following chapter, "An Inconvenient Growth: Watching Child Actors, Growing Up, Sideways and Backwards in Contemporary British Film and Television", Karen Lury analyses the different ways in which child actors are shown to grow alongside their fictional characters in Michael Winterbottom's 2012 film *Everyday* and the BBC sitcom *Outnumbered* (2007–2014). Lury demonstrates that by highlighting the differences of and between children, contemporary British film and television offer a pluralist picture of children's growth. In the subsequent chapter, "Adults Looking at Children: Books, Bodies and Buying in Children's Book Covers", Jessica Medhurst examines the 2014 cover for the Penguin Modern Classic's edition of *Charlie and the Chocolate Factory*. Approaching the cover and its paratexts from a feminist-constructivist perspective, Medhurst analyses the ways in which commentators perceive the girl on the cover and thereby perpetuate certain notions of childhood and appropriateness. The final essay in this section, "Reflections on British and American Images of and for Children" by Ellen Handler Spitz, discusses how recent visual art in the UK and the US, including picture books, installations and paintings, construct childhood in diverse ways and contexts.

The third section "Historical and Social Dimensions of Childhood in Contemporary Britain" takes off with Angela Davis's chapter "Childcare for the Under-Fives in Post-1945 England: Contemporary Reflections on Past Childhoods". Davis demonstrates how childcare for very young children has evolved in Britain since the second half of the twentieth century and critically reflects upon the potentials and limits of using oral history in research about contemporary childhoods. Erica Burman's contribution "Contingent Connections: Between German and British Childhoods – Marion Daltrop" reconstructs the biography of Marion Daltrop who was born in Germany and came to Britain as a child on the last Kindertransport of 1939, where she later became a philanthropist, artist and activist working with children.

The final section of this volume consists of three chapters on "Contemporary British Childhoods between Rights and Regulations". Nigel Parton's "The Politics of Child Protection in Contemporary England: Towards the 'Authoritarian Neoliberal State'" provides a critical survey of recent changes in child protection policy and practice in contemporary England. Since the late 2000s, Parton argues, England has followed an authoritarian neoliberal approach to child protection and child welfare more generally, which can be seen, for instance, in a new emphasis on parental responsibility as well as severe reductions of welfare services. The next chapter, "Dressing up for School: Beyond Rights and Welfare" by Daniel Monk, explores school dress and its place within current public and legal debates about bullying, discipline, sexuality and consumerism in the UK. Monk shows that school dress is a highly contested topic in contemporary Britain, which reveals anxieties toward children's autonomy. In the final chapter of the volume, "The Recognition and Distribution of Children's Agency in the UK", Michael Wyness addresses a rather recent paradigm in the study of childhood, that is, the notion that children are active agents. Wyness tackles the question of to what extent the theoretical notion of children's agency is reflected and practiced in schools, homes and politics and how socio-economic factors have an impact on the distribution and recognition of children's agency in contemporary Britain.

Acknowledgements

The editors would like to thank the Bielefeld Centre for Interdisciplinary Research for funding the conference from which this volume emerges. The Centre's unique programme and setting proved the ideal venue for an encounter among the different disciplines engaged in the study of childhood.

Notes

1 See, for instance, Brooks (2006, 5–18), Buckingham (2000, 61–122; 2011, 5–24), Kehily (2013), Krinsky (2008) and Wyness (2012, 107–19).
2 See, for instance, Coveney (1967), Kuhn (1982), Pattison ([1978] 2008), Plotz (2001) and Rowland (2012).
3 See, for instance, Coveney (1967), Cunningham (1991, 1995), Fletcher (2008), Heywood (2001), Higonnet (1998), MacFarlane (1986), Shorter (1976) and Stone (1977).
4 See, for instance, Cox (1996), Hendrick (1994, 1997), Locke (2011) and Pifer (2000).
5 Sandra Dinter completed her PhD thesis "Childhood in Contemporary English Fiction: Contesting the Last Vestige of Essentialism" at Bielefeld University in 2016. She is currently preparing a monograph on the same subject for publication. A three-year research project funded by the Deutsche Forschungsgemeinschaft (German Research Foundation) on "Children and Childhood in Literature: Theory, Narratology, Criticism" is taking up work in June 2017 at Bielefeld University, under the supervision of Ralf Schneider and with Katharina Pietsch and Tyll Zybura as researchers.

References

About a Boy. 2002. DVD. Directed by Chris Weitz and Paul Weitz. Universal Pictures.
Anita and Me. 2002. DVD. Directed by Metin Hüseyin. BBC.
Ariès, Philippe. (1960) 1973. *Centuries of Childhood*. Translated by Robert Baldick. London: Cape.
Ashworth, Andrea. 1998. *Once in a House on Fire*. London: Picador.
Ball, Stephen J. 2008. *The Education Debate: Policy and Politics in the Twenty-First Century*. Cambridge: Polity Press.
Beck, Ulrich. 1992. *Risk Society: Towards a New Modernity*. Translated by Mark Ritter. London: Sage.
Billy Elliot. 2000. DVD. Directed by Stephen Daldry. Universal Pictures.
Boy A. 2007. DVD. Directed by John Crowley. The Weinstein Company.
Bradshaw, Jonathan. 2011. "Child Poverty and Deprivation." In *The Well-Being of Children in the UK*, 3rd ed., edited by Jonathan Bradshaw, 35–64. Bristol: Policy Press.
Brooks, Libby. 2006. *The Story of Childhood: Growing Up in Modern Britain*. London: Bloomsbury.
Buckingham, David. 2000. *After the Death of Childhood: Growing up in the Age of Electronic Media*. Cambridge: Polity Press.
———. 2007. "Childhood in the Age of Global Media." *Children's Geographies* 5 (1–2): 43–54.
———. 2011. *The Material Child: Growing Up in Consumer Culture*. Cambridge: Polity Press.
Burman, Erica. 2008. *Deconstructing Developmental Psychology*. 2nd ed. London and New York: Routledge.

Butler, Catherine, and Kimberley Reynolds. 2014. *Modern Children's Literature: An Introduction*. 2nd ed., Basingstoke: Palgrave Macmillan.

Byatt, A.S. (2009) 2010. *The Children's Book*. London: Vintage.

Coveney, Peter. 1967. *The Image of Childhood: The Individual and Society: A Study of the Theme in English Literature*. Harmondsworth: Penguin.

Cox, Roger. 1996. *Shaping Childhood: Themes of Uncertainty in the History of Adult-Child Relationships*. London and New York: Routledge.

Cunningham, Hugh. 1991. *The Children of the Poor: Representations of Childhood since the Seventeenth Century*. Oxford: Blackwell.

———. 1995. *Children and Childhood in Western Society since 1500*. London: Longman.

Dinter, Sandra. 2016. "Childhood in Contemporary English Fiction: Contesting the Last Vestige of Essentialism." PhD diss., Bielefeld University.

Dodou, Katherina. 2012. "Examining the Idea of Childhood: The Child in the Contemporary British Novel." In *The Child in British Literature: Literary Constructions of Childhood: Medieval to Contemporary*, edited by Adrienne E. Gavin, 238–50. Basingstoke: Palgrave Macmillan.

Donoghue, Emma. (2010) 2011. *Room*. London: Picador.

Dorling, Danny. 2014. "'What Have the Romans Ever Done for Us?' Child Poverty and the Legacy of 'New' Labour." In *Thatcher's Grandchildren? Politics and Childhood in the Twenty-First Century*, edited by Stephen Wagg and Jane Pilcher, 89–100. Basingstoke: Palgrave Macmillan.

Doyle, Roddy. (1993) 1999. *Paddy Clarke Ha Ha Ha*. London: Vintage.

Durham, Martin. 1991. *Sex and Politics: The Family and Morality in the Thatcher Years*. Basingstoke: Macmillan.

Enright, Anne. 2007. *The Gathering*. New York: Black Cat.

Falconer, Rachel. 2009. *The Crossover Novel: Contemporary Children's Fiction and Its Adult Readership*. London and New York: Routledge.

Fass, Paula S., ed. 2013. *The Routledge History of Childhood in the Western World*. Abington, UK and New York: Routledge.

Fink, Janet. 2002. "Private Lives, Public Issues: Moral Panics and 'the Family' in 20th Century Britain." *Journal for the Study of British Cultures* 9 (2): 135–48.

Fletcher, Anthony. 2008. *Growing Up in England: The Experience of Childhood 1600–1914*. Newhaven, CT and London: Yale UP.

Foer, Jonathan Safran. (2005) 2006. *Extremely Loud & Incredibly Close*. London: Penguin.

Franklin, Bob. 2002. "Children's Rights and Media Wrongs: Changing Representations of Children and the Developing Rights Agenda." In *The New Handbook of Children's Rights: Comparative Policy and Practice*, edited by Bob Franklin, 15–42. London: Routledge.

Gavin, Adrienne E., ed. 2012. *The Child in British Literature: Literary Constructions of Childhood, Medieval to Contemporary*. Basingstoke: Palgrave Macmillan.

Giddens, Anthony. 1991. *Modernity and Self-Identity: Self and Society in the Late Modern Age*. Cambridge: Polity Press.

Graham, Allan. 1999. "Introduction." In *The Sociology of the Family: A Reader*, edited by Allen Graham, 1–7. Oxford: Blackwell.

Haddon, Mark. (2003) 2004. *The Curious Incident of the Dog in the Night-Time*. London: Vintage.

Hendrick, Harry. 1994. *Child Welfare: England 1872–1989*. London: Routledge.
———. 1997. *Children, Childhood and English Society 1880–1990*. New Studies in Economic and Social History. Cambridge: Cambridge University Press.
Heywood, Colin. 2001. *A History of Childhood: Children and Childhood in the West from Medieval to Modern Times*. Cambridge: Polity Press.
Higonnet, Anne. 1998. *Pictures of Innocence: The History and Crisis of Ideal Childhood*. London: Thames and Hudson.
Ishiguro, Kazuo. (2005) 2006. *Never Let Me Go*. London: Faber & Faber.
James, Allison, and Adrian James. 2012. *Key Concepts in Childhood Studies*. 2nd ed. London, SAGE.
James, Allison, and Chris Jenks. 1996. "Public Perceptions of Childhood Criminality." *British Journal of Sociology* 47 (2): 315–31.
James, Allison, Chris Jenks, and Alan Prout. 1998. *Theorizing Childhood*. Cambridge: Polity Press.
James, Allison, and Alan Prout. 2006a. "A Paradigm for the Sociology of Childhood? Provenance, Promise and Problems." In *Constructing and Reconstructing Childhood: Contemporary Issues in the Sociological Study of Childhood*, 2nd ed., edited by Allison James and Alan Prout, 7–33. London: Routledge Falmer.
———. "Introduction." 2006b. In *Constructing and Reconstructing Childhood: Contemporary Issues in the Sociological Study of Childhood*, 2nd ed., edited by Allison James and Alan Prout, 1–5. London et al.: Routledge Falmer.
Jenkins, Henry, ed. 1998. *The Children's Culture Reader*. New York: New York University Press.
Jenks, Chris. 2005a. "The Postmodern Child." In *Children in Families: Research and Policy*, edited by Julia Brannen and Margaret O'Brien, 13–25. London and Washington, DC: Falmer Press.
———. *Childhood*. 2005b. 2nd ed. London: Routledge.
Jones, Ken. 2015. *Education in Britain: 1944 to the Present*. 2nd ed. Cambridge: Polity Press.
Kehily, Mary Jane, ed. 2010. *An Introduction to Childhood Studies*. Maidenhead: Open University Press.
———. 2013. "Childhood in Crisis? An Introduction to Contemporary Western Childhood." In *Understanding Childhood: A Cross-Disciplinary Approach*, edited by Mary Jane Kehily, 1–52. Bristol: Policy Press.
Kelman, Stephen. 2011. *Pigeon English*. London: Bloomsbury.
Krause, Michael. 2011. "The Public Death of James Bulger: Images as Evidence in a Popular Tale of Good and Evil." *Journal for the Study of British Cultures* 18 (2): 133–48.
Krinsky, Charles, ed. 2008. *Moral Panics over Contemporary Children and Youth*. Farnham: Ashgate.
Kuhn, Reinhard. 1982. *Corruption in Paradise: The Child in Western Literature*. Hanover: UP of New England.
Lebeau, Vicky. 2008. *Childhood and Cinema*. London: Reaktion.
Lesnik-Oberstein, Karín, ed. 1998. *Children in Culture. Approaches to Childhood*. Basingstoke: Palgrave Macmillan.

———, ed. 2011a. *Children in Culture Revisited: Further Approaches*. Basingstoke: Palgrave Macmillan, 2011.

———. 2011b. "Introduction: Voice, Agency and the Child." In *Children in Culture Revisited: Further Approaches to Childhood*, edited by Karín Lesnik-Oberstein, 1–17. Basingstoke: Palgrave Macmillan, 2011.

Litt, Toby. 2001. *deadkidsongs*. London: Penguin.

Locke, Richard. 2011. *Critical Children: The Use of Childhood in Ten Great Novels*. New York: Columbia University Press.

Lord of the Flies. 1990. DVD. Directed by Harry Hook. Castle Rock Entertainment.

Louv, Richard. 2010. *Last Child in the Woods: Saving Our Children from Nature-Deficit Disorder*. Chapel Hill, NC: Algonquin.

Lury, Karen. 2010. *The Child in Film: Tears, Fears and Fairytale*. London and New York: Tauris.

MacFarlane, Alan. 1986. *Marriage and Love in England: Modes of Reproduction 1300–1840*. Oxford: Basil Blackwell.

Mallan, Kerry, and Clare Bradford, eds. 2011. *Contemporary Children's Literature and Film: Engaging with Theory*. Basingstoke: Palgrave Macmillan.

McCourt, Frank. 1996. *Angela's Ashes: A Memoir*. New York: Scribner.

McEwan, Ian. (2001) 2003. *Atonement*. 2001. New York: Anchor Books.

Micklewright, John, and Kitty Stewart. 2000. *The Welfare of Europe's Children*. Bristol: Policy Press.

Oliver Twist. 2007. DVD. Directed by Coky Giedroyc. BBC One.

Oppenheim, Carey, and Ruth Lister. 1996. "The Politics of Child Poverty 1979–1995." In *Thatcher's Children? Politics, Childhood and Society in the 1980s and 1990s*, edited by Jane Pilcher and Stephen Wagg, 114–33. London and Washington DC: Falmer, 1996.

Palmer, Sue. 2006. *Toxic Childhood: How the Modern World Is Damaging Our Children and What We Can Do About It*. London: Orion.

Parton, Nigel. 2006. *Safeguarding Childhood: Early Intervention and Surveillance in Late Modern Society*. Basingstoke: Palgrave Macmillan.

———. 2014. *The Politics of Child Protection: Contemporary Developments and Future Directions*. Basingstoke: Palgrave Macmillan.

Pattison, Robert. (1978) 2008. *The Child Figure in English Literature*. Athens: Georgia University Press.

Pifer, Ellen. 2000. *Demon or Doll? Images of the Child in Contemporary Writing and Culture*. Charlottesville and London: University Press of Virginia.

Pilcher, Jane, and Stephen Wagg, eds. 1996. *Thatcher's Children: Politics, Childhood and Society in the 1980s and 1990s*. London: Falmer.

Plotz, Judith. 2001. *Romanticism and the Vocation of Childhood*. Basingstoke and New York: Palgrave.

Postman, Neil. (1982) 1994. *The Disappearance of Childhood*. New York: Vintage.

Qvortrup, Jens, ed. 2005. *Studies in Modern Childhood: Society, Agency and Culture*. Basingstoke: Palgrave Macmillan.

Qvortrup, Jens, William A. Corsaro, and Michael-Sebastian Honig, eds. 2011. *The Palgrave Handbook of Childhood Studies*. Basingstoke: Palgrave Macmillan.

Rowland, Ann Wierda. 2012. *Romanticism and Childhood: The Infantalization of British Literary Culture*. Cambridge: Cambridge University Press.
Rudd, David. 2014. "A Coming of Age? Children's Literature at the Turn of the Twenty-First Century." In *Thatcher's Grandchildren? Politics and Childhood in the Twenty-First Century*, edited by Stephen Wagg and Jane Pilcher, 118–39. Basingstoke: Palgrave Macmillan.
Schneider, Ralf. 2006. "Literary Childhoods and the Blending of Conceptual Spaces: Transdifference and the Other in Ourselves." *Journal for the Study of British Cultures* 13 (2): 147–60.
Scraton, Phil. 1997. "Whose 'Childhood'? What 'Crisis'?" In *'Childhood' in 'Crisis'?*, edited by Phil Scraton, 163–86. London: UCL Press.
Shorter, Edward. 1976. *The Making of the Modern Family*. London: Collins.
Shriver, Lionel. (2003) 2010. *We Need to Talk About Kevin*. London: Serpent's Tail.
Smith, Carmel, and Sheila Greene, eds. 2014. *Key Thinkers in Childhood Studies*. Bristol: Policy Press.
Stearns, Peter N. 2011. *Childhood in World History*. 2nd ed. London and New York: Routledge.
Stone, Lawrence. 1977. *The Family, Sex and Marriage in England 1500–1800*. London: Weidenfeld and Nicolson.
Tew, Philip. 2004. *The Contemporary British Novel*. London: Continuum.
Tsiolkas, Christos. (2008) 2011. *The Slap*. London: Atlantic Books.
Wagg, Stephen, and Jane Pilcher. 2014a. "Introduction: Sociology, Politics and Childhood – the Contemporary Landscape." In *Thatcher's Grandchildren? Politics and Childhood in the Twenty-First Century*, edited by Stephen Wagg and Jane Pilcher, x–xvi. Basingstoke: Palgrave Macmillan.
———, eds. 2014b. *Thatcher's Grandchildren? Politics and Childhood in the Twenty-First Century*. Basingstoke: Palgrave Macmillan.
Ward, Lucy. 2005. "'Child-Unfriendly' England Served Notice: First Children Commissioner Wants to End Marginalisation." *The Guardian*, March 2. Accessed 30 September 2013. www.theguardian.com/society/2005/mar/02/childrensservices.politics.
Woodhead, Martin. 2009. "Childhood Studies: Past, Present and Future." In *An Introduction to Childhood Studies*, 2nd ed., edited by Mary Jane Kehily, 17–34. Maidenhead: Open University Press.
Wyness, Michael. 2012. *Childhood and Society*. 2nd ed. Basingstoke: Palgrave Macmillan.
Zelizer, Viviana A. Rotman. 1994. *Pricing the Priceless Child: The Changing Social Value of Children*. Princeton, NJ: Princeton University Press.

Section I
Childhood in Contemporary British Literature and Literary Criticism

1 Writing Plural Childhoods – Some Thoughts Concerning the Recent Carnegie Medal Shortlists

Anja Müller

An assessment of childhood in contemporary Britain would certainly be incomplete without taking into account contemporary children's literature because it is a truth universally acknowledged that children's literature is a good index for childhood concepts. Children's literature scholars agree unequivocally that children's literature does not simply respond to the 'true nature of children. Together with school and the family, it has become an integral actor when it comes to defining and conceptualising childhood (Buckingham 2000, 7–9). Accordingly, the development of children's literature throughout the ages coincides with the historical contingency of childhood concepts. Charles Frey and John Griffith therefore maintain that children's books "provide a reading of children and of childhood" (1987, vii), whereas John Stahl, when contemplating canon formations in children's literature, believes that "[t]he task of establishing a canon is analogous to determining the nature of childhood" (1992, 12). By implying their readership through selections of topics, characters and narrative techniques, however, children's books not only reflect, they also participate very actively in shaping notions of childhood or rather 'childhoods'. Taking the plural form as a cue, the following chapter explores whether and in how far contemporary children's literature indeed conceptualises childhood as plural.

Since the bulk of contemporary children's literature is so vast that it is impossible to gauge it in its entirety, I have decided to resort to literary prizes in order to select my material. I am aware that books that have received institutional appraisal may not necessarily be those that also enjoy the highest sales numbers or the largest readership. Nevertheless, literary prizes condense, as it were, socially and institutionally legitimated norms, values and interests (Dücker 2013, 217). In the case of children's literature, such value systems include social constructions of childhood, as books that are included in the shortlists of literary awards tend to reflect ideas of what children ought to read, hence, what is believed to be adequate reading matter during childhood today (Kidd 2007; Stevenson 2009).[1]

My particular focus in this essay lies with the Carnegie Medal shortlists from 2012 to 2014. The Carnegie Medal is arguably the most prestigious children's book award in the UK (comparable to the Newbery

Medal in the US) and thus representative of what is supposed to be 'good' reading matter during childhood and adolescence in Britain. In what follows, I am first going to present the Carnegie Medal's criteria of selection in order to gauge in how far these criteria already hint at the concepts of childhood implied and supported by the respective award committee. I am then going to situate this conceptualisation within current discourses on childhood in children's literature research, before finally discussing the shortlisted books with regard to their acknowledgement of plurality.

According to the Carnegie website, the Carnegie Medal "was established in 1936, in memory of the [...] Scottish-born philanthropist Andrew Carnegie (1835–1919)", who greatly supported the implementation of libraries. Today the medal is awarded by the Chartered Institute of Library and Information Professionals (CILIP), which also co-ordinates the nomination process and recruits the jury. Apart from its high reputation, this particular award offers itself to further academic enquiry because the Carnegie's criteria are, in comparison to most other awards, made very transparent on its website.[2] There, one can read the following requirements for becoming a Carnegie Medal winner:

> The book that wins [...] should be a book of outstanding literary quality. The whole work should provide pleasure, not merely from the surface enjoyment of a good read, but also the deeper subconscious satisfaction of having gone through a vicarious, but at the time of reading a *real* experience that is retained afterwards. (emphasis in original)

The criteria for plot construction and development, characterisation and style are then further specified (the following summary is based on the list of criteria on the Carnegie website):

Plots should be well constructed. The author ought to be "in control of the plot, making definite and positive decisions about the direction events take and the conclusions they reach". Events ought to "happen, not necessarily logically, but acceptably within the limits set by the theme", culminating in a credible, final resolution. Characters must be believable, convincing, rounded and dynamic. Interaction between characters ought to be as convincing and consistent as characters' behaviour and speech. An effective deployment of narrative strategies, such as narration, dialogue, action and thoughts for direct and indirect characterisation is equally desired. Finally, the jury evaluates whether the handling of style (in both prose and verse) and mood are appropriate to the subject and theme of the novels, and whether the author succeeds in using literary techniques – such as narrative or poetic elements – effectively. Factual references ought to be accurate and clear. Most of these criteria are obviously not age-specific but apply to narrative fiction in general, although one can discern a general predilection for an idea of the 'good' book as a piece of art, with coherence and consistency between form and contents, very much in the sense of John Keats's "well-wrought urn".

Considering these statements, the Carnegie Medal clearly understands itself as an award for literary quality. Such an agenda may be self-evident for a book award, yet it actually is not so when it comes to children's literature. After all, children's literature has struggled for a long time, and to some extent is still struggling, to be recognised as a full member of the literary field. Whereas general literature has asserted its aesthetic autonomy since the eighteenth century (Reinfandt 1997), children's literature has always been hovering between determination by extra-literary factors (such as morality, socialisation or didacticism) and asserting its aesthetic autonomy as a literary genre (Müller 2011). The liminal literary status of children's literature is still manifest today in the fact that children's literature had, for a considerable time, been excluded from canonisation processes. By now, children's literature research may have become to some extent institutionalised in British literature departments, thanks to the pioneering work of scholars like Peter Hunt. Yet outside the few specialised research centres (for example, at the universities of Reading, Roehampton or Newcastle, the latter two being closely associated with renowned national archives) it is frequently relegated to didactics or pedagogy and, consequently, determined by the academic interests and methods of these disciplines, whereas it is often quite slow to respond to developments in general literary or cultural theory.[3] This ambiguous status of children's literature also reveals something about the concept of childhood underlying the respective institutional associations: the realm of aesthetic appreciation of (high) art is, apparently, a cultural field that does not necessarily grant childhood access to it. Consequently, children's books are seen as a concern of socialisation rather than artistic considerations. If didactic concerns are downplayed, finally, children's literature is largely appreciated for its entertaining functions without requiring particular aesthetic depths.

Whereas such characterisations of children's literature were connected with conceptualisations of childhood as a deficient state of the human being, they are today more often linked with the very opposite, namely, idealising discourses about childhood. Such idealising discourses perceive childhood as a precarious, transitory state of innocence, of authenticity, liberty from civilisational and professional restraints, freedom from the prejudices imbued by socialisation into peer groups and enviable youthfulness, imagination and optimism (Buckingham 2000, 12). As all these qualities are believed to be gradually abandoned or lost while growing up, childhood has become a utopian counterpart to the experience of the contemporary disillusionment and corruption of the adult world. In a time where the UK and other Western European countries are facing a demographic change, involving the reversal of the age pyramid, childhood seems to become even more precious, and its preservation is pursued with increasing vigour. From a historical perspective, all these are well-known developments, and one can easily recognise in today's almost obsessive concern with childhood a reverberation of the condition that engendered the Romantic cult of the child (Müller 2009, 232).

As far as children's literature is concerned, the legacy of Romantic idealised childhood, with its preservationist imperative, has the effect that strong currents in children's literature criticism call for a literature for children supporting this concept. The reactions to the Carnegie medallist of 2014, Kevin Brooks's *Bunker Diary*, which will be discussed in this chapter, are exemplary for a position believing that children's literature should offer a comfort zone or at least a safe house built on the ground rule that occurring conflicts and hardships must be harmoniously solved. No book should end without at least so much as a hopeful, if not entirely happy, ending, in order to reassure the child readers that the worlds they encounter (the fictional and, by implication, the real) are, despite all appearance, endowed with an ordered, meaningful structure. In line with this attitude are voices demanding that books for children should be written in a language strictly following all the codes of political correctness and that older texts therefore ought to be rewritten accordingly.[4] It is declared that if children grow up with a language cleansed of anything that may contain traces of discrimination, the very practice of discrimination will be extinguished, too. This quasi-magical belief in the negative creative power of language (that is, if you do not say the word, the thing does not come into existence) has triggered almost militant bouts of censorship and expurgations, especially of literary texts that were produced in the years, decades and centuries 'BPC' (before political correctness). The problem with such endeavours is, however, that they not only ignore the historical contingency of literary language and forget that discrimination first and foremost means 'distinction' (an indispensible cognitive tool for identity construction by the means of inclusion and exclusion as well as the notion of difference). Finally, and more importantly for our context, the idealising preservationist idea of childhood ultimately presupposes that children are only able to read texts literally and that they exclusively approach texts via identification. Children are thus believed to be unable to distinguish fiction from reality, to distance themselves from a text and to reflect on it critically. Since distancing and critical reflection in a literary text are achieved by stylistic devices (such as narrative strategies or imagery), children ought to learn to realise or process such devices, otherwise their reading will only be for the plot, for identification and entertainment. However, if one looks at didactics for teaching literature at school, one will find that literary texts tend to be increasingly employed as mere topical starting points for general discussions. Diane Duncan's *Teaching Children's Literature* (2009) is a case in point: in order to "make stories work in the classroom" (so the subtitle of her book), she suggests dramatisations of narratives in class or asking pupils about what or whom they like or identify with. Although critical terms for literary study, such as metaphor, also surface in the book, they are by far less prominent than suggestions concerning the social skills children should learn from literary texts or the topical issues that ought to be discussed. Pupils are, hence, consistently asked to identify with characters, to wonder what might have happened if a character had decided otherwise, to visualise scenes or to complete fragments of literary texts with their own stories. Instead of providing tools that enable young readers to enter into a dialogue with literature and its alterity, the 'other' (that is, the text) is appropriated and assimilated into one's own experiences and codes. Such a didactic approach to literature may invite children to read more, yet it will also result in a self-fulfilling prophecy: while arguing that it suits the way children read, it does not sufficiently provide young readers with tools that would enable them to reveal the strategies of a text; instead, it produces child readers who fuse fictional and real worlds, who are unable to distance themselves from the text and who therefore either need careful monitoring and protection or become mindless consumers.[5]

Luckily, the zealous educationalists promoting the preservationist concept of childhood are not the only actors in the field of children's literature. Other actors, including a considerable number of authors and readers of children's books, have come to see things differently. Wouter de Nooy, for example, has diagnosed a shift in the system of literary prizes for children in the late 1980s from a 'pedagogic' to a 'literary' perspective among the juries of awards for children's literature. As a result, prizes have become more and more concerned with literary quality instead of educational considerations, and literary scholars have joined the jury boards in addition to the accustomed majority of educationalists or librarians (de Nooy, esp. 202–3 and 212). The Carnegie Medal is a very visible representative of this change in the actors defining standards in literary prizes for children. By emphasising the literary quality of children's literature, they presuppose that children's books should offer their readers more than a hopeful assurance of possible conflict resolutions. Reading should be an "experience that is retained afterwards", as the Carnegie Medal website contends. Whatever engenders this lasting impact, it certainly contains an experience that exceeds the already known. Although the listed criteria for good children's literature highlight aspects of content (plot and character) slightly more than form (style), their guiding principles are narrative coherence, plausibility and effectiveness. A good children's book, therefore, is a book that coherently follows the ground rules established in its story world. It does not need legitimation by external factors, such as ideological demands for happy endings. Nor is the language of a text bound to codes outside the story world – the use of language should effectively contribute to the aesthetic appearance of the book as a work of art. With its deliberate refusal to establish age-specific aesthetic criteria, the Carnegie Medal purports an inclusive view of childhood with regard to literary aesthetics. When it comes to literary quality, so the underlying agenda, age distinctions do not apply to literary texts, but the standards are largely the same. Such an approach to quality assessment in children's literature is, perhaps, even more prominent in the Costa (formerly Whitbread) Award. The different categories of the Costa Award (novel, first book, biography, poetry, children's book) distinguish different areas of the literary market rather than qualities. With its practice to additionally award the 'Best Book' among the winners of all categories, including children's literature, the Costa Award is the only award with a direct competition of books for adults and children. Against the objection that this practice is only possible because Costa emphasises entertainment, whereas the prestigious Booker Prize, for instance, emphasises literary quality, one can always hold the fact that books frequently appear on the shortlists on both awards.

To return to my particular example, the books shortlisted for the Carnegie Medal illustrate concern with the literary quality of children's books as well as the plurality of childhood concepts. On the level of content, the books leave the immediate experiential world of their readers, confronting them with a plethora of geographical or historical settings with extreme situations of crisis.

Among the books shortlisted for the Carnegie Medal from 2012 to 2014, for instance, Julie Berry's *All the Truth That's in Me* and Susan Cooper's *Ghost Hawk* are set in an unspecified colonial North America. The plots of Elizabeth Wein's *Code Name Verity*, Sonya Hartnett's *The Midnight Zoo* and Ruta Sepetys's *Between Shades of Grey* unfold in Continental Europe (France, Germany, Lithuania/Siberia) during World War II, highlighting hitherto neglected issues such as the involvement of women in war activities, the genocide of gypsies or the deportations of Lithuanians under the Soviet regime. Katherine Rundell's *Rooftoppers* leads its survivor of the Queen Mary shipwreck to Paris. Nick Lake's *In Darkness* and Andy Mulligan's *Trash* deal with life in slums in Haiti and the Philippines, respectively; the former shuttles between the story of a young gangster of today and that of the nineteenth-century Haitian freedom fighter Toussaint L'Ouverture. Ali Lewis's *Everybody Jam* takes its readers to the Australian Outback, whereas Rachel Campbell-Johnston's *The Child's Elephant* deals with the plight of child soldiers in Uganda. William Sutcliffe's *The Wall* examines the problems of Israeli settlements in Gaza. The almost mythic cycle of stories in Marcus Sedgwick's *Midwinterblood*, all set on a remote island in the North, travels from the present to the ancient Nordic past. The dystopic world of Sally Gardner's *Maggot Moon*, finally, at first sight reminds one of representations of totalitarian states like Nazi Germany, the GDR or other Communist countries but soon reveals itself as a future Britain under a government that might have risen had Hitler won the Second World War.

In sum, 14 of the 24 books on the Carnegie shortlists of those three years confront their readers with an experience of alterity in historical or geographical terms. This alterity also includes a plurality of childhood concepts, the common denominator of which is that these childhoods are far from safe. The – to Western European/British contemporary child readers – unfamiliar settings generally represent a potential threat to the childhoods represented within them. However, it is not the alterity of the settings as such that generates the threat. The books do not insinuate that childhood thrives best in the surroundings a Western European middle-class affective family ideally provides. The conflicts the protagonists encounter are brought about by political, social or economic crises as well as by natural catastrophes. It is significant that all these crises are not represented as intrinsic to the alterity of the setting; therefore, the resolutions of the conflicts do not necessitate an assimilation of the different space or time to the condition of the contemporary readers' experiential world, either. Instead, the texts convey to their readers that childhood exists in a plurality of appearances and that these different shapes of childhood have equal validity and legitimation.

Besides, the notion of crisis in the shortlisted books is by no means confined to the alterity of settings. In general, almost all novels relate stories of extreme experience, exposing their characters to what may be called the 'darker' sides of life. Take, for instance, the Carnegie shortlists of 2013: In Sarah Crossan's verse novel *The Weight of Water*, young Polish immigrant Kasienka strives to begin a new life in a world (the UK) where she is not welcome, whereas her mother must realise that she has been abandoned by her husband. In Roddy Doyle's *A Greyhound of a Girl*, four generations of Irish women ultimately re-establish lost family bonds over a common *Trauerarbeit*. Standish, the underdog hero in *Maggot Moon*, engages in a desperate but futile fight against a totalitarian regime. *In Darkness* gives voice to gangster kid Shorty, who has been trapped after an earthquake and reflects on his life, and his memories are linked to the history of a nineteenth-century freedom fighter. *Midwinterblood* recycles a story of love, violence and sacrifice through the centuries. August, the grossly disfigured protagonist of R.J. Palacio's *Wonder* struggles for acceptance among his peers. The heroines in *Code Name Verity* experience torture and death during their missions in Nazi-occupied France. Even Dave Shelton's *A Boy and a Bear in a Boat* exposes its eponymous protagonists to increasing deprivation as the book turns out to be a boy-and-a-bear-in-a-boat version of *Waiting for Godot*.

Similar bleakness characterises the list of 2014: *All the Truth That's in Me* tells the story of Judith, a girl who was abducted from her Puritan settlement home for two years, then sent back with her tongue cut, who is now shunned by the entire village community, including her own family. *The Child's Elephant* and *The Wall* plunge their protagonists into deadly danger caused by political conflicts: they respectively address the plight of African child soldiers and the poisoned relationship between Palestinians and Israelis. The cultural conflict between Native Americans and colonial settlers lies at the heart of *Ghost Hawk*. Anne Fine's *Blood Family* is more domestic: it deals with traumatisation through child abuse. Even the two most light-hearted books on the list, *Rooftoppers* and Rebecca Stead's *Liar & Spy* take their protagonists through the anxieties of the potential bereavement of a parent and the feeling of being an outsider in the community. The Carnegie medallist of 2014, Kevin Brooks's *The Bunker Diary,* is perhaps the darkest story of all: said diary records the protagonist's last weeks of life, which he spends in a bunker where he and five other characters have been abducted and incarcerated by a mysterious stranger. Nothing is revealed about the identity or motivation of the man who seems to enjoy watching and torturing anxious beings in his very own perverse, subterranean Big Brother container.

The list of experiences to which characters and readers are exposed in these books includes bereavement, grief, social isolation, illness and handicap, displacement, violence, domestic abuse, war, crime, drug addiction, extreme poverty, exposure to arbitrary violence and oppression, abduction, loss of home, friends or parents. Not only are the characters frequently confronted with death, in five books the protagonists eventually die: *Midwinterblood* is a constant cycle of death and life; in *Code Name Verity*, one protagonist must shoot the other; in *Ghost Hawk*, the first-person narrator dies halfway through the book, and the other protagonist dies at the end; and medallists of 2013 (*Maggot Moon*) and 2014 end with the deaths of their protagonists while the environment that has caused their deaths remains apparently unchanged and largely unscathed. With such a body count, the books on the Carnegie shortlists certainly do not endorse a view of childhood that advocates sparing the child from dark topics unless some hope is offered in the end. They not only represent worlds in which childhood is not a safe place, they also unsettle the notion of safety as such among their readership who is expected to be able to process and cope with stories that challenge accustomed values, experiential frames and story plotlines. In other words, the novels on the Carnegie list are 'novels' in the very sense of the literary genre that developed in the attempt to present readers with new experiences.

The challenge to the child readers' cognitive, intellectual and affective abilities and competence also applies to the narrative techniques deployed in the books. With its focus on the literary quality of its listed books, the Carnegie Medal supports writing for young readers that explores the entire range of possibilities of narrative strategies contemporary literature offers without regard to readers' age. Even the most cursory glance at contemporary British children's literature reveals that narration in this literature is far from simple: fragmented narratives with a non-linear handling of time (*All the Truth*), multiperspectival narration (*Blood Family, In Darkness, Wonder, Trash, Code Name Verity*) or unreliable narration (*Liar & Spy, Code Name Verity*) are some of the narrative modes that have by now assumed a firm place in contemporary literature for children and young adults. Other techniques include verse narrative (*Weight of Water*), iconotextual narration in word and image (Patrick Ness's *A Monster Calls* or the embedded flip graphic tale in *Maggot Moon*), multigeneric narration (see the shift of genres in *Midwinterblood*) and the extreme reductionism of *The Bunker Diary* or the Beckettian *A Boy and a Bear in a Boat*, in which nothing actually happens, while the characters are gradually deprived of almost any object that could distract them on their existential journey.

Since prize lists like the Carnegie shortlist explicitly favour such demanding techniques of storytelling, they simultaneously create an implied readership able to face the challenges of complex narrative structures. Through their criteria and selection, they construe readers who – no matter how young they are – engage critically with the narratives instead of merely consuming books for entertainment. They are expected not to trust the narrator, not to trust the obvious on the text's surface but to explore connotations. The readers of those books are invited to assume a vantage point observing plot, characters and setting rather than getting fully absorbed into the story. In other words, the Carnegie shortlists favour texts presupposing readers who are veritable agents, active readers rather than passive consumers. Such readers can make a distinction between fictional worlds and reality. They may empathise with protagonists, thus processing and assimilating vicarious experiences of alterity, but they do not mindlessly identify with the characters or worlds they encounter. The concept of childhood behind such ideal readers is one of a rational childhood with high cognitive capacities that may prove to need less sheltered protection and more challenges than commonly assumed.

The choice of narrators in those novels further encourages this reflective, critical attitude. Almost all the listed books use homodiegetic first-person narrators, but the respective novels exemplify succinctly the falsity of the assumption that first-person narrators automatically ask for identification, especially in books for children. The opposite seems to be the case for the books on the Carnegie lists: here, the first-person narrators first and foremost insist on their own alterity as they introduce themselves as special, hence different. They may ask other characters as well as readers for empathy; however, they hardly ask the readers to identify with them but insist on their uniqueness as individuals. This renders them 'others', not only for their community in the story world but also for their readers. The narrators tend to invite the readers (either directly or implicitly) to adapt a critical distance to the related events, actions or characters and to find a way to face alterity and plurality while neither rejecting nor idealising them. In the narratives, this stance may be supported by the use of multiple focalisation or unreliable narration, which makes the readers question the narrator as an instance and leaves them to their own critical judgement.

More significantly, the plots told in the respective novels are not necessarily plots of inclusion because these plots do not actually aim at finally integrating a former outsider into the happy embrace of a community. The novels rather emphasise consistently the individual agency of the outsider protagonist, whose peculiarities are precisely the desirable assets of the characters, which should be supported and enhanced instead of being watered down by assimilating the protagonist into a community. The integrative plot pattern of the traditional *Bildungsroman* or novel of initiation is at least partly abandoned when the plot endings of the shortlisted novels describe the formation of alternative communities or, more radically, even favour the protagonist's death over an all-too-neat dissolution of the self into a community. The denouements in *Liar & Spy*, *All the Truth*, *Rooftoppers*, *The Wall* or David Almond's *My Name Is Mina*, for instance, do not jettison the outsider character of their respective protagonists, but allow the protagonists to find new communities for themselves, fostering alternative values than those of the general community, which is often presented in a very critical light. The novels thus favour a radical individualism, juxtaposed to the common call for inclusion into a society where differences are levelled as much as possible. This radical individualism lays great emphasis on ethical choices; it may be considered a counterpoise to the notion of what has been called post-individualism: that is, the definition of self through one's inclusion into social communities or networks rather than identification via distinctions. This radical individualism entails a veritable imperative for plurality as it demands readers accept the existence not only of diverse identities but also of the legitimacy of diverse family structures, peer group relationships and, in the end, concepts of childhood.

Having said this, I ought to add that embracing a plurality of childhood concepts in the Carnegie shortlists necessarily also includes the traditional childhood concept, which I previously called idealised, Romantic or preservationist. After all, some of the listed books do contain happy endings, integrative solutions to conflicts or glimpses of hope. Such consolatory endings can be found, for example, in the intergenerational reunion in *A Greyhound of a Girl* or in the harmonious conflict solutions in Lissa Evans's *Small Change for Stuart* or Annabel Pitcher's *My Sister Lives on the Mantelpiece*. *In Darkness* and *Wonder* even bend the plotlines into almost *tour de force* happy endings. The tearful moral conversion of teenage gangster Shorty, who after his rescue forsakes his criminal career and asks his mother for forgiveness, comes so abrupt it appears a contrived, inconsistent and quite dissatisfying ending to the otherwise bleak worlds of *In Darkness*. In *Wonder*'s concluding chapters, the school headmaster awards the grotesquely disfigured protagonist August at the school year's closing ceremony with a prize for the best personality – very much like Albus Dumbledore's yearly giveaway of extra points for special heroism that help Gryffindor win the Hogwarts House Cup. This sugary ending, reminding readers that true beauty lies within and that marginalised characters are most likely to turn out to be morally outstanding, has already been prepared for because *Wonder*, despite using multiperspectival narration, has only given voice to those characters who eventually accept August and support his integration into the community. The few characters who refuse to accept August until the very end of the novel are not given a voice; they thus remain the actual outsiders of a narrative of which the inclusion plotline is largely a self-fulfilling prophecy. In *Wonder*, the imperative for a happy, hopeful ending therefore creates a narrative that deliberately limits its own potential. Is it a coincidence that most of the traditional happy endings are provided by US American authors? This is, of course, a rhetorical question; yet it would be interesting to explore it further, because it seems indeed as if European authors are more daring in this respect. A striking example of unmonitored multiperspectival narration is, for instance, German author Kristen Boie's *Erwachsene reden, Marco hat etwas getan*. This short novel for ten-year-old readers records the statements of various inhabitants of a small town where a home for asylum seekers had been set to fire, causing the death of some refugees. The statements present a wide range of opinions from racist supporters of the arsonist to advocates of the refugees. As the novel abstains from a third-person narrative voice that comments on or even just connects the statements, the readers are asked to take position without external monitoring.

Conclusion

Contemporary children's and young adult books on recent Carnegie Medal shortlists provide experiences of alterity and plurality in various ways. They present childhoods in different historical, cultural and social constellations. While doing so, they make no attempt at homogenising these different manifestations and experiences of childhood but highlight the plurality and contingency of childhoods as well as of individual experiences. However, the Carnegie Medal's approach to children's literature and its concomitant endorsement of a plurality of childhoods is not uncontested. The common mingling of prestige and scandal one can find in the context of any cultural prize (English 2005, esp. Chapter 9) is not unfamiliar when it comes to literary prizes for children, either. Reviews of the Carnegie Medal's shortlisted books have continuously voiced harsh criticism of the jury's supposed predilection for dark books that are, according to the reviewers, actually unsuitable for children. When Kevin Brooks's *Bunker Diary* won this year's Medal, critic and novelist Amanda Craig announced she "refused to review it on publication", because the novel is devoid of hope: "It is the latest in a trajectory for the Carnegie prize which nobody who loves children's books can possibly applaud". Lorna Bradbury, in another review, calls the book a "uniquely sickening read", and reminds her readers that Brooks had difficulties finding a publisher because of its hopeless ending. She deplores the fact that the book had been published without flagged warnings about its content and fears that the Medal will increase its readership. Her explicit appeal to adults (she uses an unspecified "we") to control what their children watch and read, and her admission that the book may have its place in monitored reading groups as a basis for discussing hostage-taking or abuse precisely identifies her as an advocate of the preservationist childhood concept I mentioned earlier. Her view of childhood, which she apparently shares with a considerable number of others, is one that demands a safe comfort zone for at least this period of life – and if one considers the current discussions evolving around trigger warnings at universities, one may wonder if that safe space, traditionally associated with childhood, is supposed to be expanded – and childhood with it, too.

Besides, Bradbury chastises the book for presenting only the bunker scenario, which is "extremely close to real life, for one thing – or to what it might hold at one troubling extreme. And there's no distancing alternative-world scenario at work". In other words, Bradbury presupposes a reading of the text that perceives the story world as a reality that will inevitably be connected with the reader's reality. Hence, the absence of an alternative to the bleak, represented world may lure the readers into believing their reality is as bleak as Brooks's fiction. That a narrative can create distance through other means than the mere story contents (see my previous elucidations on narrative strategies) is all too easily overlooked by critics who similarly confine children's reading experience to the reception of a story. Apparently, Craig's and Bradbury's concept of childhood implies a readership with considerably less developed cognitive faculties, literacy skills and critical potential than the Carnegie Medal. I argue that it is a great asset of the Carnegie Medal that it does not endorse such a homogenising, universalising view of childhood as a well-protected comfort zone. The focus on the literary value of children's books detaches the books from legitimation by external factors and asserts their place within the field of literature as a form of art. More importantly, such a take on children's literature allows for a plurality of childhood concepts in the represented stories as well as in the readership it envisages. By awarding books that deliberately deviate from traditional, especially from idealising, views of childhood, the Carnegie Medal encourages a literature for children that counters debilitating idealisations and instead offers a challenge to its readers, taking them seriously and demanding from them the ability to tackle the plurality of their world. If children's literature only provided safe havens and comfort zones, on the other hand, it would run the risk of becoming a mere mirror of Narcissus, obliterating the alterity and plurality confronting contemporary children and childhood.

Notes

1 This general relevance of children's book awards is, of course, not restricted to Britain. See, for instance, the essays by Anne Morey or Erica Hateley on the impact of literary prizes on various cultural fields in the US or Australia, respectively.
2 For instance, the two other highly prestigious awards for children's books in Britain, the Costa Children's Book Award and the Guardian Children's Fiction Prize, do not include similar criteria checklists on their otherwise quite elaborate websites. Instead, they emphasise their own special features, namely that the Costa Award has children's books and books for adults compete on equal terms for the Costa Book of the Year Award and that the Guardian Children's Fiction Prize is an award whose jury entirely consists of other children's writers. The Children's Book Prize (formerly Red House Book Award) takes pride in being entirely voted for by readers, yet its criteria, too, remain uncertain as the shortlists basically emerge from an online voting system.
3 The list of postgraduate programmes on children's literature in the UK, compiled by Pat Pinsent and Kimberley Reynolds for Charles Butler's *Teaching Children's Fiction* (2006), accordingly mentions nine such programmes. Only three of them focus exclusively on children's literature, two are specialisations within general English Literature programmes and four are situated within Master of Education programmes (177–80).
4 The most prominent example from Western European children's literature that has fallen under this verdict is probably Astrid Lindgren's *Pippi Longstocking*.
5 Whereas such didactics have already become firmly rooted in some German curricula (for instance in North Rhine-Westphalia), in the UK, the National Curriculum may yet prevent the most dire consequences if it continues – as it does at present – retaining certain standard procedures of literary criticism among its major goals in the subject of English – if only at later stages.

References

Almond, David. 2010. *My Name is Mina*. London: Hodder.
Berry, Julie. 2013. *All the Truth That's in Me*. London: Templar.
Boie, Kristen. 1994. *Erwachsene reden, Marco hat etwas getan*. Hamburg: Oetinger.
Bradbury, Lorna. 2014. "The Bunker Diary: Why Wish this Book on a Child?" *The Telegraph*, June 24. Accessed 9 September 2014. www.telegraph.co.uk/culture/books/10920101/The-Bunker-Diary-why-wish-this-book-on-a-child.html.

Brooks, Kevin. 2013. *The Bunker Diary*. London: Puffin.
Buckingham, David. 2000. *After the Death of Childhood: Growing Up in the Age of Electronic Media*. Cambridge: Polity.
Campbell-Johnston, Rachel. 2013. *The Child's Elephant*. Oxford: David Fickling Books.
CILIP Carnegie Medal. 2016. Accessed 8 October 2016. www.cilip.org.uk/.
Cooper, Susan. 2013. *Ghost Hawk*. London: Bodley Head.
Craig, Amanda. 2014. "The Bunker Diary: Should Books Have Happy Endings?" *The Independent*, June 25. Accessed 9 September 2014. www.independent.co.uk/arts-entertainment/books/features/the-bunker-diary-should-books-have-happy-endings-9560752.html.
Crossan, Sarah. 2012. *The Weight of Water*. London: Bloomsbury.
de Nooy, Wouter. 1989. "Literary Prizes: Their Role in the Making of Children's Literature." *Poetics* 18: 199–213.
Department for Education. 2013. *The National Curriculum in England: Key Stages 1 and 2 Framework Document*, September. Accessed 9 September 2014. www.gov.uk/government/uploads/system/uploads/attachment_data/file/425601/PRIMARY_national_curriculum.pdf.
Doyle, Roddy. 2011. *A Greyhound of a Girl*. London: Marion Lloyd Books.
Dücker, Burckhard. 2013. "Literaturpreise und -wettbewerbe im deutsch- und englischsprachigen Raum." In *Handbuch Kanon und Wertung: Theorien, Instanzen, Geschichte*, edited by Gabriele Rippl and Simone Winko, 215–21. Stuttgart: Metzler.
Duncan, Diane. 2009. *Teaching Children's Literature: Making Stories Work in the Classroom*. London: Routledge.
English, James F. 2005. *The Economy of Prestige: Prizes, Awards, and the Circulation of Cultural Value*. Cambridge, MA: Harvard University Press.
Evans, Lissa. 2011. *Small Change for Stuart*. London: Doubleday.
Fine, Anne. 2013. *Blood Family*. London: Doubleday.
Frey, Charles, and John Griffith. 1987. *The Literary Heritage of Childhood: An Appraisal of Children's Classics in the Western Tradition*. Westport, CT: Greenwood Press.
Gardner, Sally. 2012. *Maggot Moon*. London: Hot Key Books.
Hartnett, Sonya. 2010. *The Midnight Zoo*. London: Walker.
Hateley, Erica. 2016. "Visions and Values: The Children's Book Council of Australia's Prizing of Picture Books in the Twenty-First Century." In *Canon Constitution and Canon Change in Children's Literature*, edited by Bettina Kümmerling-Meibauer and Anja Müller, 205–21. London: Routledge.
Kidd, Kenneth. 2007. "Prizing Children's Literature: The Case of Newbery Gold." *Children's Literature* 35: 166–90.
Lake, Nick. 2012. *In Darkness*. London: Bloomsbury.
Lewis, Ali. 2011. *Everybody Jam*. London: Andersen.
Morey, Anne. 2016. "The Junior Literary Guild and the Making of New Canonical Works: The Case of Waterless Mountain." In *Canon Constitution and Canon Change in Children's Literature*, edited by Bettina Kümmerling-Meibauer and Anja Müller, 189–204. London: Routledge.
Müller, Anja. 2009. *Framing Childhood in Eighteenth-Century English Periodicals and Prints, 1689–1789*. Farnham: Ashgate.

———. 2011. "Identifying an Age-Specific English Literature for Children." In *Mediating Identities in Eighteenth-Century England: Public Negotiations, Literary Discourses, Topography*, edited by Isabel Karremann and Anja Müller, 17–30. Farnham: Ashgate.
Mulligan, Andy. 2010. *Trash*. Oxford: David Fickling Books.
Ness, Patrick. 2011. *A Monster Calls*. London: Walker.
Palacio, R.J. 2012. *Wonder*. London: Bodley Head.
Pinsent, Pat, and Kimberley Reynolds. 2006. "Children's Literature at Postgraduate Level in the United Kingdom." In *Teaching Children's Fiction*, edited by Charles Butler, 172–80. Basingstoke: Palgrave.
Pitcher, Annabel. 2011. *My Sister Lives on the Mantelpiece*. London: Orion.
Reinfandt, Christoph. 1997. *Der Sinn der fiktionalen Wirklichkeiten: Ein systemtheoretischer Entwurf zur Ausdifferenzierung des englischen Romans vom 18. Jahrhundert bis zur Gegenwart*. Heidelberg: Winter.
Rundell, Katherine. 2013. *Rooftoppers*. London: Faber & Faber.
Sedgwick, Marcus. 2011. *Midwinterblood*. London: Indigo.
Sepetys, Ruta. 2011. *Between Shades of Grey*. New York: Penguin.
Shelton, Dave. 2012. *A Boy and a Bear in a Boat*. Oxford: David Fickling Books.
Stahl, John Daniel. 1992. "Canon Formation: A Historical and Psychological Perspective." In *Teaching Children's Literature: Issues, Pedagogy, Resources*, edited by Glenn Edward Sadler, 12–21. New York: The Modern Language Association of America.
Stead, Rebecca. 2012. *Liar & Spy*. London: Andersen Press.
Stevenson, Deborah. 2009. "Classics and Canons." In *The Cambridge Companion to Children's Literature*, edited by Andrea Immel and Matthew Grenby, 108–23. Cambridge: Cambridge University Press.
Sutcliffe, William. 2013. *The Wall*. London. Bloomsbury.
Wein, Elizabeth. 2012. *Code Name Verity*. London: Electric Monkey.

2 The Adult within the Literary Child
Reading Toby Litt's *deadkidsongs* as an Anti-*Bildungsroman*

Katharina Pietsch and Tyll Zybura[1]

Introduction

In this chapter, we read Toby Litt's novel *deadkidsongs* (2001) as representative of a trend in British novels to negotiate the constructedness of children and childhood. We argue that *deadkidsongs*, which presents a child reader responding to an adult author's fatally failing attempt to construct his own childhood as nostalgic and whole, makes contrastive use of tropes associated with the *Bildungsroman* genre to deconstruct hegemonic notions of childhood. Through its extravagant formal experimentation, the novel exposes ideological investments in the concept of childhood and forces readers into a position of reflexive sense-making that disturbs and questions their own conceptions of childhood.

Representations of childhood in British literature marketed to adults not only increased quantitatively toward the end of the twentieth century (Dinter 2016, 2–3; Dodou 2012, 238; Schneider 2006, 148), they also became increasingly self-aware and critical of the category of childhood itself (Dodou 2012, 238, 249). As Sandra Dinter argues, such contemporary British novels, as an effect of late modern destabilisation of certainties as well as heightened anxieties concerning childhood in Britain since the Thatcher years, tend to scrutinise hegemonic notions of childhood and highlight its constructedness (2016, 1–8). A literary form that has come under critical investigation is the *Bildungsroman* ('novel of formation') – the genre in which childhood was predominantly represented in British literature in the tradition of Charles Dickens's *David Copperfield*, *Great Expectations* and Charlotte Brontë's *Jane Eyre* before the recent diversification and complication. Closely tied to the grand narratives of development, maturation and refinement, the *Bildungsroman*'s formation plot negotiates the distinctly modern importance growing up has for our understanding of what it means to be fully human and thus contributes to the constitution of the adult–child opposition as one of the fundamental cultural binaries of modern Western societies: in modernity, adulthood is conceived of as the arrival at a state of stability, a fixing of identity after the risky developmental time of childhood.

While, as Georgia Christinidis (2016, 307) points out in her study of the history of the genre, the *Bildungsroman* was already critical of the possibility for self-realisation and actualisation, it nevertheless retains the utopian ideal of *Bildung* and features a step-by-step progression of the protagonist's path toward maturity. In its diachronic focus on children as "human becomings" (Qvortrup 1985, 132) and the utopian privileging of the adult's status as a valuable member of society, the classical *Bildungsroman* reinforces the idea of childhood as a glorious phase of innocence and ignorance that must be left behind, under pains of adapting to the social context, to become a 'full' human being. While the developmentalist view on childhood and adulthood privileged in modernity is an integral part of the *Bildungsroman* genre even through its historical and contemporary transformations (Boes 2006, 239), in late modernity those modern notions of childhood and adulthood come into question, and "the aspect of development […] fades from the spotlight" (Dinter 2016, 3).

As Anja Müller observes in her contribution to this volume, contemporary children's literature increasingly focuses on protagonists in opposition to society instead of on their integration and assimilation. In literature written by and marketed for adults, Margarida Morgado even sees the transition from the *Bildungsroman* to a new genre of the 'child novel', beginning with Henry James's *The Turn of the Screw*, which focuses on adult negotiations of children's world views and voices, "revolv[ing] around a child protagonist or group of children who usually do not grow up into adulthood" (1998, 210). However, this new genre cannot be neatly separated from the *Bildungsroman*: nor has the *Bildungsroman* been uniform and without self-critical experimentation nor have novels of growth and formation gone out of fashion. Rather, it is useful to think of many contemporary novels about childhood as showing a thematic and formal awareness of the tropes of the *Bildungsroman* as foil and as positioning themselves in contrast or even opposition to those tropes. Many works do not reference the *Bildungsroman* – as expert scholars of the genre would – with appreciation of the complexities and self-reflexivity already inherent in the genre but rather use its stereotypical features and tropes that establish patterns of contrast and correspondence to a sufficient degree to be recognisable in order to then defamiliarise and subvert them.

On the one hand, formation stories of queer and/or migrant protagonists in novels like Jeanette Winterson's *Oranges Are Not the Only Fruit* (1985), Hanif Kureishi's *The Buddha of Suburbia* (1990), Meera Syal's *Anita and Me* (1996) or Diana Evans's *26a* (2005) defamiliarise the typically white, Western and male maturation plot. On the other hand, we can observe a thematic change toward a critical investigation of *Bildungsroman* tropes themselves as well as an increase in formal complexity that subverts the linearity of the formation trope or the idea of coherent teleological development and stages the thematic critique in terms of form. Doris Lessing's *The Fifth Child* (1988) defies all expectations pertaining to the enculturation of its title character Ben into society through social institutions, mainly the nuclear family he lives in, the asylum and the education system. Even more importantly, the novel refuses to make Ben's subjectivity accessible through internal focalisation or to deliver an explanation for his 'condition' and to resolve the problem he poses to the social order through narrative progression and character development while highlighting the violent aspects of the enculturation and normalisation processes to which he is subjected (Dinter 2016, 135). A.S. Byatt's *The Children's Book* (2009) is structured in three parts that follow a reversed mythical order of decline instead of maturation from "The Golden Age" through "The Silver Age" to "The Age of Lead". This structure corresponds to the character arcs of most of the novel's child characters. While their childhoods, constructed as carefree and blissful Golden Ages, are full of potential, their growing up ends when they are traumatised, maimed or killed in the First World War or end up as collateral damage of their parents' artistic ambition. Instead of attaining self-realisation, the child characters in *The Children's Book* are self-realisations of adults. In highlighting adult investment in children as opposed to the hegemonic conception of growing up as a fulfilment of human potential, *The Children's Book* is highly critical of the *Bildungsroman*'s coming-of-age plot. Toby Litt's *deadkidsongs* launches a similar criticism as is already suggested in the naming of its four parts "Summer", "Autumn", "Winter" and "Winter, Also", which frustrates the expectation of 'Spring' as the optimistic closure to a tumultuous coming-of-age journey. Instead, in its adult author's failure to construct and cohere his own childhood narrative after *Bildungsroman* fashion, *deadkidsongs* foregrounds the violence of adult investment in childhood.

Opposing the literary utopia of self-realisation, these novels refuse to buy into a developmentalist ideology of adult betterment and self-actualisation but rather present a dystopic view of the adult–child binary: instead of representing childhood as an inherently linear progression from innocence to experience, ignorance to knowledge and dependency to autonomy, they foreground how childhood is determined by the power structures of the generational order. For these protagonists, growing up means being subject to adult investments, in a violently destructive sense.

Scholarship on literary childhoods usually focuses on the thematic deconstruction of childhood, but, as Morgado has argued, "[t]he complexity and relevance of fictional children are approachable only when one considers the thematic significance *together with* the modes of its construction in the text, content and form" (1998, 225, emphasis in original). While the dominant formal features of classical *Bildungsroman* novels support the coherence of the formation plot, many contemporary novels about children break up the linear, teleological narrative patterns readers associate with stories of development and maturation (Christinidis 2012, 472) through formal complexities and subversions. The first-person narrator of Dickens's *David Copperfield* (1850), who overtly writes his own coming-of-age story from the position of a mature and stable adult identity, is typical for the *Bildungsroman* and its emphasis on an individual's subjectivity as the centre of narrative coherence. Even the modernist stream-of-consciousness experimentation in, for instance, James Joyce's *A Portrait of the Artist as a Young Man* (1916) is meant to reflect the growing complexity and maturity of the protagonist's world view and mind in his struggle for emancipation and autonomy. In contrast, contemporary fictionalisations of children and childhood which complicate and subvert narrative forms typical for the *Bildungsroman* critically expose the very constructedness and contingency of current meanings of 'adult' and 'child'. Thus, the novelty of these texts is not merely their nondevelopmentalist view on childhood but that through their negotiation of literary conventions of representing children and childhood they facilitate a meta-perspective of childhood as a construction. In order to do justice to the intricacies of form that are part and parcel of literary investigations of childhood, we therefore need not only thematic deconstructions of childhood informed by insights from childhood studies and critical theory but also a focus on detailed narratological analysis.

In this chapter, we explore how this is done by reading Toby Litt's novel *deadkidsongs* thematically and narratologically as an anti-*Bildungsroman* which questions hegemonic notions of growing up as attaining a stable and autonomous adult identity. In foregrounding how adulthood is constitutive for childhood, the text deconstructs the adult–child binary and its *Bildungsroman* ideal of self-realisation. Taking our cue from critical investigations of other fundamental binaries like man–woman, white–black, heterosexual–homosexual and so on, we assume that 'adult' defines itself by denying, dismissing and subordinating its opposite, the 'child'. Thereby, it constitutes itself as the privileged position, which grants it the right to be represented as normal, universal, superior, prestigious and unmarked, whereas the other, the child, is represented as inferior, special, deviant, abnormal and marked. We go beyond an understanding of this binary as a mutual, symmetrical construction and trace how adulthood is not only constitutive for childhood as its opposite but also as its very founding principle within the construction of the child and childhood, deliberately looking for the 'adult within' the literary child.[2] Underlying this approach is the formal analysis, which shows how this construction work inherently relies on a complex constellation of communicative frames, narrative voices, perspectives or ways of presenting consciousness, narratorial contradictions and omissions and genre references. In combination, these formal features fundamentally constitute the novel's adult investments in children and childhood.

Childhood as Found Manuscript

Deadkidsongs's complex narrative structure begins with the introduction of a frame narrator, Matthew, who finds a manuscript in his father's desk after his father hanged himself on the day before Matthew's fourteenth birthday. The following embedded narrative is the content of this manuscript, which we read along with Matthew, who returns as a frame narrator in a second short section before the last chapter and again in a third at the very end to conclude the narrative (the frame narrative is unpaginated and will be referred to as first, second and third sections).

The manuscript portrays the childhood of four young English boys: Andrew, Matthew, Paul and Peter, who have formed "Gang", with capital G and no article, a group with military-like structures and procedures, to prepare themselves for an imaginary impending war. Led by 'Sergeant' Andrew, the four members of Gang live a stereotypical boys' childhood: they climb trees, ride bicycles, enact battles with toy planes, go on secret missions, build fires and equip themselves with matches, Swiss Army knives, catapults and chocolate bars. When Matthew suddenly dies of meningitis, Andrew, Paul and Peter blame his grandparents (who raised him and his sister Miranda) and develop a revenge plan to kill them. The narrative performs the constant identity construction of Gang and the negotiation of its meaning. Gang as a "foursquareness" (Litt 2001, 291) and unity that lends the four boys strength and specialness they lack on their own *is* childhood in this text, a childhood the four boys as characters and as narrators construct for themselves as up against everything and everyone else: "The world was definitely out to get us. The only thing that could protect us from being got by the world was Gang" (181). Soon, however, Gang becomes the story's main contested issue: who controls it, who defines it, who belongs to it. In reading *deadkidsongs* as a text that provides a meta-perspective on childhood, the text's constant contestation of Gang foregrounds how childhood itself is its main contested issue. This contestation takes place not only among the four boys as characters but also on the level of narrative construction: the embedded narrative's switching from Gang as a first-person plural narrator who speaks and perceives as a coherent unit to a first-person singular, and eventually, third-person narrator attests not only to the breaking up of Gang's unity but also to a struggle for representational authority.

Although there is inconclusive and contradictory information in the manuscript, there is evidence that the frame narrator's father is either Paul or Peter, now a grown-up, and that he named his own son after

Matthew the member of Gang. While Matthew the frame narrator is not sure what to believe of it (second section), he accepts the manuscript as autobiographical material. The embedded narrative of the manuscript thus serves not only the father as an endeavour to make sense of his own childhood, but it also serves the son to make sense of his father and their relationship. In an attempt to find stability and closure, to close off his adulthood to the past, Matthew's father tries to write the story of Gang as his own formation plot – but fails as becomes apparent in the deterioration of the narrative on several levels, leading up to his eventual suicide.

The most obvious structural *Bildungsroman* reference is what appears to be the title of the manuscript: "Summer–Autumn–Winter–Spring" (1), which implies a stereotypical seasonal progression from happiness to hardship and by overcoming despair to an eventual new beginning in hope. But while chapters 1–4, 5–8 and 9–11 are divided by the respective seasonal epigraphs from summer to winter, chapters 12–14 bear the epigraph "Winter, Also", signifying the breakdown of teleological progression and undermining the possibility of new beginnings. The story ends with two different last chapters: chapter 14 is titled "Chapter Thirteen, Also" and bears a note from Matthew's father saying that this is the "true version", which is supposed to replace the first Chapter Thirteen. Although both Chapters Thirteen provide endings to the storyline narrated in the manuscript, neither chapter can be accepted at face value. In the first one, Andrew brutally kills Matthew's sister Miranda and their grandparents before committing suicide, while all four are still alive in the second chapter thirteen; this alternative ending presents a war scenario of a Nazi invasion of England in which the boys are rounded up and interrogated by enemy forces about the killing of Matthew's grandparents' dog as a part of their revenge plan.

Analogously to the formal-structural indicators, the narrative refuses resolution on the content level. The novel undermines notions of developmental progress that are usually used to legitimise the adult–child binary; it infuses the adult present with disturbing childhood pasts that lead to its self-obliteration and stresses – by means of the frame narrative of Matthew as reader of his father's failed sense-making – that these deadly disturbances live on in subsequent generations. The overt reference to teleological developmental narratives reminds us that narrative structure is used to support adult investment in adulthood as much as in childhood. Consequently, we will analyse three 'adults within' *deadkidsongs*: Andrew's father as the "Major-General" of Gang, whose abuse lies at the heart of how the boys conceptualise their own childhood as a training for war; Matthew's father as the author of the manuscript: and the reader, who is equally forced into a position of sense-making with regard to the notions of childhood and adulthood the novel explores.

Temporal Constructions of the Adult–Child Binary

The grand narrative of modernity, which is reproduced in the *Bildungsroman*, that is, the narrative of the development of the rational, responsible, morally refined, competent and mature subject, upholds itself in opposition to the child. Childhood as "a foundational product of the modern episteme" (Wallace 1995, 286) is a transitory state of both incompetence and innocence that is meant to be out-grown on a journey into the adult future and glorified in nostalgic reverence of the paradisiacal past (Alanen 2005; Nodelman 1992; Prout 2005).

In the embedded narrative of *deadkidsongs*, this adult–child temporality is upheld and complicated at the same time: the boys' self-conception is still structured along the familiar diachronic axis of growing up as a training for later life, the young as heirs to the future and of children as essentially different from adults. Gang's portrayal as performing such stereotypical children's activities as climbing trees, roaming outdoors, making grandiose plans and playing war employs hegemonic representations of children as immature and belonging to a world different from that of the domestic adults. At the same time, the temporal dimension of the adult–child binary in the embedded narrative is mainly constructed around the notion of a war between grown-ups and the young, with their parents and other adults imagined as "the enemy" (Litt 2001, 20, 40, 177). After Matthew's sudden death, it becomes imperative for the identity construction of Gang not to buy into the adult narrative that Matthew's death was a tragedy. In the story the boys construct for themselves, Matthew's death was caused by his grandparents' negligence to call the doctor in time. For Gang, Matthew is "[a] casualty in a war. The war between the Young and the Old" (349). Consequently, Andrew, Paul and Peter frame their revenge against Matthew's grandparents as "Operation Extinction" (ch. 8) after the extinction of ill-adapted dinosaurs in natural catastrophe, which then gave rise to the evolution of mammals and, eventually, humans (196–200). While, as Paul puts it, "[w]e are *Homo sapiens*. We are what survives and triumphs" (200), all adults inevitably become casualties: "Like the dinosaurs, they would fail to adapt, and like the dinosaurs, they would die" (101). Through the dinosaur metaphor, the adult–child temporality that the embedded narrative establishes on the story level is literally one of different species and thus undermines the hegemonic notion of biological and cultural reproduction in which children ensure the continuation of their parents' and culture's identity but instead emphasises the conflicting and violent aspects of the succession of the young. On the one hand, the two last chapters – Andrew's killing spree and the Nazi invasion fantasy – in their respective ways cater to the idea that children out of adult control become destructive because they lack adult morality and understanding (Schneider 2006, 152–3). On the other hand, the values that incite and structure Gang's destructive actions – honour, camaraderie, sacrifice, vengeance – are crucial to the adult, and especially masculine, ideology with which they grow up.

In sum, Matthew's father, in his childhood account, upholds the logic of developmental progression toward maturity but exposes how this logic fails: the boys do not grow out of their 'childishness' but rather remain caught up in 'adult' fantasies of war; their childhood cannot be conceived of as in any way independent of adult investment. Adult nostalgia for childhood innocence must break down because childhood in this novel turns out to be neither innocent nor so inconsequential that one can easily outgrow it and build a stable adult identity on overcoming it. What transcends and undermines the temporal dimension of the adult–child binary in *deadkidsongs* is abuse, violence and (self-)destruction, from which no emancipation is possible.

The Adult within: The Best Father

On the story level, the seemingly clear-cut binary opposition of children and adults is undermined most by the influences and investments of Andrew's father. We already learn on the second page of the embedded narrative that fathers play a crucial role in the hierarchy of Gang:

> The highest up the tree was Andrew, because we were all agreed that he had the best father. Then came Paul, whose father was a teacher. Then Matthew, whose father, as well as whose mother, was dead. Last and lowest of all was Peter, whose father came home late every day except Friday.
> (Litt 2001, 10)

In the course of the novel, it emerges that this hierarchy of fathers is based on their involvement in their sons' lives. In directly linking this involvement to the spatial hierarchy of the boys, the very first scene already deconstructs the division between the boys' self-created social unit in opposition to the adult world on which the childhood nostalgia of the manuscript's author is built, since it undermines the notion that Gang is established as independent of adult and parental involvement.

Andrew's father is the adult least distant from the boys' lives in several respects: he is involved in the boys' war games as the "Major-General", who sends Gang on mock military missions (40–57) and shapes the boys' ideology of hierarchy, punishment and strength-based masculinity. He teaches the boys how to build a fire, an activity of highly symbolic value, and he initiates the uniqueness of Gang as marked by the omission of an article. That this role constitutes Andrew's father as the most vital part of Gang is recorded in the rules of Gang: "6. Do not trust grown ups, except Andrew's Father who is the Secret Head of ~~the~~ Gang" (ch. 8, crossing out in original). In terms of narrative structure, Andrew's father is crucially involved in the story's turning point at which Gang decides to take revenge for Matthew's death. He provides the boys with the information that Matthew's grandparents should have called the doctor much sooner, and his social-Darwinian teachings of "survival of the fittest" are the source for Peter's dinosaur analogy.

The most significant influence the "Best Father" has on Gang, however, is his infectious violence. Andrew's father regularly and brutally abuses and tortures Andrew and his wife. Although the violence of Andrew's father against his son is regularly suggested, there is only one scene in which we witness it. This passage is foregrounded because part of it is told in stream-of-consciousness narration – tellingly the only instance where this stylistic device is used in the novel:

> I am stupid and inconsiderate and don't know how lucky I am and will go up to bed right now without having any of this lovely supper that my mother has cooked me look at that and just you wait and how did it happen anyway? (I reply, I explain about the fire-putting-out practice.) What am I trying to do, get myself killed? Not that anyone would give a shit anyway. I'm not exactly going to be a great loss to the world, am I? [...]
>
> (340)

This narrative technique of the interior monologue is commonly associated with modernist representation of a character's subjectivity and the ways in which this subjectivity perceives the world. While we find an individual and unique subjectivity in modernist stream-of-consciousness writing with the protagonist's mind at the centre – as, for instance, in Joyce's *A Portrait of the Artist as a Young Man* – here we find the father, the adult within: the text evokes Andrew's subjectivity and then shows us that it consists of his father's abusive and debasing words. He repeats in his mind what his father says to him in the first person, making his father's assertions his own, making them the truth about himself. In the rare instances when Andrew speaks himself, this is put in parentheses, marking it as insignificant. The singular use of this stylistic device highlights that something vitally important is happening here: the narrative blending of Andrew and Andrew's father represents how the adult is reproduced through his child; the son is obliterated and is only able to speak of himself in the abusive words of his father. This blending of Andrew and Andrew's father is the linchpin for the formation of Gang, for the seeming division of adulthood and childhood and for the war of adults against children. Andrew is created by his father's power to assert himself on and in Andrew so violently that Andrew becomes his creation: Andrew's strength, his will to inflict violence and his need to pass on violence and humiliation, his need to uphold the hierarchy of Gang and be leader all stem from his father's treatment of him. The novel declines both the idea of a rational and self-determined subject and the possibility of emancipation from the father, which are, again, tropes of the *Bildungsroman*. While for Joyce, stream-of-consciousness narration is the means to represent Stephen Dedalus's inner emancipation processes, in *deadkidsongs* it is used to show that for Andrew all attempts at self-realisation are in vain since his subjectivity only exists in relation to his father: there is no boy Andrew without this specific father.

However, the father's power creates more than Andrew as the boy he is. Gang only exists as the effect of that power. Not only is Andrew's father directly invested in Gang as the Major General and the "Secret Head of Gang", Gang is constituted out of Andrew's need to pass on the pain his father inflicts on him. This – not the playful forming of a children's social unit in opposition to the adult world – is Gang's raison d'être. Andrew's father's abuse of his son is the reason for Andrew's strong need to command and humiliate, which, as a "willingness to do more, to do worse, than the others would ever dare" (252) and an ability to tolerate violence done to him, translates, in the meaning-making of Gang, into a strength the other boys lack, as Paul remarks: "He doesn't mind being hit. I do. I blame my father for this. He hasn't taught me about pain like Andrew's father has" (190). Andrew as leader of Gang thus not only spreads his father's abuse but also represents the superiority of its ideology: "Through Andrew, the Best Father passed on his lessons to all of us" (54). This also undermines the novel's seeming alliance with the usual trivialisation of children's games: Gang, its activities, military ranks and the struggles for its hierarchies and meaning are deadly serious because they are founded in the ideological value system of Andrew's father and are upheld by Andrew to pass on the abuse he receives. In Andrew, parental abuse combined with an ideology of a masculine will to violence proves so pervasive that it constitutes Gang's hierarchical structure, its rituals of punishment and torture, its meaning as a fighting force and the inevitability of the boys' framing their lives as war. Since Gang is the tangible representation of childhood in this novel, the consequences for the adult–child binary are vast: Gang/childhood become evident as the vested interest of an abusive adult and abused child.

Although Andrew's father is by far the most obvious 'adult within', he does not actually constitute the exception in terms of adult investment in childhood in *deadkidsongs*. This comes into view in the recurring punishment theme: not only Andrew, but all the boys live in constant fear and expectation of being punished by their parents and other adults. This directly aligns Andrew's father with adult power in general and makes him and his investment in Gang representative of adulthood and the adult investment in childhood. In *deadkidsongs,* the power to punish, more than anything else, connects adults to children and *makes* children by the power structures of the generational order.

Authorial Investments: Matthew's Father

So far we have almost exclusively looked at the embedded narrative; now we will take the frame narrative and the rhetorical context in which it is produced into account, acknowledging that "narrative is not just story but also action, the telling of a story by someone to someone on some occasion for some purpose" (Phelan 1996, 8). As outlined above, the frame narrator Matthew finds the embedded narrative as a manuscript authored by his father, who is likely Gang's Paul or Peter. The questions of why the embedded story is being told and the effect it has on its reader, Matthew, introduce another 'adult within' to the literary childhood of *deadkidsongs*. In the second section of the frame narrative, we learn that Chapter Thirteen, Also "was handwritten, hastily", which lets Matthew assume that his father had written this last chapter directly before his suicide. This connects the question of which of the two ending chapters is the 'true' one directly to Matthew's father's suicide and hence to the whole act of writing the manuscript: what are Matthew's father's stakes in writing the story of Gang? Why did he write two completely contradictory versions of the last chapter? Why did he kill himself shortly after having finished the second Chapter Thirteen? Why does he eventually address the narrative to his son?

The inconsistencies of the embedded story – first among them the large variety of narrative situations, several factual contradictions and ominous omissions and especially the conflicting Chapters Thirteen – point toward the struggle of Matthew's father to produce a coherent narrative account of Gang (which also means a coherent account of his childhood). This narrative turns out to be unsuccessful, especially because the two conflicting endings do not provide closure. That the embedded story is told by a variety of different narrators stands in contrast to the *Bildungsroman*: Matthew's father does not manage to construct a narrator whose adult subjectivity provides stability and coherence to the narrative. As already indicated, another aspect that highlights the embedded narrative's lack of closure is that "Spring", the text's projected closing optimistic ending, is missing in the epigraphic seasonal progression. Matthew speculates that his father might have wanted to replace the first Chapter Thirteen with the second one but had "simply run out of time" (second section). This remark makes Matthew's father's suicide seem inevitable and out of his control rather than voluntary, an effect either of his unsuccessful attempt to produce a coherent narrative of his childhood or of his having been a member of Gang. As a member of Gang, Matthew's father inherited Andrew's father's violence and values, which stand in stark contrast to the nostalgic view on childhood – as a "time when life was that rarest of all things: truly good" (11) – he wants to narrate. His narration does not manage to uphold this "truly good" childhood, however, and as it finally collapses in the confused double ending, so does his life collapse in a suicide that parallels Andrew's suicide in the first Chapter Thirteen, which is also caused by Andrew's father's abuse and his ideology of violence. Paul, as narrator of this chapter, tells us how Andrew's suicide precisely follows the logic of Andrew's father's teachings:

> I knew his [Andrew's father's] heart must be filled with unbelievably immense pride. It was him, as the Major-General, who had told us never to allow the enemy to catch us alive. […] And there Andrew was, not caught, never caught.
>
> (418)

Again, as in the stream-of-consciousness passage in the previous chapter, Andrew's father's teachings assert themselves violently in Andrew, now obliterating him completely and inevitably.

If we read the embedded narrative as Matthew's father's attempt to write the story of Gang as his own *Bildungsroman* plot, then its ending should provide narrative closure in a stable identity of adulthood and fatherhood, a state of being that signifies full personhood and humanness and enables the self-realised subject to leave behind childhood as essentially different and worthy of nostalgia. But this is obviously what the embedded narrative fails to achieve: instead of leaving a glorious summer to overcome adolescent tumult and hardship of autumn and winter and to finally be reborn into a stable adult identity, the fourth part of the novel with its two conflicting endings prevents both the stabilising of narrative structure and the stabilising of the adult–child binary. In its refusal to follow the narrative pattern of the *Bildungsroman*, *deadkidsongs* also foregrounds the stabilisation of the adult–child binary as a main purpose of established *Bildungsroman* narratives.

Reader Investments: Matthew as Narratee

Deadkidsongs's deconstruction of tropes of emancipation and self-realisation becomes even more disturbing when we look more closely at the three short sections of the frame narrative. That Matthew is the ultimate addressee of his father's manuscript is apparent from a "security clearance" (first section) for Matthew, which his father added to the manuscript and which passes the task of sense-making on to his son – what he as author could not accomplish is supposed to fall to his son as reader now. This is an act of bequeathing and reproduction: children inherit their parents' meaning making because they themselves are always a vital part of it. By issuing clearance and clarifications as to how Matthew should regard certain parts of the manuscript, his father is no longer invested just in the writing, i.e. in his struggle for authorial control. He is also invested in Matthew as his reader.

That Matthew's relationship to his father changes through his reading of the manuscript becomes evident in the contrast between the first section of the frame narrative – before Matthew starts reading – and the third section – after he has finished. In the first section, Matthew is "hoisting [his] feet up onto [his father's] oh-so-sacred desk", suggesting a rather distanced relationship to his father in which, instead of an emotional reaction to his death, Matthew enjoys an act of transgression and irreverence. In the third section, when Matthew has finished reading the manuscript, he is eager to declare his father "was the best father to me. Just like *the* Best Father" (emphasis in original). On the one hand, he compares his father to Andrew's father because of the military jargon his father had used: "'Ignore all previous dispatches'. (My father had often talked to me like this, and now I understood where it came from: the Major-General.)" (third section). Since for Andrew's father the military jargon is a direct expression of his values and abuse, it can be assumed that Matthew's father shared these traits, most importantly the parental abuse. This parallel is emphasised by Matthew's eager triple repetition of the vindicating phrase "my father was a great man" (third section), which Andrew uses in the embedded narrative right after his father calls him "a little shit" and chides him for letting a girl break his nose: "I am grateful that my father is such a great and generous man" (366). In the same way that Andrew's father is the Best Father to the members of Gang because of his investment in the constitution of Gang, Matthew's father becomes the best father through his investment in his son's reading of the manuscript.

The frame narrator Matthew, too, is a boy created as the boy he is by his father's power: the power of storytelling, of providing a narrative where before there was just a "top secret" locked drawer, the power of disclosure. Matthew, too, only exists as the effect of that power, as the effect of his reading the manuscript, his father's attempt at the construction of a sense-making account of his childhood. In the same way that Andrew ends up as an epitome of his father's values, teachings and orders, cutting his own throat (418), Matthew's father is the adult within Matthew's reading of the text he leaves for him and within the boy that Matthew becomes through his meaning making of the embedded story. In the context of the *Bildungsroman,* this is another chilling and cynical reflection on enculturation and maturation as the process of continued violence and its vindication by the following generation: no generation seems to have the chance of self-actualisation, but every new generation is determined by an abusive imprinting of the former's broken narratives.

Conclusion

Set within the literary tradition of novels concerned with childhood and adulthood, most notably the traditional *Bildungsroman* it self-consciously references, the contemporary formal experimentation of *deadkidsongs* exemplifies the depriviliging of the monadic subject's individual development and instead stresses the protagonists' hierarchical dependencies, which exert extreme force to shape their lives. Adults, nominal representatives of the 'mature', self-actualised utopia, are manically self-obsessed in their attempts to shape their children in their own image, and the adult world is deconstructed as impossible to live in, not only for the children, but also for the adults. In *deadkidsongs*, read as an anti-*Bildungsroman*, identity is not stable, not something to grow into, not something in need of transformation or something that is *yours* at all: it is easily penetrated, violated, de- and reconstructed, falling apart, held together in its fragments by violence. Children *and* adults are possessed, invaded and obliterated by – paternal and paternalistic – rhetoric and narrative; but a narrative that fails in easy sense-making and in imposing structural unity on identity. Characters, authors and readers are exposed as being nothing but 'character' in someone else's story, ultimately giving up any naïve hope of self-actualisation. More than other novels, *deadkidsongs* exposes how modernity's grand narrative of the adult rational self depends on the stabilisation of the adult–child binary and by deconstructing the latter also deconstructs the former. Both the narrative form, which Matthew's father fails to gain control over, and the defamiliarising diegetic crassness of action disturb and overwhelm hegemonic notions of developmental progression and societal order traditionally associated with the *Bildungsroman*.

Not only Matthew is set the task to make sense out of the found manuscript – we as readers are also challenged to invest ourselves in a construction of the novel's children and childhood that allows for a meaningful, coherent interpretation of the novel. When readers try to answer the questions posed by the text, for instance, whether they believe that a child could commit the brutal murders and subsequent suicide in the first Chapter Thirteen and what the reasons for those actions might be, they inevitably construct children in a way that allows for their answer. As opposed to thematically similar narratives of male child violence and fall from innocence, like William Golding's *Lord of the Flies* (1954), which employs a conventional authorial and authoritative narrator, Litt and other contemporary novelists, by disturbing the narrative form, innovatively expose the problems of adult meaning making in the construction of literary children and childhoods. The text of *deadkidsongs* itself with its many instances of defamiliarisation constantly challenges its readers' attempts to reconcile hegemonic notions about childhood and adulthood with the narrative. Therefore, in its most radical strategy of providing a meta-perspective on childhood, it invites us to take note of our own meaning making and thus foregrounds *our* construction that is actually playing out here. The text exposes adult investment in the construction of the child precisely because, by referencing both familiar narrative structures of the *Bildungsroman* plot and a barrage of childhood stereotypes before frustrating both, it asks us as adult readers to invest ourselves in the construction of the children and childhood of the novel. Then it makes it very hard for us *not* to see how this investment is an attempt at meaning making that ultimately belongs to the reader, not the text, because the text refuses to comply with the reader's need to resolve the contradictions. Thus, the text lets us see that reading is never innocent, never free of power; in other words, meaning making is in itself power. With its overt narrative constructedness, Litt's novel challenges us *not* to resolve the inconsistencies because every conclusion about the 'nature' of children – which also means a conclusion about how children *should* be – implicates each of us as an 'adult within', as an authoritative instance with vested interests in the formation of the child.

Notes

1 This chapter was written in the context of the research project "Children and Childhood in Literature: Theory – Narratology – Criticism" at Bielefeld University, Germany, which is headed by Ralf Schneider and funded by the German Research Foundation (DFG). Parts of the textual analysis of *deadkidsongs* were first developed in Katharina Pietsch's MA thesis, Bielefeld University, 2016.
2 While proponents of the new sociology of childhood systematically distinguish between 'children' and 'childhood' – with children defined as social actors and childhood as a socially constructed category – (Corsaro 2011, 4; Honig 2009, 62), we do not adhere to this distinction here, because we treat both children and childhood and sometimes 'the child' (Wallace 1994, 173) as representations, endowed with the same set of cultural meanings.

References

Alanen, Leena. 2005. "Women's Studies/Childhood Studies: Parallels, Links and Perspectives." In *Children Taken Seriously: In Theory, Policy and Practice*, edited by Jan Mason and Toby Fattore, 31–45. London: Jessica Kingsley Publishers.
Boes, Tobias. 2006. "Modernist Studies and the Bildungsroman: A Historical Survey of Critical Trends." *Literature Compass* 3 (2): 230–43.
Byatt, A.S. 2009. *The Children's Book*. New York: Alfred A. Knopf.
Christinidis, Georgia. 2012. "Radical Transformation: Angela Carter's Adaptation of the *Bildungsroman*." *Textual Practice* 26 (3): 467–87.
———. 2016. "Genre, Canon-Formation, and Bildung: Transformations of a Critical Category." In *The Institution of English Literature: Formation and Mediation*, edited by Barbara Schaff, Johannes Schlegel, and Carola Surkamp, 295–310. Göttingen: V&R unipress.

Corsaro, William. 2011. *The Sociology of Childhood*. 3rd ed. Thousand Oaks, CA: Pine Forge Press.
Dickens, Charles. (1850) 2004. *David Copperfield*. London: Penguin Books.
Dinter, Sandra. 2016. "Childhood in Contemporary English Fiction: Contesting the Last Vestige of Essentialism." PhD diss., Bielefeld University.
Dodou, Katherina. 2012. "Examining the Idea of Childhood: The Child in the Contemporary British Novel." In *The Child in British Literature: Literary Constructions of Childhood, Medieval to Contemporary*, edited by Adrienne E. Gavin, 238–50. Basingstoke: Palgrave Macmillan.
Evans, Diana. 2005. *26a*. London: Vintage.
Golding, William. (1954) 1971. *Lord of the Flies*. London: Faber & Faber.
Honig, Michael. 2009. "How Is the Child Constituted in Childhood Studies?" In *The Palgrave Handbook of Childhood Studies*, edited by Jens Qvortrup et al., 62–77. Houndmills: Palgrave Macmillan.
Joyce, James. (1916) 2000. *A Portrait of the Artist as a Young Man*. London: Penguin Books.
Kureishi, Hanif. 1990. *The Buddha of Suburbia*. London: Faber & Faber.
Lessing, Doris. 1988. *The Fifth Child*. London: Cape.
Litt, Toby. 2001. *deadkidsongs*. London: Penguin.
Morgado, Margarida. 1998. "The Season of Play: Constructions of the Child in the English Novel." In *Children in Culture: Approaches to Childhood*, edited by Karín Lesnik-Oberstein, 204–30. Houndmills: Macmillan.
Nodelman, Perry. 1992. "The Other: Orientalism, Colonialism, and Children's Literature." *Children's Literature Association Quarterly* 17 (1): 29–35.
Phelan, James. 1996. *Narrative as Rhetoric: Technique, Audiences, Ethics, Ideology*. Columbus: Ohio State University Press.
Prout, Alan. 2005. *The Future of Childhood: Towards the Interdisciplinary Study of Children*. London and New York: RoutledgeFalmer.
Qvortrup, Jens. 1985. "Placing Children in the Division of Labour." In *Family and Economy in Modern Society*, edited by Paul Close and Rosemary Collins, 129–45. Houndmills: Macmillan.
Schneider, Ralf. 2006. "Literary Childhoods and the Blending of Conceptual Spaces: Transdifference and the Other in Ourselves." *Journal for the Study of British Cultures* 13 (2): 147–60.
Syal, Meera. (1996) 2004. *Anita and Me*. London: Harper Perennial.
Wallace, Jo-Ann. 1994. "De-scribing the *Water Babies*: 'The Child' in Post-colonial Theory." In *De-scribing Empire: Post-colonialism and Textuality*, edited by Chris Tiffin and Alan Lawson, 171–84. London: Routledge.
———. 1995. "Technologies of 'the Child': Towards a Theory of the Child-Subject." *Textual Practice* 9 (2): 285–302.
Winterson, Jeanette. (1985) 2014. *Oranges Are Not the Only Fruit*. London: Vintage.

3 The Child Narrator in Contemporary British Fiction and Literary Criticism
The Case of Stephen Kelman's *Pigeon English*

Sandra Dinter

Introduction

Contemporary British fiction for adults not only features numerous novels about childhood, but it also abounds with first-person child narrators. Toby Litt's *deadkidsongs* (2001), Ali Smith's *The Accidental* (2005) and *There but for the* (2011), John Harding's *Florence & Giles* (2010), Claire King's *The Night Rainbow* (2013) and Kate Hamer's *The Girl in the Red Coat* (2015) are only a few examples of this trend. Ian McEwan's latest work *Nutshell* (2016) even retells Shakespeare's *Hamlet* from the point of view of a foetus in the womb. In British literary history, the child narrator is indeed a rather recent phenomenon. As Margarida Morgado explicates, "representational attempts to capture the intrinsic qualities of a child, its point of view, its voice, its language, its rhythms" (1998, 207) have only occurred on a larger scale since the second half of the twentieth century. Similarly, Katherina Dodou identifies the "ambition to represent the child's interiority" (2012, 247) as a distinct feature of contemporary British fiction.

The interest of this chapter arises from the discrepancy between the large variety of first-person child narratives contemporary British fiction offers on the one hand and the surprisingly homogenous ways in which they have been theorised in literary criticism on the other hand. Despite the current popularity of the constructivist paradigm in the study of childhood, most narratological criticism concerned with child narrators perpetuates essentialist conceptions of childhood. In a close reading of Stephen Kelman's Booker contender *Pigeon English* from 2011, this chapter aims to demonstrate how first-person child narrators in contemporary fiction can be approached from a constructivist perspective. This chapter intends to identify the literary devices *Pigeon English* employs to construct its child protagonist's narrative voice as well as the assumptions that are made about childhood in this process.

At the centre of *Pigeon English* stands 11-year-old protagonist and first-person narrator Harri Opoku, who has recently arrived from Ghana and now lives in an inner-city housing estate in London. After an unnamed boy is murdered in the neighbourhood, Harri and his friend Dean undertake a secret investigation: they interview potential witnesses and collect evidence. Their inquiry provides insights into various contemporary pressing social issues in Britain, including the precarious status of immigrants, knife crime, teenagers' sexual promiscuity, 'failing' schools and surveillance culture. The boys eventually find out who the murderer is, but before they can inform the police, Harri is attacked by one of the members of the 'Dell Farm Crew' gang and bleeds to death.

Kelman's novel is timely in several respects: it combines various semiotextual elements (e.g. representations of drawings, lists, pictograms and handwriting) with a detective plot and first-person child narration.[1] This formula had already struck a chord with readers in Mark Haddon's *The Curious Incident of the Dog in the Night-Time* (2003) and Jonathan Safran Foer's *Extremely Loud & Incredibly Close* (2005). Furthermore, *Pigeon English* picks up the popular theme of children's migration experiences in Britain, as previously found in Meera Syal's *Anita and Me* (1996), Zadie Smith's *White Teeth* (2000), Diana Evans's *26a* (2005), Alex Wheatle's *Brixton Rock* (1999) and Chris Cleave's *Little Bee* (2008). The novel is also loosely based on an actual event, that is, the tragic murder of ten-year-old Damilola Taylor on a North Peckham estate in 2000. The acknowledgements in the first edition of *Pigeon English* make this connection explicit. They include links to the websites of the *Damilola Taylor Trust* and *Families United*, a charity that is dedicated to families who have lost relatives to youth violence. In this section, Kelman also expresses his "deepest gratitude and sympathy" "to the children and their families" who suffered similar fates (2011). In an interview, Kelman explains:

> He [Damilola Taylor] seemed to me to be such a genuinely good kid and a bright kid with so much potential and I'm sure he would have gone onto become a great man and do some real good in the world. For me to have that potential ripped away in such a brutal senseless way was tragic and I was deeply saddened.
>
> (Lawless 2016)

These statements can be read as calls for political initiative and change embedded within the novel's paratextual apparatus. In my analysis of *Pigeon English*, I will treat Kelman's ethical impetus as a crucial prerequisite for his construction of Harri's narrative point of view. I regard *Pigeon English* as a novel that aims to alert a middle-class readership to the problematic conditions of children living in poor areas in England by forming Harri's narrative voice according to the hegemonic discourse of childhood as an innocent and vulnerable state, which is constantly at risk.[2]

Child Narrators in Literary Criticism

Overall, narratology has not paid much attention to child narrators. Either the child narrator serves as a prototypical example of the concept of the unreliable narrator (e.g. Riggan 1981, 144–70) or s/he is solely assessed in terms of authenticity. As Silke von Sehlen notes in *Poetiken des kindlichen Erzählens* (2015), one of the few studies in the field, many scholars and reviewers ignore the fictional quality of child narrators and instead focus on the question of to what extent their narrative voices represent those of 'real' children (18–9). The issue of the child narrator is therefore all too often a normative one that proceeds on an essentialist notion of childhood as a homogenous identity that is claimed to be 'naturally' different from adulthood. Hence, it does not come as a surprise that most scholars agree upon the factors that distinguish the child narrator from its adult counterpart. For Maria Nikolajeva, for instance, the child narrator's voice and perspective are characterised by "the profound difference in life experience as well as linguistic skills" (2000, 173). Similarly, Mechthild Barth assumes that the child narrator's point of view is limited because s/he is unable to articulate complex thoughts and, due to what she sees as the child's inherent naiveté and lack of experience, poses more gaps for the reader to fill than an adult narrator (2009, 31, 233). According to Fiona Björling, child narrators even contradict the very notion of childhood because "[t]he ability to organize narrative material hierarchically seems to incur a level of sophistication which young children have not yet achieved" (1983, 7).

The reviews of *Pigeon English* are a case in point. Upon its release, most critics reacted to the novel by focusing on the question of whether Harri is a credible narrator or not. While Rachel Aspeden found his narrative voice "laboured and faux-naïf" (2013), Lewis Jones appreciated "the miraculous voice of Harrison 'Harri' Opoku, aged 11" (2011). Rebecca Caldwell posited that although "[i]t can be difficult to write in the voice of a child without sounding cloying, [...] the author captures Harri brilliantly" (2011). Olushola Ojikutu accentuated "clever tricks by Kelman to root his first person narrative more firmly in a child's milieu, especially that of the West African child" (2011). Susie Thomas applauded Harri's voice because his "partial understanding of the world around him means that Kelman can allow the reader to infer what is going on without having to spell it out" (2011). The issue of credibility was equally raised in many interviews with the author. In fact, Kelman himself admitted that the authenticity of Harri's voice was one of his central concerns:

> There were certainly challenges along the way. There were a few times I had to ask myself 'would a child act this way and talk this way when faced with a certain situation?' I was lucky as I was

surrounded by kids like Harri and was able to absorb the way they spoke to each other and the things they were preoccupied by.

(Lawless 2016)

Along with his reviewers, Kelman approaches Harri's voice as a form of representation that can (and should) be traced back to a 'real' child who exists outside the literary text. As Karín Lesnik-Oberstein and Stephen Thomson have shown, this is how most criticism engages with 'the child'. Instead of conceiving of the child as "the product of a given history and culture [that] emerges from competing ideologies of class, ethnicity, nationality", the child often appears as "an *anti-theoretical* moment, resistant to analysis, itself the figure deployed *as* resistance. The child as a figure that operates through repetition, and therefore as the repeating figure, is made to found the 'real' beyond language as the always retrievable already-there" (2002, 36, emphasis in original).

Accordingly, many scholarly accounts present the construction of a child's narrative voice as a significant challenge or problem for the adult author to master. Barth, for example, understands the creation of a child narrator as an "exceptionally difficult endeavour" in which the author must employ certain strategies in order to "verify himself as a credible narrator" (2009, 31, my translation). Similarly, in *Infant Tongues: The Voice of the Child in Literature*, Elizabeth Goodenough, Mark Heberle and Naomi Skoloff propose:

> In the end, how to present a child's voice that is genuinely mimetic or rhetorically significant is a problem faced by every writer who creates characters and invents a language for them. The relative inarticulateness of children makes any representation of their consciousness necessarily a tentative and fundamentally artificial construction of adult writers and audiences [...].
>
> (1994, 3)

Here the "relative inarticulateness" of what can easily be read as *all* children appears as a given fact. Fictional accounts of these voices can, at least potentially, be "genuinely mimetic", which implies that fictional voices can, under the right (but here unspecified) circumstances, do justice to a 'real' counterpart. This implies that the narrative voice of a child character would have to, at least partly, reflect the child's 'natural' inarticulateness to be 'convincing'. However, the authors' gestures toward representational modes stand at odds with the connotations of the terms "invented" and "artificial" language. These adjectives suggest that the language that is given to a child narrator by an adult writer can never be mimetic in the first place. It is striking that the creation of a child narrator is seen by so many scholars to be a fundamentally different process from that of the making of an adult narrator if we consider that *all* narrators are, in the end, literary constructs. However, in view of the anti-theoretical tendency of the study of childhood as outlined by Lesnik-Oberstein and Thomson, this argumentative inconsistency is perhaps not surprising.

Such essentialist conceptions of the child narrator lead to another trope commonly found in narratological criticism, that is, the understanding of a child character's point of view as a defamiliarising device. Barth claims that children look at the world in a different manner because they have an "unusual" point of view (2009, 232, my translation). The child narrator, she maintains, bears an innovative potential, as it "allows us to examine our historically saturated body of knowledge from a new perspective. It is a perspective that has become foreign but once was ours" (16, my translation). In contemporary fiction, she argues, the child's new point of view serves to re-examine and re-evaluate established literary themes (234). Barth's argument again rests on the ideas that children are inherently different from adults and that all adults perceive literary texts in the same way.

For a constructivist approach to child narrators, it is vital to rephrase the points above: because we can only ever access the child's narrative voice as a construct in the first place, the question of authenticity becomes irrelevant. Rather, the task is to look at how a narrative voice is constructed and which hegemonic discourses of childhood are and are not at work in it. Simply put, the question should not be whether it is credible that a child narrator understands a certain matter to a full extent or not, but what assumptions about childhood are made, for instance, by ascribing an inferior level of awareness to a child narrator. This is exactly how I want to approach Harri as a narrator. I argue that, once we take into account the ethical and political agenda of Kelman's novel, Harri emerges as a character who does not provide his readers with a new or defamiliarising perspective. As a child character whose point of view perpetuates hegemonic principles of childhood derived from Romanticism, including naivety, innocence and ignorance, Harri's voice has – despite what may appear as its linguistic non-conformity – a *familiarising* function. He provides his readers exactly with what they may expect from a child narrator and this is, in turn, how readers are invited to sympathise with him.

Harri as a Child Narrator and Protagonist in *Pigeon English*

Although *Pigeon English* is a literary work about ethnic minorities and the 'underclass', a contentious label that gained notoriety in Britain in the 2000s and 2010s, it is written by a white author and addresses, as Kelman himself puts it, a "middle-class readership – a white liberal

The Child Narrator

readership" (Lawless 2016). In his article "The Race Problem with the Booker", Alex Wheatle addresses this conflict. He praises *Pigeon English* as a work that raises awareness because "depictions of the black underclass in the UK are so rare in literary fiction", although he wonders "why it had to take a white author to explore the black underprivileged to finally attract the attention of a major award" (Wheatle 2011). As Barbara Korte and George Zipp maintain in *Poverty in Contemporary Literature*, council estate novels like *Pigeon English* involve various

> social symmetries – or more often asymmetries – between the characters depicted as poor in the textual world, and the agents in the text's circulation, which include not only authors and publishers, but also readers. For the question as to who listens to and ideally understands and empathises with what is being articulated, is, in social terms, at least as important as the question of voice.
>
> (2014, 14)

This constellation is central to Harri's narrative voice. I claim that *Pigeon English* constructs Harri's position as first-person narrator and protagonist as an outsider in an 'underclass' environment. Kelman endows him with characteristics that will appeal particularly to middle-class readers. As a migrant, Harri is in the same position as many of his readers are: he observes other characters interacting with each other without being too complicit in or familiar with what happens around him. Just as Harri asserts that when he first arrived in London, "there were so many new things it even made my eyes go blurry. I never suspected to see so many new things just in one day" (Kelman 2011, 79), the 'underclass' milieu depicted in the novel will be 'new' to most readers but becomes tangible through its predictable innocent child protagonist. Harri's voice effectively functions as a bridge to the council estate.

The majority of Harri's first-person narration consists of associative interior monologues and alternates freely between the present tense and the past tense, which gives his narrative voice an immediate and transparent quality. An obvious linguistic marker of it is code-switching. Harri tells his story in English but habitually employs lexical items of Ghanaian or Ghanaian-English origin. Frequent examples are "asweh" (Kelman 2011, 4), "adjei" (9), "hutious" (12), "red-eyes" (12), "bo-styles" (13), "obruni" (43) and "donkey hours" (51). Readers can easily infer the meanings of these words from context. A striking grammatical feature is Harri's use of reduplications to signal emphasis or comparatives, as in the sentences "[a]djei, the wind came back quick quick" (24) or "he ran away sharp-sharp" (25). The novel's title *Pigeon English*, a homophone of the linguistic term 'pidgin English', frames Harri's narrative and encourages readers to read his language as a contact language, which is indicative of his transcultural perspective. Moreover, Harri's syntax is predominately paratactic. He mostly employs short and simple sentences, which often contain anaphora. He rarely uses subordinating conjunctions. A typical example is the novel's opening paragraph: "You could see the blood. It was darker than you thought. It was all on the ground outside Chicken Joe's. It just felt crazy" (3). Such features can be read as an indication of the novel's conception of childhood as a simple, naive and less sophisticated state than adulthood.

A largely mimetic narrative mode underlines Harri's role as an innocent child character. As Anjali Pandey demonstrates, many passages in *Pigeon English* read more like a filmic screenplay or drama than a novel, particularly the dialogues (2014, 54). A typical example appears in the opening scene: "Jordan: 'I'll give you a million quid if you touch it.' / Me: 'You don't have a million.' / Jordan: 'One quid then'" (Kelman 2011, 3). As the narrative abstains from the classic insertion of 'she/he said', Pandey concludes, "we sort of 'see' who does the talking in this novel – just as we would 'watch' a slowly unfolding filmic scene, for instance" (2014, 54). This narrative mode underpins the hegemonic conception of childhood as one of emotional and perceptual immediacy, as opposed to the association of adulthood with complexly structured narratives. Furthermore, this specific presentation of dialogues allows Kelman to implement Harri's innocence on a formal level of the text, whereby he is marked out as a 'child at risk' in an environment that is otherwise dominated by 'risky children'. This becomes evident in the dialogues that contain obscene language and 'indecent' content, for example, when the Dell Farm Crew mug Dean and Harri:

X-Fire wouldn't let us past. They were waiting outside the cafeteria. They were all standing in our way and they wouldn't move. You didn't know if it was a trick or for real.

DIZZY: 'What's up, pussy boys?'
CLIPZ: 'I heard you failed the test. That's weak, man.' […]
X-FIRE: 'Don't worry, Ghana. I'll think of something easier for you next time, you'll be alright. What you got then, Ginger?'
Dean went all stiff. My belly went cold. […]
DEAN: 'I've got a quid, that's it. I need it.'
DIZZY: 'Yeah well, shit happens, innit.'
He took Dean's quid. There was nothing you could do to stop it. He was very sad, you could tell. […]
DEAN: 'F-ing hell, man.'
DIZZY: 'Don't be fronting me you little bitch, I'll batter you.'
(Kelman 2011, 65)

Here, as well as in numerous other episodes, Harri remains detached from the Crew's aggressive behaviour. Strictly speaking, he does not even quote them in direct or indirect speech; their derogatory language is merely 'shown' and obviously contrasts with Harri's neutral words.

In this way, the novel leaves open the possibility that Harri does not fully understand the connotations of their language, which again underscores his innocence.

Pigeon English also dissociates Harri from the contemporary moral panic concerning children's 'premature' exposure to pornography and rising rates of sexual promiscuity. In the novel, sexually explicit material is constantly available to the child characters through the new media and is implicated in their language. Conor Green, for instance, casually mentions that he watched "this video once of a woman shagging a dog" (65). Sexual references pervade in the screenplay-like dialogues. "'Pervert!'" (54), "'Dog-er!'" (54), "'You f-ing skank!'" (176) and "'Bum-licker!'" (159) are only a few examples. Notably, this register is again limited to other child characters. When Harri relates to sexual content or employs sexualised language, he frequently does it incorrectly and, thus, with a potentially comic effect for the reader: "Miquita and Chanelle are both dey touch, they're always bluffing about all the boys they've sucked off (it means harder kissing)" (28), "Prossie and hooker and tutufo all mean the same. In England if a girl has a tattoo she's a tutufo" (130), "Orgasm is just another word for the sneeze of a mouse. It's my favourite word of today" (174). The same technique is employed when two pages in the novel show rather than let Harri tell what his classmates write on their t-shirts at the end of the term, e.g. "MR PERRY SUCKS DOG COCKS" (256, capitalisation in original) and "I STINK OF JIZZ" (257, capitalisation in original). Harri's crush on his classmate Poppy Morgan is similarly marked by innocence. Whereas many of the other child characters engage in sexual acts, Harri's adoration for Poppy is always respectful and asexual (23–4, 163–4, 258–60). These examples suggest that *Pigeon English* constructs Harri and his voice in deliberate contrast to most of the other child characters on the estate.

Another distancing element is Harri's appropriation of the role of detective, which showcases his moral integrity and reinforces his position as a 'naturally good' child character. "Detectives catch the bad guy" (139), Harri proclaims. Being a detective raises the well-established associations of childhood with exploration, play and creativity. Moreover, Harri's appropriation of an adult profession infers that he will at some point become a working adult. The novel suggests that Harri holds a social and economic potential for society, thus placing him firmly within the discourse of the child as the "citizen-worker of the future" (Williams 2004, 408), which arose in Britain in the 2000s under New Labour. His diligence obviously demarcates Harri from the other idle truants and criminals on the estate. At the same time, his role as a detective serves an element of social criticism. Harri only assumes his mission because the local authorities are apparently not interested in solving the murder of the young boy. The state is only represented on the estate through the CCTV cameras and danger signs, which do not prevent any crimes. In

Pigeon English, the state fails to assume its moral and practical responsibility for its citizens, particularly the children at risk. One of the girls on the estate is known among the children for walking "funny" and being "quiet like a rabbit" (Kelman 2011, 165) because her grandfather rapes her but nobody ever helps. In the end, Harri dies because he assumes precisely this kind of responsibility.

In addition, *Pigeon English* constructs countless scenarios in which Harri directly proves his moral integrity. Harri happily abjures a series of temptations. In case other children offer him a cigarette, he tells himself: "I'll just say no thanks, I'm trying to give up, doctor's orders (it's the best way to get out of anything)" (98). When Jordan encourages Harri to obtain a knife, he responds: "'No thanks. I don't really need one'" (132). While Jordan's favourite gun is a Glock because "[i]t's what all the toughest gangsters use" (186), Harri cannot think of anything else than a harmless "supersoaker" (186). Harri's conviction that "laughing is the best way to make them [girls] admire you" (180) affirms his role as a 'naturally' good child in the Rousseauian tradition.

Moreover, the Dell Farm Crew want Harri to carry out two specific dares. The first one consists of falsely activating the fire alarm at his school. From the start, Harri is aware of the consequences:

> If it's a false alarm and they find out who did it they go to jail. It's a crime to set off the alarm if there's no real fire because while the firemen are checking there could be a real fire somewhere else and somebody could die.
>
> (56)

His strong physical reactions ("I could feel my heart going proper fast like a crazy drum, my mouth tasted like metal" (56)) suggest that Harri has a strong super ego. He obviously values most of the legal regulations, which the other child characters on the estate routinely disregard. He finally attempts the dare but does not manage to finish it:

> I bashed the alarm. I did it proper hard but the glass wouldn't break. It just made my hand go funny. I wanted a hammer. I wanted to run. I looked around for help but X-Fire and Dizzy were gone, all I could hear was them laughing in the distance. Dizzy: 'Pussy boy!' I just went red-eyes. I bashed the glass again. It was no good. I just didn't have the blood. I just wanted to get away before somebody saw me. I ran down the stairs and under the bridge to the Humanities block. I made it to the toilets. Safe. My belly felt proper sick. I think the Dell Farm Crew are my enemy now. That's what happens when you fail your mission.
>
> (57)

Harri is caught between legal and moral obligations and the expectations of his violent peer group. The introspective mode and the lexical and syntactic repetitions in this passage foreground Harri's moral dilemma. The same pattern recurs in Harri's second dare, the mugging of his neighbour, Mr Frimpong. Here, the introspective narrative mode ("Dizzy and Killa ran together. I just followed them", "'It wasn't me it wasn't me it wasn't me!' (I just said it inside my head.)" (118)) once again sets Harri apart as a passive observer who finally escapes.

Harri's role as an exceptionally moral character extends to his family. In contrast to the socially decayed recurring characters on the estate, including Terry Take Away and Fag Ash Lil, Harri's mother has an honourable profession as a midwife. Harri notes several times that "Agnes couldn't come with us because Mamma has to work all the time" (9) and complains that "Mamma has to work at night as well" (69). Similarly, his father can only speak to them on the phone from Ghana because he needs to work there (171). The Opokus are presented as a respectable and religious working-class family. Within the boundaries of their small flat, the family actively shuts itself off from its neighbours: "We always keep the chain on the door and the locks locked up so the invaders can't get in" (27). Despite the mother's long workdays, the family is indeed poor; they must purchase many of their belongings from the charity shop. Nonetheless, they are extremely modest. The Opokus serve as an antithesis to the influential discourse of welfare scrounging in contemporary Britain. Equally countering the prevalent discourse of child abuse as, for instance, epitomised by the tragic death of Victoria Climbié in 2000, Harri's mother is affectionate, responsible and caring. She always encourages her children to follow rules and to moderate their language (20, 35). When she catches Harri and Jordan throwing stones at a bus, she tells her son: "If I see you around this boy again there'll be big trouble'" (190). She does not tolerate the kind of behaviour that the other children on the estate have cultivated.

Another important element in Harri's position as an exceptionally moral outsider is the novel's setting. Harri lives in a neglected periphery that has nothing to do with the iconic centre of London with which most of his readers are familiar. The Dell Farm Estate is depicted as an extremely hostile environment that is unsuitable for the Romantic tradition of childhood that Harri epitomises. The school and the youth club are run down, and the church is vandalised. As Harri casually remarks, "[t]here's always drug needles around the playground" (98), and the junkies sleep on the stairs (153). The fact that a group of children set fire to the play area speaks for itself. Harri explains: "The playground was dying but nobody was trying to save it" (250). The fire symbolises the way in which the entire community witnesses what the novel conceives as the destruction of a 'naturally' innocent childhood without doing anything about it. While the local authorities have obviously lost control over public space, the gangs, as Ulla Rahbek puts it, "possess the power to erect borders and to dictate modes of behaviour. Part of their power game is to let non-members believe that there are safe places" (2013, 434).

The estate poses a serious risk to Harri. In the end, he dies because he believes that the stairs are the last remaining safe place on the estate.

As Owain Jones shows, "[i]n the UK, concerns for the conditions of modern childhood are particularly articulated *through visions of the child in urban environment*" (2002, 17, emphasis in original). These concerns are, he argues further, grounded in a symbolic disjunction between hegemonic constructions of childhood and of the urban. More specifically, urban environments are incompatible with the Romantic construction of childhood as an innocent state (7–20). Based on the Romantic construction of childhood, Jones illustrates, it is still general consensus that "the innocence of childhood is more at home, and can survive longer, in rural settings where children have contact with 'nature' and are away from the problems and unnatural sophistications of the urban" (20). In turn, it is assumed that "[c]ity children can also become 'too knowing', too sophisticated and clued up" (24). *Pigeon English* draws precisely on this discourse, for it laments the lack of 'natural' spaces for children and links this to the moral corruption of the estate's children. Harri emerges as a child character in the Romantic tradition not least because he is drawn to dying 'natural' spaces. An illustrative example is the river, which Harri visits with Dean. Harri observes that the river is

> only dark. It's too small for swimming and the water is acid, if you fell in all your skin would burn off. There's a platform that goes over the shit pipe that's big enough for both the two of you to sit on. You can just sit there and watch all the things in the river go past. It's usually just sticks or cans or paper. Whoever sees a human head first gets a million points. [...] There's even no fish in the river. It made me feel proper sad. There should be fish even if they're not tasty ones. There's no ducks left either, the smaller kids killed them with a screwdriver. The babies just got crushed.
> (Kelman 2011, 47–8)

The polluted river is life threatening in every respect. Furthermore, this passage establishes a link between the destruction of nature and the young peoples' moral decay. The polluted river, Harri testifies, prevents the children on the estate from swimming, which is here implicitly assumed to be one of their 'natural' preferences. As this is no longer possible, they are corrupted; they revert to destructive activities. Harri is again exempt from this because he is the narrative instance and regrets this development. Moreover, Harri and Dean's game of watching the objects that go past in the river attests to their creativity and innocence. This scene recalls a key piece of British children's literature: A.A. Milne's famous character Winnie the Pooh also likes to play 'pooh sticks'.

Harri equally laments the clearing of the trees on the estate: "I hated the sawmen. They were very mean, you could tell. It felt like the tree was being tortured. [...] It made me proper sad, I don't even know why" (85–6). Once again, the delicate trees can be read as symbols of the Romantic conception of childhood. The violent and organised removal of the trees, which Harri can only helplessly witness, causes him pain; it is depicted as an act of plunder. The uprooting of the trees visualises the erosion of the 'naturally' innocent core of childhood in the novel. Like the trees, childhood is presented as at risk; it requires systematic protection. Kelman's novel integrates the discourse of the disappearance of childhood as once put forward by Neil Postman in *The Disappearance of Childhood* (1982). Like Postman, the novel here presupposes that the Romantic innocent child is a norm that is under threat in the light of new developments. Harri is constructed as a remnant of Romantic childhood, which has otherwise died out on the estate. *Pigeon English* naturalises Harri's Romantic childhood.

Another device that ties in with the novel's post-pastoral imagery and positions Harri as a child in the Romantic tradition is his friendship with the pigeon. Harri declares: "I just want something that's alive and that I can feed and teach tricks to" (Kelman 2011, 25) and "I love all the birds, not just pigeons. I love them all" (82). The choice of a bird as Harri's companion is significant. As Marie-Luise Egbert points out with reference Percy Bysshe Shelley's "To a Skylark", John Keats's "Ode to a Nightingale" and William Wordsworth's "To the Cuckoo", "the Romantics [...] gave pride of place to birds both in their poetry and poetics" (2015, 9). In this way, Harri is thus further associated with the Romantic tradition.[3] Harri's pigeon is, just like the trees and the river, constructed as one of the few remnants of nature on the estate.

For most of the estate's inhabitants, the pigeon is an irritating and unwanted intruder. As the pigeon itself puts it:

> *You go to such lengths to keep us out. You blockade our favourite roosting sites with steel mesh and spikes. You shoot us with .22-calibre rifles where the law allows, poison us with strychnine, coat your flypaper and watch us do the mashed potato as we try to unstick ourselves.*
>
> (Kelman 2011, 102, italics in original)

Harri sees beyond the pigeon's negative reputation. Thereby, the novel affirms once more the Rousseauian trope of Harri's 'naturally' good disposition. He does not prejudge the pigeon as the adult characters do. For Harri, the pigeon has the qualities that are usually associated with its more 'respectable' relative, the dove: peace, faithfulness and moral integrity (Lengiewicz 2012, 440–1).

The pigeon assumes a central role in the novel, not least because it accompanies Harri as a second first-person narrator. Harri's first-person narration is interspersed with poetic and philosophical passages narrated by the pigeon, which are stylistically and typographically distinct from Harri's musings. They are important because they validate Harri's moral integrity from an external narrative perspective. It is from the perspective of the pigeon that Harri looks "*so blameless*" (26, italics in original). Moreover, the pigeon voices social criticism. It remembers the dead boy (26, 191) and condemns violence (62). The pigeon therefore acts as a prophet, a symbolic role that has frequently been bestowed upon birds in literature (Egbert 2015, 10). In some instances, Harri and the pigeon even enter direct dialogues; at other times, a spiritual exchange unites them.

The pigeon and Harri share a precarious and marginalised status on the estate. Like Harri, the pigeon is constantly at risk. It is harassed by the magpies the, "*[s]tupid creatures*" who "*think I'm one of them*" (Kelman 2011, 119, italics in original). It is more than obvious that the devious magpies bear resemblance to the Dell Farm Crew. This analogy emerges more clearly when the magpies attack the pigeon: "*They came from nowhere, I didn't have a chance to get ready*" (227, italics in original). This incident foreshadows the manner in which Killa eventually sneaks up behind Harri before he stabs him: "I didn't see him. He came out of nowhere" (262), Harri thinks shortly before he dies. In an environment that lacks effective protection, Harri and the pigeon watch out for each other. Harri shoos away the magpies before his pigeon is seriously hurt. Likewise, after the mugging of Mr Frimpong, the pigeon urges,

> *I just wanted to get your attention, Harri, get you out of another mess. I'm trying to help you while I still can, I'm trying my best but there's only so much I can do from here. It's down to you, you have to keep your eyes open, watch for the cracks in the pavement.*
>
> (119, italics in original)

Whereas the institutions of childhood, including Harri's school, his family and the security apparatus, fail to recognise and prevent the impending danger he is in, the pigeon occupies a position from which it can watch over Harri in virtually all contexts. For Pandey, the pigeon therefore obtains the "aerial positionality [that] really 'sees' everything – a type of vision which Kelman seems to insinuate, we as a society can ultimately truly rely on" (2012, 130). Harri's friendship with the pigeon envisions a reconnection with a set of values the novel obviously considers to be missing in English society. Yet in the end, the pigeon cannot prevent Harri's death either, even if it stands by him when he bleeds to death on the stairs to his flat.

Although *Pigeon English* is in many respects consistent in its essentialist construction of Harri as an innocent child narrator in the Romantic tradition, it contains a self-conscious moment. Noticing that his mother is apparently addicted to the news, Harri remarks that

> Mamma likes it best when it's a child who died. That's when she prays the hardest. She prays proper hard and squeezes you until you think you're going to burst. Grown-ups love sad news, it gives them something special to pray for.
>
> (53)

Here, Harri alludes to the spectacle of child abuse that has pervaded the British media since the 1980s. Read as a self-referential device, this passage implies that Kelman's novel is aware of what it invests in childhood as a literary work and showcases this awareness ironically in this passage. At the end of the novel, Harri dies just like the children his mother watches on TV. In this sense, then, it could be argued that *Pigeon English* at least briefly reflects what Dodou sees as another trend in contemporary British fiction, that is, "the prevalence of the aim to scrutinize the idea that the child in inherently innocent and that this innocence is precious and worth protecting" (2012, 239).

Conclusion

This chapter attempted to make a case for a constructivist approach to the child narrator, who appears frequently in contemporary British fiction for adults. Rather than reiterating the normative debate on the child narrator's accuracy and authenticity as found in many academic studies on the subject, I sought to outline how literary works construct childhood by letting their child protagonists narrate the story in a certain way. By focusing on *Pigeon English* as an illustrative example, I showed that the assumption that childhood is an innocent, asexual and creative state that must be protected can be implemented through various narrative and thematic devices, such as mimetic presentations of dialogues, moral dares and pastoral elements. With regard to Kelman's humanist agenda, this is an effective strategy: because Harri is innocent, it becomes almost impossible not to pity him. This sympathy, in turn, is precisely what generally underpins initiatives against child poverty and gang crimes. As a first-person child narrator and protagonist, Harri therefore functions as an ethical anchor for the novel. *Pigeon English* may be a disappointment in view of the many contemporary British novels that radically deconstruct hegemonic notions of innocent childhood or even approach childhood from a constructivist perspective.[4] However, it is a novel that points to the limits of constructivism by indicating that ethical and political practice always necessitate essentialist conceptions of identity, in this case, a fixed idea of an essence that all children have in common.

Notes

1 For an extensive analysis of the novel's semiotextual elements, see Pandey (2012, 2014).
2 In doing so, I follow Barbara Korte and George Zipp's brief reference to *Pigeon English* in their book *Poverty in Contemporary Literature* (2014). They look at the novel as an example of the council estate novel, a genre that "centre[s] on young protagonists who are subjected to deprived circumstances without having any personal responsibility for their situation" and propels "the view that child poverty is a form of marginalization that deserves special attention and effort" (2014, 60).
3 At the same time, Thomas remarks, *Pigeon English* echoes Black British writing in the twentieth century (2011). A pigeon actually features in one of the most iconic Black British texts on migration: Sam Selvon's *The Lonely Londoners* (1956). In this novel, Galahad is so hungry that he catches and eats a pigeon.
4 See Katharina Pietsch and Tyll Zybura's contribution to this volume as well as my doctoral thesis "Childhood as Contemporary English Fiction: Contesting the Last Vestige of Essentialism" (2016).

References

Aspden, Rachel. 2013. "*Pigeon English* by Stephen Kelman – Review." *The Guardian*, March 13. Accessed 4 March 2016. www.theguardian.com/books/2011/mar/13/pigeon-english-stephen-kelman-review.
Barth, Mechthild. 2009. *Mit den Augen des Kindes: Narrative Inszenierungen des kindlichen Blicks im 20. Jahrhundert*. Heidelberg: Winter.
Björling, Fiona. 1983. "Child Narrator and Adult Author: The Narrative Dichotomy in Karei Poláček's *bylo nás pět*." *Scando-Slavica* 29: 5–19.
Caldwell, Rebecca. 2011. "U.K. Immigrant Tale Cuts Like a Knife." *The Globe and Mail*, June 1. Accessed 31 March 2016. www.theglobeandmail.com/arts/books-and-media/pigeon-english-by-stephen-kelman/article582048/.
Cleave, Chris. (2008) 2010. *Little Bee*. New York: Simon and Schuster.
Dinter, Sandra. 2016. "Childhood in Contemporary English Fiction: Contesting the Last Vestige of Essentialism." PhD diss., Bielefeld University.
Dodou, Katerina. 2012. "Examining the Idea of Childhood: The Child in the Contemporary British Novel." In *The Child in British Literature: Literary Constructions of Childhood, Medieval to Contemporary*, edited by Adrienne E. Gavin, 238–50. Basingstoke: Palgrave.
Egbert, Marie-Luise. 2015. "Introduction." In *The Life of Birds in Literature*, edited by Marie-Luise Egbert, 9–20. Trier: WVT, 2015.
Evans, Diana. 2005. *26a*. London: Vintage.
Foer, Jonathan Safran. 2005. *Extremely Loud & Incredibly Close*. Boston, MA: Mariner.
Goodenough, Elizabeth, Mark Heberle, and Naomi Skoloff. 1994. "Introduction." In *Infant Tongues: The Voice of the Child in Literature*, edited by Elizabeth Goodenough, Mark Heberle, and Naomi Sokoloff, 1–15. Detroit, MI: Wayne State University Press.
Haddon, Mark. (2003) 2004. *The Curious Incident of the Dog in the Night-Time*. London: Vintage.

Hamer, Kate. 2015. *The Girl in the Red Coat*. London: Faber & Faber.
Harding, John. 2010. *Florence & Giles*. London: Blue Door.
Jones, Owain. 2002. "Naturally Not! Childhood, the Urban and Romanticism." *Human Ecology Review* 9 (2): 17–30.
Jones, Lewis. 2011. "*Pigeon English* by Stephen Kelman: Review." *The Telegraph*, March 7. Accessed 31 March 2016. www.telegraph.co.uk/culture/books/bookreviews/8362385/Pigeon-English-by-Stephen-Kelman-review.html.
Kelman, Stephen. 2011. *Pigeon English*. London: Bloomsbury.
King, Claire. 2013. *The Night Rainbow*. London: Bloomsbury.
Korte, Barbara, and George Zipp. 2014. *Poverty in Contemporary Literature: Themes and Figurations on the British Book Market*. Basingstoke: Palgrave.
Lawless, Stephanie. 2016. "So That's What Hutious Means! Stephen Kelman, Author of *Pigeon English*, in Interview." *Three Monkeys Online: A Curious, Alternative Magazine*. Accessed 31 March 2016. www.threemonkeysonline.com/so-thats-what-hutious-means-stephen-kelman-author-of-pigeon-english-in-interview/.
Lengiewicz, Adam. 2012. "Taube." In *Metzler Lexikon Literarischer Symbole*, 2nd ed., edited by Günter Butzer and Joachim Jacob, 440–1. Stuttgart and Weimar: Metzler.
Lesnik-Oberstein, Karín, and Stephen Thomson. 2002. "What Is Queer Theory Doing with the Child?" *Parallax* 8 (1): 35–46.
Litt, Toby. 2001. *deadkidsongs*. London: Penguin.
McEwan, Ian. 2016. *Nutshell*. London: Jonathan Cape.
Morgado, Margarida. 1998. "The Season of Play: Constructions of the Child in the English Novel." In *Children in Culture: Approaches to Childhood*, edited by Karín Lesnik-Oberstein, 204–30. Basingstoke: Macmillan.
Nikolajeva, Maria. 2000. "Imprints of the Mind: The Depiction of Consciousness in Children's Fiction." *Children's Literature Association Quarterly* 26 (4): 173–87.
Ojikutu, Olushola. 2011. "Writing across the Colour Margin (On Booker Prize Longlister, *Pigeon English*)." *Miss Ojikutu…Writes African Literature, Music & Art*. Last modified September 2. https://missojikutu.wordpress.com/2011/09/02/writing-across-the-colour-margin-on-booker-prize-longlister-pigeon-english/.
Pandey, Anjali. 2012. "Is Big Brother Watching? State-Sanctioned Voyeurism Visualized in a Booker Contender: A Semiotic Analysis." *Ravenshaw Journal of Literary and Cultural Studies* 2 (1): 118–47.
———. 2014. "Picturizing Narrative Innovation: A Bird's Eye View of Hypervisualized Intertextuality in Stephen Kelman's *Pigeon English*." *Visual Communication* 13 (1): 51–74.
Postman, Neil. (1982) 1994. *The Disappearance of Childhood*. New York: Vintage.
Rahbek, Ulla. 2013. "'Repping Your Ends': Imagined Borders in Recent British Multicultural Fiction." *Literature & Theology: An Interdisciplinary Journal of Theory, Criticism and Culture* 27 (4): 426–38.
Riggan, William. 1981. *Pícaros, Madmen, Naïfs, and Clowns: The Unreliable First-Person Narrator*. Norman: The University of Oklahoma Press.
Selvon, Sam. (1956) 2006. *The Lonely Londoners*. London: Penguin.

Smith, Zadie. 2000. *White Teeth*. London: Penguin.
Smith, Ali. 2005. *The Accidental*. New York: Anchor Books.
———. *There but for the*. (2011) 2012. New York: Anchor Books.
Syal, Meera. 1996. *Anita and Me*. London: Flamingo.
Thomas, Susie. 2011. "Review: Stephen Kelman, *Pigeon English*, Bloomsbury 2011." *The Literary London Journal* 9 (2). Accessed 31 March 2016. www.literarylondon.org/london-journal/september2011/thomas2.html.
von Sehlen, Silke. 2015. *Poetiken kindlichen Erzählens: Inszenierte Kinder-Erzähler im Gegenwartsroman aus komparatistischer Perspektive*. Würzburg: Königshausen & Neumann.
Wheatle, Alex. (1999) 2004. *Brixton Rock*. London: Arcadia.
———. 2011. "The Race Problem with the Booker." *The Independent*, October 17. Accessed 31 March 2016. www.independent.co.uk/arts-entertainment/books/features/the-race-problem-with-the-booker-2371944.html.
Williams, Fiona. 2004. "What Matters Is Who Works: Why Every Child Matters to New Labour. Commentary on the DfES Green Paper *Every Child Matters*." *Critical Social Policy* 24 (3): 406–27.

4 Children's Literature, Cognitivism and Neuroscience
Karín Lesnik-Oberstein

In much of the world, including Britain, the so-called 'neuro-turn' has in recent decades become a predominant narrative accounting for human emotions, cognition and behaviours.[1] The beginning of such an interest can be and has been located at many different points, ranging from nineteenth-century ideas of heredity and phrenology to Charles Darwin's writings in and of themselves, to developments in evolutionary psychology of which British geneticists Hilary and Stephen Rose wrote in 2001 that they had "grown dramatically" "[o]ver the last ten years", (1) to American cultural and literary critic Jonathan Kramnick's observation that the "[a]cademic year 2008–2009 was something of a watershed moment for literary Darwinism"[2] (2011, 315) due to the twin publication of Denis Dutton's *The Art Instinct: Beauty, Pleasure, and Human Evolution* and Brian Boyd's *On the Origin of Stories: Evolution, Cognition, and Fiction*. Similarly, in a lead comment article in the English newspaper *The Observer* in 2013, a pre-eminent scientist and philosopher of science, Raymond Tallis, wrote that

> [t]he grip of neuroscience on the academic and popular imagination is extraordinary. In recent decades, brain scientists have burst out of the laboratory into the public forum. They are everywhere, analysing and explaining every aspect of our humanity, mobilising their expertise to instruct economists, criminologists, educationalists, theologians, literary critics, social scientists and even politicians.
>
> (2013, 31)

Tallis added: "It does, however, make you wonder why the pronouncements of neuroscientists command such a quantity of air-time and even credence" (ibid.). Tallis's article goes on to explain how deeply scientifically dubious the many and wide-ranging claims of neuroscience and brain-imaging are, but he continues to struggle to understand the popularity and persistence of those claims in contemporary Britain.

In this chapter, I will be exploring ways of accounting for the power of the neuro-turn narratives in contemporary Britain through drawing parallels between this widespread interest in cognitivist and neuroscientific approaches in evolutionary psychology and certain investments in childhood. My interest, unlike that of critics such as Tallis, lies primarily not just in analysing the problematic nature of the science that this kind of work claims, but in analysing what is at stake in such approaches. Specifically, I too am puzzled by the popularity of these kinds of claims when both the scientific and the philosophical frameworks they rest on are, at best, questionable and not in any sense new or original, neither philosophically nor scientifically speaking. I argue here, following theorist Neil Cocks's formulation, that neuroscientific accounts of cognition recover and maintain thought as scan, brain and figure: an object of scrutiny and exchange.[3] Therefore, these cognitivist and neuroscientific studies are about, as theorist Jacqueline Rose puts it in relation to childhood and children's literature specifically,

> a conception of both the child and the world as knowable in a direct and unmediated way, a conception which places the innocence of the child and a primary state of language and/or culture in a close and mutually dependent relationship.
> ([1984] 1992, 9)

This chapter demonstrates, then, further implications of reading the child as *textuality* rather than constituting it as a 'merely' textual reflection or representation of a prior and primary sociological or anthropological entity. In these terms, my reading engages with how the child – as with the neuro-turn – is an instance of the capitalist insistence as it operates in Britain today on the object *as* object, even while the child also is made to police a capitalist marketplace defined by the child's placement as outside that market. Both in discussing the child as a produced object (and any object as produced) and in reading the child *as* text, the same drive is here for me at work in, as Slavoj Žižek puts it, questioning

> the properly fetishistic fascination of the 'content' supposedly hidden behind the form; the 'secret' to be unveiled through analysis is not the content hidden by the form (the form of commodities, the form of dreams) but, on the contrary, *the 'secret' of this form itself.*
> ([1989] 2008, 3; emphasis in original)

My interest then is not to ask, what a child is, but rather *why and how* the question 'what is the child?' persists. As part of this question, finally, I will go on to explain in this chapter how and why children's literature criticism must by definition continue either (advertently or inadvertently) to ignore or misread Jacqueline Rose's famous arguments in her book *The Case of Peter Pan or: The Impossibility of Children's Fiction*, just as neuroscientific accounts of cognition, whether or not in relation to literature specifically, must ignore or suppress the arguments of previous theorists of science (especially, although not only, feminist theorists of science) such as Donna Haraway.[4]

Rose, then, argued that children's literature and its criticism are necessarily produced by one self-defined identity – adults – on behalf of a defined 'other' – the child. Rose reads the investment in childhood in these areas (and beyond) as the desire for a 'real' that defeats language and the unconscious in accessing self-identical objects, including the child defined as such:

> Children's fiction rests on the idea that there is a child who is simply there to be addressed and that speaking to it might be simple. [...] *Peter Pan* stands in our culture as a monument to the impossibility of its own claims – that it represents the child, speaks to and for children, addresses them as a group which is knowable and exists for the book, much as the book (so the claim runs) exists for them. [...] Children's literature is impossible, not in the sense that it cannot be written (that would be nonsense), but in that it hangs on an impossibility, one which it rarely ventures to speak. This is the impossible relation between adult and child.
>
> ([1984] 1992, 1)

Rose made this argument almost 30 years ago, but David Rudd and Antony Pavlik, the editors of the 2010 special issue of the *Children's Literature Association Quarterly* to mark the twenty-fifth anniversary of the publication of *The Case of Peter Pan*, note that in children's literature studies still "references to Rose's work are, more often than not, *en passant*, and once made, the critic then proceeds as though it were 'business as usual'" (2010, 225). The special issue contributions themselves however, to my reading, also "then [proceed] as though it were 'business as usual'," even where overtly claiming to be in agreement with Rose. Gabrielle Owen, for instance, writing on "Queer Theory Wrestles the 'Real' Child", understands Rose to be implying

> a child who is moving, who escapes, and I want to suggest that this movement, this disappearing, is what happens when the child is depicted not as empty, but as a powerful, unpredictable, desiring agent. [...] This disappearing refers literally to the ways we fail to see what is powerful, sexual, or adult about the children around us. [...] The idea of the child as memory and fantasy comes from psychoanalysis, [...] I believe Rose offers not only a theory of what happens in and around the idea of children's fiction, but a theory of how the stories we tell ourselves about what happens – or even, what *can* happen – so often operate independently of the lived reality right in front of us. [...] And thinking of *child* in the usual ways – where it functions as an empty category ready to be filled with our desires,

> projections, and disavowals – makes it impossible to really see either the child or ourselves.
>
> (2010, 256–7; emphasis in original)

I read here a reading different from my own, not only of Rose's arguments about the child and psychoanalysis, but also of what is at stake in the whole debate. Owen invokes Rose to *correct* misunderstandings about the child: it is "not [...] empty" but "a powerful, unpredictable, desiring agent" that can be thought of as "fail[ed]" to be seen; this is the "lived reality right in front of us", which is recognisable as separate from "stories we tell ourselves", which make "it impossible to really see either the child or ourselves". In other words, "the child" and "ourselves" are already known to be *there* to be "really" seen, if only the stories did not get in the way; the "lived reality", moreover, is also separate from the "us" it is "right in front of" as the "ourselves" are separate from the "we" who tell them the stories.

Three core issues are at stake here for me: first, that Rose's arguments about the child are neither about a child as 'actual' nor about a child as 'fictional' or 'ideal' and, in that sense, not about 'the child' 'as such' and, therefore, not about the possibility of 'correcting' the child. Second, it is precisely the assumption of necessary, knowable separations between 'stories' and 'lived reality', 'the child' and 'ourselves', and the 'us' and 'stories' and 'lived reality' that constitute the 'real' that Rose puts into question. Finally, and as a necessary corollary to the first two issues, I argue here that the investments in the 'real' that Rose reads through children's fiction are not about 'just' children's fiction or childhood, but rather extend to any claims about the 'real'.

To explore further what is at stake in the child, I want to turn now to some further specific issues in readings of the child: readings that declare an overt interest in considering childhood and history, but that, at the same time, just as with children's literature criticism and with neuroscientific claims about science and literature, can be seen always already to know the child and history as a *content* that defeats a history as/of difference. To draw out some of the implications of this, I want to read closely as a typical example Paul Sharrad's "Turning the Screw Again: The Precocious Colonial Child in Henry James's Story". Sharrad starts his article

> by asking two questions to which the voluminous scholarship on Henry James's *The Turn of the Screw* has seemingly not paid full attention. First, from where does Flora learn her shocking language? Second, in a tale whose details are inspected from as many angles as critics can devise, what weight might we give to the Indian origin of the two children who provide an extra turn to the storytelling

screw? My argument here is that a postcolonial reading of the text can provide us with answers.

(2012, 1)

As with contemporary children's literature criticism, the child here has a language and an origin, for Flora has a "shocking language" that is "her[s]", although at the same time that language is learnt elsewhere; the two children here are seen to have an "Indian origin" that may have "weight" and "provide an extra storytelling screw" despite not having hitherto been inspected by critics. Sharrad adds to his claims about Flora's language by arguing that the "'my dear' language that precocious Miles employs in more intimate moments with his governess is that of the rake seducing a maiden" (2012, 6). Sharrad combines these concerns about languages and origins in terms of the children having originally lived in India:

> In *The Secret Garden*, the tyrannical Anglo-Indian Mistress Mary first appears swearing, calling her Ayah a 'Daughter of a Pig' for not responding immediately to her call (Burnett 7). This is a direct translation of a common invective picked up from the Indian parlance of Mary's servants and suggests an answer to the question of where Flora gets her bad language from. Mary, through her contact with wholesome English housekeepers and gardeners, is brought to a selfreflective civility (Phillips 177, 179, 187), at which point she loses some of her more "Indian" characteristics. But we recall that the dialect-speaking Yorkshire folk in *The Secret Garden* are likened to 'native' Indians (Phillips 185), and that children raised abroad learned vernacular before English (McMaster 27). Bad language, then, takes on added meaning. From a postcolonial viewpoint, we can see the Master as a distant Prospero; the governess, perhaps, as a dangerously innocent Miranda; Miles as an Ariel killed for playing both sides; and Flora as a Caliban, hauled away cursing like a native (380–1).

(9)

Language here, then, both belongs to the children and is not their own: Sharrad sees the language as being the voices of Miles and Flora, although "[t]he most debated question of *The Turn of the Screw* so far has been whether or not the governess is delusional [...] it has been taken for granted in the story itself and amongst critics that Mrs Grose is a reliable figure, who, even if convinced by the governess, maintains a steady hold on reality" (2012, 8). Mrs Grose's "steady hold on reality" means for Sharrad that no matter how delusional or convincing the governess may be, Mrs Grose can be relied upon to speak the truth, including the truth about the children's language, which here amounts to the same thing as

72 *Karín Lesnik-Oberstein*

the children speaking themselves. Sharrad can read the children's language as "bad" and "shocking" to the reliable Mrs Grose because it is not English, adult and of a "low" class: he parallels Flora's language to Mary's swearing as a "direct translation of a common invective picked up from the Indian parlance of Mary's servants" and "the children raised abroad learned vernacular". For Sharrad this is what is at stake in the "added meaning": that the inappropriate speaking of these children is not just about being "precocious", but that it is about being raised originally in a non-English and lower-class environment. Moreover, that environment and its language is one Sharrad can identify and know from and as its reality too, a reality above and beyond what is included in the texts; as he concludes, "[y]et it was these pagan, child-marrying underclasses, steeped in stories of divine sexual activities, who had daily contact with colonial children" (7).

The child (and the Indian and the servant) here is, then, constituted as a first-person narration that apparently requires no interpretation but constitutes a pure communication of the self, albeit an inappropriately non-child self: here we have a representation that is not a representation *for* or *to* anyone. As theorist Sue Walsh argues in her analysis of the child and the animal:

> [I]t is not the case that the construction of the 'real object' (the child/animal) somehow immune to the 'corruption' of language is something that is exclusive to children's literature criticism and animal advocacy. It is something that occurs routinely in critical and philosophical positions that speak of 'representation', and of 'ideology' and in doing so root themselves in the presumed knowable 'real'.
>
> (2002, 162)

Following this inescapable logic of representation,[5] Sharrad continues throughout his article to note critical propositions about complexities and ambiguities of interpretation in relation to James's text, but, as with the child and the Indian, directly overcomes them all to retrieve a transparent and neutral reality or history nonetheless. For instance, as it is nowhere mentioned in *The Turn of the Screw* itself that the children lived in India, it is a stable and knowable history supplying the argument that

> prior to the systematizing of colonial administration that followed the 1857 Indian Mutiny it was common for East India Company soldiers to take mistresses and wives in India. So it is entirely probable that the children are not completely English.
>
> (2012, 3)

Equally, through the claim that "[i]n line with James's story, which will and will not 'tell' […], the brother may not have died or even lived in

India, so a postcolonial scenario is just one more possibility amongst many" (3), James's "not 'tell[ing]'" is produced as the repression of specific possibilities that nonetheless remain as possibility: this is a repression, therefore, which is known and overcome as such.

Indeed, throughout Sharrad's article, the child, the servant and the Indian are – as Walsh's analysis explains – necessarily preserved as a real that is beyond perspective (narration), or, to put it differently, implies that perspective is only ever partial, that there is always something that remains outside that is not itself subject to perspective. For Sharrad, therefore,

> Miles – described suggestively as 'exquisite' (361) – 'says things' to school mates he likes and is expelled as a result (James 392–3). If he has taken on some aspect of transgressive sexuality, whether that be simply knowing too much about sex of any kind, or tempting other boys into sexual 'perversity', the colonial Indian origins of James's children provide a discursive context in which this makes sense and allow us to infer other elements of threat to the English status quo than mere accidental personal deviance. The governess says of Miles, 'they are not of your own sort' (James 354). It is primarily his colonial origins that make this true: Miles is not quite child or adult, not quite gentry but belonging to it, too exquisite to be simply masculine but too male to be seduced by his governess. Ultimately, he is not quite child and not quite 'white'.
>
> (2012, 8)

Miles and his transgressive sexuality are here assumed as prior to, and exceeding, perspective in being able to be known from his "saying things" and being "expelled as a result", just as they are excessive in being simultaneously prior and post-narration in being part of "a discursive context" that "makes sense" of what would otherwise be "mere accidental personal deviance". Without "the colonial Indian origins", Miles's saying would here not be able to be made "sense" of, and Miles's being of his "own sort" too is underpinned "primarily [by] his colonial origins". The colonial is the source of inappropriate or perverse sexuality to the child as Miles has possibly "taken [it] on"; in other words, even in India it was not initially his. For Sharrad, then, Miles is a known uncertainty, where the uncertainty itself is further overcome by the certainty of the "colonial Indian origins".

What is also entirely consistent within Sharrad's position is his particular interpretation of Shoshana Felman's article "Turning the Screw of Interpretation" ([1977] 1982a), which the title of his own article so pointedly references. I can read Sharrad's version of Felman as consistent with the misreadings of Jacqueline Rose in both the *Children's Literature Association Quarterly* special issue and more widely in children's literature criticism and elsewhere and with the absence of Haraway from cognitivism and neuroscience in evolutionary psychology and literary studies. For Felman, Rose and Haraway's arguments are closely connected in their adherence to reading perspective as *inescapable*. Indeed, this very argument is precisely at stake, of course, in "Turning the Screw of Interpretation". For Sharrad,

> Admitting Shoshana Felman's thesis about the indeterminate nature of the text and of reading, we might suggest that one area that a psychoanalytic reading of James '*understate,* leave open' [sic] (Felman 119) in focusing on ghosts, madness and sexuality, is the *political* unconscious. In *The Turn of the Screw*, as in *The Secret Garden*, the country house can be read as a figure for British empire, and the Indian reference allows us to extend the metonym and read its master as an absentee colonial ruler [...].
>
> (9, emphasis in original)

For Sharrad and the critics he cites further, James's "indeterminacy" and "open[ness]" can after all be determined and closed as much as the child, the Indian, the servant, sexuality and identity can be determined and closed. Indeterminacy here is, then, a lack of absolute certainty about a knowable truth, which can be tolerated through filling that lack with the known possibilities or probabilities, including removing the indeterminacy altogether by ultimately settling on one of the known possibilities: here, that is "the *political* unconscious", which is not about "ghosts, madness and sexuality" but about "the country house [...] as a figure for the British Empire".

For Felman, crucially, this is precisely not the status of indeterminacy, the unconscious and sexuality. Instead, indeterminacy is that which remains irresolvable because there is no view available from which any possibility can be seen as, after all, 'correct'; in this sense, this is 'perspective':

> 'The difficulty itself is the refuge from the vulgarity,' writes James to H. G. Wells [...]. What is vulgar, then, is the '*imputed* vice,' the 'offered example,' that is, the explicit, the specific, the unequivocal and immediately referential 'illustration.' *The vulgar is the literal* [...] because it *stops* the movement constitutive of meaning, because it blocks and interrupts the endless process of metaphorical substitution.
>
> ([1977] 1982a, 106–7, emphasis in original)

What is centrally at stake here for both Rose and Felman is a certain reading of Freud: a reading elaborated by Felman throughout "Turning the Screw of Interpretation" and offered by Rose in *The Case of Peter Pan* in the first chapter, which starts by asserting that "We have been reading the wrong Freud to children" (12). This psychoanalysis is the psychoanalysis which resists the 'vulgar' and the 'literal' of which Felman writes through her reading of James:

> The specific complication which, in Freud's view, is inherent in human sexuality as such. The question here is less that of the meaning *of* sexuality than that of a complex *relationship between sexuality and meaning*; a relationship which is not a simple *deviation* from literal meaning, but rather, a *problematization of literality as such*.
> ([1977] 1982a, 110, emphasis in original)

In this sense, Sharrad's understanding of Felman's "psychoanalytic reading" as one that could identify and retrieve lack as a "*political* unconscious" separate from or other to an identifiable and known sexuality is still "reading the wrong Freud to children".

I will now consider how the neuroscience of evolutionary psychology in contemporary Britain too relies on the child and the object as "something that can be scrutinised and assessed", as described by journalist Zoe Williams in 2014 in the English newspaper *The Guardian*:

> 'Neuroscience can now explain why early conditions are so crucial,' wrote [English politicians] Graham Allen and Iain Duncan Smith in their 2010 collaboration, *Early Intervention: Good Parents, Great Kids, Better Citizens*. 'The more positive stimuli a baby is given, the more brain cells and synapses it will be able to develop.' Neuroscience is huge in early years' policy. This week, in what's been characterised as the largest shake-up of family law in a generation, the 26-week time limit for adoption proceedings has come into force, much of it justified by the now-or-never urgency of this set of beliefs, that the first three years (or sometimes first 18 months) hardwire a baby's brain, either give it or deny it the capacity for a full life. This is the engine of what is known as the First Three Years movement, which has transfixed politicians from across the spectrum. Allen and Duncan Smith's report opened with an illustration of the 'normal child's' large brain and the shrivelled, walnut brain of the neglected child.
> (2014)

In her new 1992 introduction to the reprint of *The Case of Peter Pan*, "The Return of Peter Pan", Rose argues that "Peter Pan, it seems, always provokes a crisis of precedence because of the tension between his eternal repetition and his status as a 'once and for all'" (x). This repetition, which both must and yet cannot be read as such, finds yet another return in Jonathan Gottschall's 2012 book, *The Storytelling Animal: How Stories Make Us Human*, where, in line with the numerous claims in contemporary Britain about the evolutionary embeddedness of 'story' (and related aspects) in the human brain,[6] he claims that

> [s]cience *can* help explain why stories [...] have such power over us. *The Storytelling Animal* is about the way explorers from the sciences and humanities are using new tools, new ways of thinking, to open up the vast terra incognita of Neverland. [...] It's about deep patterns in the happy mayhem of children's make-believe and what they reveal about story's pre-historic origins. [...] It's about how a set of brain circuits – usually brilliant, sometimes buffoonish – force narrative structure on the chaos of our lives. [...] *Why* are humans addicted to Neverland?
>
> (2012, xvii, emphasis in original)

Peter Pan's Neverland is instantly recognised here as the "vast terra incognita", and the child too is the repetition that is instantly known as such. Neverland's *appropriateness* as "terra incognita" lies in its already being vulnerable to "open[ing] up" by the "new tools" and "new ways of thinking" of the "explorers from the sciences and humanities", just as the "happy mayhem of children's make-believe" *constitutes* the "deep patterns" that provide the revelation of "story's pre-historic origins". Moreover, it is the literary text *Peter Pan* which for Gottschall provides the origin – Neverland – upon which the new tools and thought will come to act to "open [it] up"; Neverland is always already known to be there as the secret to be "opened", just as children's literature and the child are always already there as the secret to be opened, the mystery to be resolved. Although the brain circuits have to "force" "narrative structure on the chaos of our lives", nevertheless "humans" are "addicted to" Neverland: chaos resists narrative structure, but the human, which does not have Neverland, constantly knows and craves it as a supplement to itself; humans, then, know the story of story before they have story, as they have also made that story they know they do not have but are, after all, addicted to.

A "confusion of tongues"[7] here is absolute: children's literature is here what "humans" are "addicted to", because it is about "deep patterns in the happy mayhem of children's make-believe", which in turn "reveal" something "about story's pre-historic origins". The child, in other words, is here, as it always must be, the origin for both its own origin and that of the entirety of the "human", but designated as such by another, beside or outside any of this; neither child nor human, past nor present, real nor make-believe, science nor literature, neither brain circuit nor chaotic life or narrative structure, but able to anticipate and recognise them all. As with Gabrielle Owen's child, story and lived reality in children's literature studies, Gottschall's brain can simultaneously know about the "chaos of our lives", which is outside itself, whilst having "circuits" that impose a narrative structure upon that chaos: a binocular vision maintained by the brain both of itself and what lies outside itself absolutely. In other words, which brain can know that the brain knows what it is claimed forcibly to prevent itself from being able to know?

Owen and Gottschall's assumed separations of story, history, the child and lived experience or the chaos of our lives also underpin the mirror neuron research,[8] which in turn is made to underpin many claims in evolutionary psychology (and the literary criticism which engages with it) about the overcoming of a fundamentally assumed separation between a 'self' and an 'other', whether these are assigned as 'human' and 'animal', 'adult' and 'child', 'non-autistic' and 'autistic',[9] or 'reader' and 'story'. We can read this already in one of the earliest articles on mirror neurons, "Action Recognition in the Premotor Cortex", by Gallese et al.:

> We describe here the properties of a newly discovered set of F5 neurons ('mirror neurons', n = 92) all of which became active both when the monkey performed a given action and when it observed a similar action performed by the experimenter. Mirror neurons, in order to be visually triggered, required an interaction between the agent of the action and the object of it. The sight of the agent alone or of the object alone (three-dimensional objects, food) were ineffective. Hand and the mouth were by far the most effective agents. The actions most represented among those activating mirror neurons were grasping, manipulating and placing.
>
> (1996, 593)

"Mirror neurons" are "visually triggered", but under a range of restrictions: first, the "given action" of both the monkey and the agent is seen to be "performed" by each *as such*, so that both monkey and experimenter, and the observer of both, already have isolated and matched a set of intentional repetitions as what is deemed to be significant; second, "the sight of the agent alone or of the object alone were ineffective". Nevertheless, it is already known to both the experimenters and, according to them, also to the monkey, that what is there to be "observed" is an "agent" or an "object", even when "alone". In other words, although an "object" here is alternately defined as "three-dimensional objects, food", an "agent" must here then, according to the neuroscientists, be identified by the monkey as being neither "three dimensional" nor "food". This distinction between agent-ness and object-ness allows for the central cause of neural action to be isolated as the *seeing* of "an interaction between the agent of the action and the object of it": it is, therefore, "interaction" that must be *visible as such* and where further there must be an assumed, neurologically significant difference between "action" and "vision"; where seeing or observation do not count as actions.[10]

Both causality and intentionality can be seen here as *a priori* invoked by Gallese et al. to support their interpretation of mirror-neuron activity.[11]

There are subsequently several slippages in these matters too, for "[h]and and the mouth were by far the most effective agents", although it had previously been stated that "the sight of an agent alone [...] [was] ineffective" with respect to "effectivity" (that is, presumably, making the neurons active), the agent apparently *can* after all be seen "alone", separated out from within the interaction with its object. It can further be noted that "hand and the mouth" here too are excluded from being defined as "three-dimensional objects, food". Finally, there is a jump to the claim that "[t]he actions most represented among those activating mirror neurons were grasping, manipulating and placing", where "actions" are already not just actions but in shifting to being "represented" incorporate causality and intentionality. The claims made here, then, rest on assuming that the neurons innately know the difference between *different intentions* and, moreover, that intentionality and interaction can be *seen as such* in order to "visually trigger"; further, "visually trigger" *itself* is anyway already a reading of intention and cause. Several scientific critiques of mirror neuron research make different but complementary points to my analysis here: John Cartwright, for instance, in considering claims about mirror neurons and the origins of languages warns that

> the strong interpretation of mirror neurons supplying instant meaning to the observer faces one enormous problem. If it is suggested that mirror neurons only fire when the movement of an arm is directed towards some meaningful action (the grasping of an object) and replicate this meaning instantly inside the head of an observer, and not when confronted by movement alone, such as a hand moving towards a non-existent object, how does the mirror system 'know' that the former is meaningful? In essence, if meaning is supposedly presented instantly in the brain, how can the system decide to be selective before the action is complete?
>
> (2008, 142)[12]

What is going on, then, with claims about the child and evolutionary psychology, which repeat themselves and yet also repeatedly, now, claim their newness, their status as spontaneous and unique discovery? What is going on with their insistence on the object, the child as object and the story as object? The first thing to note, perhaps, is that this very question can itself be seen as a repetition, as we have already been able to see in Rose's preface to the new edition of *The Case of Peter Pan*. I want to foreground here how evolutionary psychology and children's literature criticism are by no means lone voices, but part of a current broader, pervasive, anti-theoretical tendency in wider literary and scientific studies as Carlo Salzani, amongst others, has argued, in his review of leading "literary Darwinist" Joseph Carroll's book *Reading Human Nature*:

> This *dialogue de sourds* extends far beyond the borders of literary Darwinism and characterizes the old opposition between natural sciences and humanities, which had an explosion – mainly in American academia – with the 'science Wars' of the 1990s […], but still rages in the contemporary debate about the 'crisis of the humanities'.
> (2011)

We can also see this view quite a while before Salzani's comments in one of the classic texts to critique evolutionary psychology, Hilary and Stephen Rose's *Alas Poor Darwin: Arguments Against Evolutionary Psychology*, in which they argue that the importance of their volume lies in "challenging what we feel has become one of the most pervasive of present-day intellectual myths […] evolutionary psychology […] [,] a particularly Anglo-American phenomenon" (2001, 1). *Alas Poor Darwin* was first published in 2000, and yet here we are at present, with a burgeoning academic and popular industry in evolutionary psychology (including neuroimaging) still also in Britain, which, as Rose and Rose already then wrote "claims to explain all aspects of human behaviour, and thence culture and society, on the basis of universal features of human nature that found their final evolutionary form during the infancy of our species some 100–600,000 years ago" (1). I am referring to Rose and Rose not to invoke their scientific authority with respect to the correctness (or otherwise) of my own critique of evolutionary psychology, but because they and I share a concern about the *violence* of the claims made by evolutionary psychologists, as there is also a violence in the claims made about the child as object. I read this violence not just in the insistence on the object, but also in the ignoring or repressing of the histories of fields of study and of history as difference *tout court*, as I have discussed above and which Rose and Rose also claim in stating that they each "separately felt that [evolutionary psychology] was making insupportable assertions which touched our own distinctive fields [sociology and biology]" (2001, 8). The rage against 'theory' of the literary Darwinists – but, significantly, not just the literary Darwinists – is precisely fired by the fact that they *all* understand theory somehow to 'evaporate' a natural, material world; as Joseph Carroll argues, "poststructuralism yields causal primacy to language", which for Carroll, as Salzani points out, means "it is incompatible with a 'perspective in which "life", self-replicating DNA, precedes thought, to say nothing of language'" (2011, quoting Carroll (2011), 78). Jonathan Kramnick quotes Brian Boyd as similarly asserting that "humans are not just cultural or textual phenomena but something more complex" (2012, 432).

I can trace the concern with the violence of this real also in another closely relevant volume of classic critique, this time of psychology more widely, *Changing the Subject: Psychology, Social Regulation and Subjectivity,* by Julian Henriques et al. In the "Foreword" to the 1998 re-issue of the volume, the editors argue that "the problems involved in changing the subject have always been related to a deeper question about forms of emancipation and liberation, whether at the individual or the collective level" ([2000] 2001a, xviii). The *investments* of psychology as a discipline are here made visible; as Henriques et al. state:

> [W]e assert the importance of modern psychology in producing many of the apparatuses of social regulation which affect the daily lives of all of us. However, unlike previous radical critiques we do not argue that psychology is or has been a monolithic force of oppression and distortion which constrains and enchains individuals. Rather, we contend that psychology, because of its insertion in modern social practices, has helped to constitute the very form of modern individuality. Psychology is productive: it does not simply bias or distort or incarcerate helpless individuals in oppressive institutions. [...] It is by producing explanations as well as identifying problems that psychology contributes to specific political positions.
> ([2000] 2001b, 1)

For Henriques et al., a consequence of this position for "understanding and bringing about change" is that the "opposition of individual and society and therefore of individual and social change is a view of the social domain which we shall criticize" (2), including "the deconstruction of the taken-for-granted, common-sense facts about human beings and our lived experience [, which] involves prising apart the meanings and assumptions fused together in the ways we understand ourselves in order to see them as historically specific products, rather than timeless and incontrovertible given facts" (ibid.).

Histories of history as *difference*, then, can be constituted as disrupting the real of childhood, experience, the body and materiality: everything which that for children's literature and evolutionary psychology not only is but *must* be "the taken-for-granted, common-sense facts about human beings [...] timeless and incontrovertible". Felman, Hilary and Steven Rose, Jacqueline Rose and Henriques et al. offer individual analyses of the political and cultural moments that lead to their challenging of a current "taken for granted". For Rose and Rose "[t]he last decades of the twentieth century have been a period of almost unprecedented social, economic and cultural turbulence [...] in this climate the search for new apparent certainties, something to cling to, has become urgent" (2001, 3). Differences and change demand, as Felman writes, that "the reader be patient (i.e. refrain from repressing too soon); let him suspend, for a moment, his natural disbelief in the face of the foreign (cultural and theoretical) *style*", ([1977] 1982b, 4, italics in original), and although I would not venture in turn to diagnose the history of my current moment, what I do propose through the readings in this chapter is that in several current areas of interest somehow such patience and suspension are in short supply, as exemplified in contemporary Britain above all by the insistence on what may be called "audit capitalism"[13] and by the "Brexit" referendum vote on 23 June 2016 for Britain to leave the European Union.

Notes

1 See, for a thorough and wide-ranging account of the 'neuro-turn' development and consequences, De Vos (2016).
2 There have been heated debates about literary criticism that draws on evolutionary psychology (sometimes called "literary Darwinism"); see, for instance, Karshan (2009), Kramnick (2011) and Lesnik-Oberstein (2016a).
3 Cocks, unpublished manuscript, February 2012 (quoted by kind permission); Cocks's formulation here echoes Rose's critique of the child and the unconscious as not "something separate which can be scrutinised and assessed" (1992, 13). For Cocks's wider critique of cognitivism, neuroscience and evolutionary psychology, see Cocks (2009).
4 See for my previous arguments about the misreading or ignoring of Rose: Lesnik-Oberstein (2000, 2010, 2011, 2016b, 2016c) and for my further arguments around the ignoring of Haraway as well as a wider critique of neuroscience: Lesnik-Oberstein (2015, 2016a).
5 See for reviews of how different disciplines engage with the child: Lesnik-Oberstein (1998, 2011).
6 See for British examples of such claims about 'story' and related issues, Lesnik-Oberstein (2016a).
7 I am quoting here the title of the article by the Hungarian psychoanalyst Sándor Ferenczi ([1933] 1955), which is also referred to by Rose in the subtitle of her third chapter of *The Case of Peter Pan* ([1984] 1992, 66, 148, note 3).
8 The ongoing persistence of the British investment in 'mirror neurons' and their implications is reflected, for instance, in the 2014 publication of a special issue of the *Philosophical Transactions of the [English] Royal Society* on "Mirror Neurons," compiled and edited by Ferrari and Rizzolatti or in the ongoing research at the University of Oxford by Heyes (2010).
9 For a thorough critique of evolutionary psychology's theories about autism, see Ainslie (2011).
10 My thanks to Dr. YuKuan Chen for helping me to develop my reading of the mirror-neuron claims. Not coincidentally, Chen herself is inspired in turn by Rose ([1986] 2005).
11 For a thorough discussion of the centrality of intentionality to ideas of "affect" as well as a thorough wider critique of affect, see Leys (2011).
12 See, for an excellent wider critique of the mirror neuron research from a perspective related to but different from my own, Leys (2012). Leys is also puzzled at the ongoing popularity of mirror neuron theories and their resistance to both scientific and theoretical critiques, but does not make this question the focus of her article, concluding only that "simply put, the network of

presuppositions and methods associated with the Basic Emotions View is too attractive and the laboratory methods too convenient to be given up" (6). For scientific critiques of neuroimaging research, see Button et al. (2013) and Bluhm (2013), for instance.

13 See, for a thorough analysis of contemporary British 'audit capitalism' particularly as it relates to education and childhood, Parker (2015) and Cocks (forthcoming 2017).

References

Ainslie, Helen. 2011. "Perspectives and Community: Constructions of Autism and Childhood." In *Children in Culture Revisited. Further Approaches to Childhood*, edited by Karín Lesnik-Oberstein, 90–107. Houndmills: Palgrave.

Allen, Graham, and Iain Duncan Smith. 2008. *Early Intervention: Good Parents, Great Kids, Better Citizens*. London: The Smith Institute.

Bluhm, Robyn. 2013. "Self-Fulfilling Prophecies: The Influence of Gender Stereotypes on Functional Neuroimaging Research on Emotion." *Hypatia* 28 (4): 870–86.

Boyd, Brian. 2009. *On the Origin of Stories: Evolution, Cognition, and Fiction*. Cambridge, MA: Harvard University Press.

Burnett, Frances Hodgson. (1911) 1985. *The Secret Garden*. Harmondsworth: Puffin.

Button, Katherine, John P.A. Ioannidis, Claire Mokrysz, Brian A. Nosek, Jonathan Flint, Emma S. J. Robinson, and Marcus R. Munafò. 2013. "Power Failure: Why Small Sample Size Undermines the Reliability of Neuroscience." *Nature Reviews Neuroscience* 14: 365–76. doi:10.1038/nrn3475.

Carroll, Joseph. 2011. *Reading Human Nature: Literary Darwinism in Theory and Practice*. New York: SUNY Press.

Cartwright, John. 2008. *Evolution and Human Behaviour. Darwinian Perspectives on Human Nature*. 2nd ed. Houndmills: Palgrave.

Cocks, Neil. 2009. *Student-Centred: Education, Freedom and the Idea of Audience*. Ashby-de-la-Zouch: InkerMen Press.

———. forthcoming 2017. *Higher Education Discourse and Deconstruction: Challenging the Case for Transparency and Objecthood*. Basingstoke: Palgrave.

De Vos, Jan. 2016. *The Metamorphoses of the Brain – Neurologisation and its Discontents*. London: Palgrave.

Dutton, Denis. 2009. *The Art Instinct: Beauty, Pleasure, and Human Evolution*. New York: Oxford University Press.

Felman, Shoshana. (1977) 1982a. "Turning the Screw of Interpretation." In *Literature and Psychoanalysis. The Question of Reading: Otherwise*, edited by Shoshana Felman, 94–208. Baltimore, MD: The John Hopkins University Press.

———. (1977) 1982b. "Foreword to Yale French Studies Edition." In *Literature and Psychoanalysis. The Question of Reading: Otherwise*, edited by Shoshana Felman, 4. Baltimore, MD: The John Hopkins University Press.

Ferenczi, Sándor. (1933) 1955. "Confusion of Tongues between Adults and Child." In *Final Contributions to the Problems and Methods of*

Psychoanalysis, edited by Michael Balint and translated by E. Mosbacher, 156–68. London: Hogarth Press.

Ferrari, Pier Francesco, and Giacomo Rizzolati. 2014. "Mirror Neurons: Fundamental Discoveries, Theoretical Perspectives and Clinical Implications." Special Issue of the *Philosophical Transactions of the Royal Society* 369 (1644).

Gallese, Vittorio, Luciano Fadiga, Leonardo Fogassi, and Giacomo Rizzolatti. 1996. "Action Recognition in the Premotor Cortex." *Brain* 119: 593–609.

Gottschall, Jonathan. 2012. *The Storytelling Animal: How Stories Make Us Human*. New York: Houghton Mifflin Harcourt Publishing Company.

Haraway, Donna Jeanne. 1989. *Primate Visions: Gender, Race, and Nature in the World of Modern Science*. New York and London: Routledge.

Henriques, Julian, Wendy Hollway, Cathy Urwin, Couze Venn, and Valerie Walkerdine. (2000) 2001a. "Foreword." In *Changing the Subject: Psychology, Social Regulation and Subjectivity*, edited by Julian Henriques, Wendy Hollway, Cathy Urwin, Couze Venn, and Valerie Walkerdine, ix–xix. London: Vintage.

———. (2000) 2001b. "Introduction: The Point of Departure." In *Changing the Subject: Psychology, Social Regulation and Subjectivity*, edited by Julian Henriques, Wendy Hollway, Cathy Urwin, Couze Venn, and Valerie Walkerdine, 1–9. London: Vintage.

Heyes, Cecilia. 2010. "Where Do Mirror Neurons Come From?" *Neuroscience & Biobehavioral Reviews* 34 (4): 575–83.

James, Henry. (1898) 2007. *The Turn of the Screw and Other Short Novels*. New York: Signet.

Karshan, Thomas. 2009. "Evolutionary Criticism." *Essays in Criticism* LIX (4): 287–301.

Kramnick, Jonathan. 2011. "Against Literary Darwinism." *Critical Inquiry* 37 (2): 315–47.

———. 2012. "Literary Studies and Science: A Reply to My Critics." *Critical Inquiry* 38 (2): 431–60.

Lesnik-Oberstein, Karín. 1998. "Childhood and Textuality: Culture, History, Literature." In *Children in Culture: Approaches to Childhood*, edited by Karin Lesnik-Oberstein, 1–28. Houndmills: Palgrave.

———. 2000. "The Psychopathology of Everyday Children's Literature Criticism." *Cultural Critique* 45: 222–42.

———. 2010. "Childhood, Queer Theory, and Feminism." *Feminist Theory* 11 (3): 309–21.

———. 2011. "Introduction: Voice, Agency and the Child." In *Children in Culture, Revisited: Further Approaches to Childhood*, edited by Karín Lesnik-Oberstein, 1–18. Houndmills: Palgrave.

———. 2015. "Motherhood, Evolutionary Psychology and Mirror Neurons or: 'Grammar is Politics by Other Means.'" *Feminist Theory* 16 (2): 171–87.

———. 2016a. "The Object of Literature and Neuroscience." *Textual Practice*: 1–17. doi:10.1080/0950236X.2016.1237989.

———. 2016b. "Gender, Childhood and Children's Literature: The CIRCL Approach." *Asian Women* 32 (2): 1–26. doi:10.14431/aw.2016.06.32.2.1.

———. 2016c. "Children's Literature: Sexual Identity, Gender and Childhood." *BREAC: A Digital Journal of Irish Studies*. http://breac.nd.edu/articles/69168-childrens-literature-sexual-identity-gender-and-childhood/.

Leys, Ruth. 2011. "The Turn to Affect: A Critique." *Critical Inquiry* 37 (Spring): 434–72.

———. 2012. "'Both of Us Disgusted in My Insula': Mirror Neuron Theory and Emotional Empathy." *Nonsite.org* 5: 1–25. Accessed 11 April 2013. http://nonsite.org/article/"both-of-us-disgusted-in-my-insula"-mirror-neuron-theory-and-emotional-empathy.

McMaster, Graham. 1988. "Henry James and India: A Historical Reading of *The Turn of the Screw*." *Clio* 18: 23–40.

Owen, Gabrielle. 2010. "Queer Theory Wrestles the 'Real' Child: Impossibility, Identity, and Language in Jacqueline Rose's *The Case of Peter Pan*." *Children's Literature Association Quarterly* 35 (3): 255–73.

Parker, Ian. 2015. "The Function and Field of Speech and Language in Neoliberal Education." *Organization* 23 (4): 550–66. doi:10.1177/1350508415591235.

Phillips, Gerry. 1993. "The Mem Sahib, the Worthy, the Rajah and His Minions: Some Reflections on the Class Politics of *The Secret Garden*." *The Lion and the Unicorn* 17 (2): 168–94.

Rose, Jacqueline. (1984) 1992. *The Case of Peter Pan of the Impossibility of Children's Fiction*. Philadelphia: Pennsylvania University Press.

———. (1986) 2005. *Sexuality in the Field of Vision*. London: Verso.

Rose, Hilary, and Stephen Rose. 2001. "Introduction." In *Alas Poor Darwin: Arguments against Evolutionary Psychology*, edited by Hilary Rose and Stephen Rose, 1–14. London: Vintage.

Rudd, David, and Anthony Pavlik. 2010. "The (Im)Possibility of Children's Fiction: Rose Twenty-Five Years On." *Children's Literature Association Quarterly* 35 (3): 223–29.

Salzani, Carlo. 2011. "Review of *Reading Human Nature: Literary Darwinism in Theory and Practice*, by Joseph Carroll." *Bryn Mawr Review of Comparative Literature* 9 (2). Accessed 30 December 2012. www.brynmawr.edu/bmrcl/BMRCLFall2011/Reading%20Human%20Nature,%20Literature%20after%20Darwin.htm.

Sharrad, Paul. 2012. "Turning the Screw Again: The Precocious Colonial Child in Henry James's Story." *Postcolonial Text* 7 (3): 1–16.

Tallis, Raymond. 2013. "Think Brain Scans Can Reveal Our Innermost Thoughts? Think Again." *The Observer*, "Comment Section," June 2.

Walsh, Sue. 2002. "Child/Animal: It's the 'Real' Thing." In "Children in Literature," edited by Karín Lesnik-Oberstein, Special Issue, *The Yearbook of English Studies* 32: 151–62.

Williams, Zoe. 2014. "Is Misused Neuroscience Defining Early Years and Child Protection Policy?" *The Guardian*. Accessed 16 December 2016. www.theguardian.com/education/2014/apr/26/misused-neuroscience-defining-child-protection-policy.

Žižek, Slavoj. (1989) 2008. *The Sublime Object of Ideology*. London: Verso.

Section II

Medial and Visual Constructions of Childhood in Contemporary Britain

5 Children's Television and Public Service in Contemporary Britain

Jonathan Bignell

Children's television is made by adults, not by children, and the term is used to designate programmes aimed by adults at an audience of children. This chapter focuses on how the notions of the child and childhood work as discursive constructs deployed by broadcasters and regulators. Children watch not only children's television but also other kinds of television aimed at multi-generational audiences and at adults, and the chapter discusses what actual children watch in contemporary Britain. The notion of the contemporary also requires some clarification in relation to television. It only gradually became publicly available in the mid-twentieth century, and television broadcasting exemplifies modernity in its ability to address mass audiences within a domestic space (Silverstone 2006, 19–22). Like its twentieth-century precursor, radio, television is dependent on the integration of scientific innovation with large-scale industrial production; it is a product of the capitalist mass production of commodities developing from the later nineteenth century. The television set is a consumer product intended for the home and represents modernity in that it privatises leisure. However, while the experience of viewing has become individualised, what is broadcast is available to a collective audience and is often concerned with a shared public experience of social life. Television imparts information about the public world of news, sport, popular entertainment and celebrity, for example. Much of this broadcast material is live, or at least is recent and perceived as relevant to its audiences. In the form that television takes in Britain (and in other developed societies), it has always been contemporary and participates in the definition of what 'contemporary' means.

Across its short history, television has changed dramatically in its technologies, modes of reception and institutional formations (Siune and Hulten 1998). The refinement of programme production techniques has been accompanied by improvements in image and sound definition, for example. Households own several devices capable of receiving broadcast television, as well as the ability to record, store and replay it. The number of television channels has increased dramatically, and the deregulation and globalisation of the television business has mirrored the ideologies of marketisation and consumer choice that are evident in most other sectors of contemporary culture. This chapter argues that television's identification with the contemporary, despite all the changes that have affected the medium, comes from its ability to adapt and assimilate. Like radio, television is organised and regulated at a national level, and it has inherited formats, forms and modes of address from theatre and journalism, for example. With the advent of digital communications media and the World Wide Web, television is adapting to "convergence culture" (Jenkins 2006, 2), which is characterised by "the flow of content across multiple media platforms, the cooperation between multiple media industries, and the migratory behaviour of media audiences". The chapter briefly considers this historical trajectory and the ways that the concept of 'the child' has been figured in British television very recently. As Graeme Turner (2009, 63) has suggested, "rather than witnessing the end of broadcasting or the beginning of post-national television, we are simply watching these two constitutive elements renegotiate their particular roles against an unusually volatile background of hyper-commercialisation and emerging technologies". This chapter argues that the study of children's television tells us a lot about how both childhood and television are understood in culture and how the tensions between continuity and change have affected them.

Historical Perspectives

British television broadcasting began in 1936, when the British Broadcasting Corporation (BBC), which already had a monopoly on radio from 1922, was given a charter by government that gave it the exclusive right to establish a television service. In exchange for this privileged position, the BBC was required to inform, educate and entertain the national audience (Scannell 1990). This arrangement, known as Public Service Broadcasting, meant that the BBC made programmes in a wide range of genres (entertainment, news, current affairs, sport, original drama, religious programmes, etc.) and aimed programmes at specific audience constituencies, including children. Children's television, made by adults, included programmes supporting the school curriculum, programmes for pre-school children at home with their mothers, entertainment programmes for children and programmes for a cross-generational family audience (Oswell 1995). Television is still most often watched in the private space of the home, but in the early days of British broadcasting, this was by no means the dominant way that viewers experienced the new medium. In the 1930s, public venues for watching television included railway stations, restaurants and department stores, and audiences watched collectively. Centralised production and dispersed individual reception of television became the norm after the Second World War with conflicting results. First, central production and private reception matched the democratic organisation of Europe and the US. Governments and licensed institutions could distribute information and culture universally to promote a fairer society. Public service broadcasting attempted to raise cultural, educational and social standards. The second result was the connection with the home. Standards of living rose steadily through the twentieth century, and the home became a site for the accumulation of consumer goods and the development of new patterns of domestic leisure. Commentators were concerned about how watching television might disturb family routines and waste time compared to reading or conversation, but for most viewers watching TV was a sociable experience. Most viewing was collective, in friends' and neighbours' houses, and helped to form communities. This was especially the case in the newly built suburbs of the major cities.

Television was both attacked and defended as a medium for children. The journalist Ivor Brown (1951, 17), for instance, contributed an essay to the *BBC Year Book*, an annual book-length publication chronicling the corporation's activities. Defending television and rejecting claims that it was bad for children, he wrote:

> In my boyhood there was an advertisement headed 'Keep your Boys at Home'. No force, naturally, but a voluntary and blissful incarceration was suggested. It was to be made easy and delectable by a dining-room table which could be turned into a billiard-table. Thus was erring and straying to be checked and temptation to be killed by kindness. Television, no doubt, is doing some of the same protective work and stabilizing the Englishman's home. But on my observation, there is no reason to think that boys and girls, once become viewers, will never more be quitters. The sharp pleasure of banging the door on one's parents and going out to sniff the air of liberty, even if that air be only the frowst of the cinema, is surely perennial. [...] People who view do not stop going to the play or the films or the cricket-match.

The television set became an important part of the culture of the home, often positioned next to the fireplace, where families would gather in the evening and keep warm (in the age before central heating) and share entertainment experiences. Children were part of this audience, addressed not only by television programmes but also an associated media and toy culture. Radio had already fulfilled a similar function (I. Hartley 1983, 16–73), and the household, configured by and for television, was inter-generational, commercial and social. Television's address to childhood and to children was one that promoted inclusion but also individuation, shared cultural references but also taste discrimination, and various forms of stratification, distinction and inequality through which social life was reproduced.

Regular television broadcasting for children, as opposed to the occasional programmes made in the early years, began only in 1950. There was always an anxiety that the relationship between broadcaster and listener would encourage children to be passive viewers, and the response was to stress collective viewing. One long-running programme for pre-school children was *Watch with Mother* (1953–1975) for example, while older children were expected to watch with siblings, friends or parents. Watching television physically positioned the child statically within a room, looking toward the screen, so its spatial configuration seemed to encourage physical inactivity. To counteract this, programmes for children represented children as physically and culturally active. The magazine programme *Whirligig* (1950–1953), or the long-running *Blue Peter* (1958–present), for example, featured items about children's hobbies, sport and outdoor recreation. Children were invited to interact with programmes by writing letters, taking part in charity fundraising and volunteering and participating in competitions. The rhetoric of address to the viewer supported this relationship, since presenters would directly address the camera and speak to the viewer as 'you', thus positioning the child as part of the 'we' of an audience community.

The BBC monopoly on television broadcasting was broken by the introduction of commercial Independent Television (ITV) in 1955, but ITV was bound by the same legal requirement to produce Public Service programming and to inform, educate and entertain. ITV produced children's programmes in similar forms to the BBC but with advertising breaks within and between programmes. Similarly, the introduction of BBC2 in 1964, Channel 4 in 1982 and Channel 5 in 1997 did not challenge those expectations, despite somewhat looser obligations being placed on these channels, and all five are often known collectively as Britain's main channels, traditional channels or PSB (Public Service Broadcasting) channels to reflect that continuity. The beginnings of the contemporary multi-channel environment were in the 1980s when broadcasting by satellite was introduced, but take-up was limited until 2002 when a consortium of broadcasters including BBC, ITV, Channel 4 and Sky launched Freeview. This free digital television service offered about 70 channels, including some specialising in children's television, and in 2013, analogue television was closed down.

The period since the millennium has seen significant changes in how children watch television but also continuities that make inherited ideas about national television culture important. Figures published by the national media regulator, Ofcom (2014, 4) revealed that over 98 per cent of UK children (five to fifteen-year-olds) had access to digital multi-channel television in 2013, and 69 per cent of households with children had access to pay channels as well as free ones. In 2013, there were 31 children's channels of which 11 were free to view, and although programmes for children were still available on some general-audience channels, the fragmentation of the child audience had several effects for broadcasters. One was that the total possible audience at any point during the day could be split up into numerous small constituencies, each watching a different channel. For channels funded by selling advertising time, a smaller audience is usually less lucrative than a larger one because channels charge advertisers according to how many thousand viewers a programme is expected to attract to the advertisements shown during it. For the BBC, funded not by advertising but by a licence fee levied on all owners of television sets, smaller audiences could threaten the BBC's legitimacy as a provider of programmes to the whole population and thus the political will to support its funding model.

Competition for audiences and potential loss of distinctiveness among a large roster of similar channels meant that British television institutions developed strategies to address audiences in new ways. One of them was branding, and in 2002 the BBC launched its two digital channels for children: CBBC and CBeebies, respectively for six- to thirteen-year-olds and for pre-school children. Schedules were stripped into four-hour blocks, rotating three times a day, so although there was programming throughout the day it comprised many repeated programmes. The BBC positioned its new channels as part of its Public Service remit. Offering a schedule that did not include any advertising was a means to appeal to parents who might be concerned about the commercialisation of children's television (and childhood in general). Moreover, 90 per cent of CBeebies programmes and 75 per cent of CBBC programmes were either British- or European-made, which was a considerably greater proportion than their US-owned competitors such as the Cartoon Network or the Disney Channel. Ofcom (2014, 6) reported that 85 per cent of parents regarded Public Service Broadcasting of children's programmes as important, and over three-quarters of parents believed that BBC in particular was offering a range of high-quality, British-made programmes. The BBC's strategy for children's television in the digital world enabled it to identify itself as a reliable, trustworthy institution that had the best interests of children at heart. This relatively conservative, mainstream ideology demonstrated continuity with the BBC discourses from much earlier decades.

Clearly, there has been change since the monopoly period when BBC was Britain's only television channel. The great majority of children (71 per cent) had access to the World Wide Web via a tablet computer in 2013 (Ofcom 2014, 4) and over half of Britain's children reported that they like to watch video from YouTube as much as or more than watching television. But Ofcom's analysis of national viewing showed that children still watch television in Britain in traditional ways. Watching television was the most common media activity for children of all ages, and children less than eight years old spent about twice as many hours watching television than they spent engaged with other media such as the Internet or video games (Ofcom 2014, 5). Children watched almost 17 hours of television per week each, but almost two-thirds of that time was spent watching programmes aimed at an adult or family audience rather than programmes aimed specifically at children. When watching children's programmes, British programmes were watched 45 per cent of the time (Ofcom 2014, 10) despite the fact that only 20 per cent of children's television (in terms of programme hours) across all channels is UK-made. The largest audience of children watches in the early evening, with adults, using the household's main TV set. The most popular programmes among children (Ofcom 2014, 226–8) were both shown in the evening and were not aimed specifically at children; they were the BBC science fiction drama *Doctor Who* (2005–present) and the primetime talent contest on the commercial ITV channel, *Britain's Got Talent* (2007–present). Among younger children, the most-viewed programme was BBC's screening of the Disney animated film *Up* (2009), but for both younger children (four to nine years old) and older ones (10–15) the BBC comedy drama for children, *Gangsta Granny* (2013), was among the top 20 most viewed and attracted half of the total child audience. It is not true that children no longer watch television or that they watch alone or that they largely spend their time on interactive computer devices. Continuities with the past are as significant to an understanding of television as apparent ruptures, breaks or revolutions.

British Television Culture in a Global Context

Britain has always been relatively unusual in that its television channels mainly show programmes made in Britain. Some British programmes sell overseas, either subtitled or dubbed, and such programmes aimed at children include the BBC's rebooted *Doctor Who* (2005–present), sold to 28 countries including Australia, Canada, France, Germany, Israel, Italy, New Zealand, Sweden, Thailand and the SyFy channel in the US. The animation *Peppa Pig* (2004–present), has been screened in over 180 countries. BBC Worldwide is the commercial arm of the BBC that distributes British programmes overseas and invests in programmes that it then exports. Worldwide invested £14.5 million in the pre-school programme *In the Night Garden* (2007–2009) to build on the export success of its predecessor, *Teletubbies* (1997–2001), for example. Nevertheless, since the 1950s, American television has far exceeded British or any other television in export revenue and coverage, and well-known examples include *Lassie* (1954–1973), *Scooby-Doo, Where Are You?* (1969) and *He-Man and the Masters of the Universe* (1983). Throughout the history of British television, there has been strong resistance to US programmes because of the fear of Americanisation. This applies especially to children, who are considered more vulnerable to the influence of the consumerism embodied in many US toy-based series and susceptible to the violent content in US children's programmes, especially cartoons. Across Europe, there are shared assumptions that children enjoy puppetry and animation, that they identify with anthropomorphised animals and child-like characters, and that they enjoy songs and music. A fundamental conception of childhood, originating in the late eighteenth century, links the great majority of programme producers, television programme buyers and executives and the parents, politicians and commentators who have shaped children's television in Europe. Children's programmes can only be so successfully internationally because of the existence of transnational institutions and technologies for sharing television programming and a shared sense of what childhood is. Britain has played a leading role in making domestic programmes for children that can be assimilated into the commercial networks of television trading.

One specific example is the television series *If You Were Me* (1971) screened sporadically on the main BBC1 channel. It was scheduled at 5.15 p.m., when most children would have recently returned home after school. In total, there were 22 half-hour episodes, shown in 1971, 1972 and 1975. The premise was summed up in the strapline printed in the BBC's listings magazine, *Radio Times* (1971, 36): "You stay in my house I'll stay in your house. You sleep in my bed I'll sleep in your bed. You come to my school I'll come to your school [...]". Thirteen-year-old boys and girls from different countries swapped lives and were filmed at home and at school. The programme was a co-production and comprised films made for television by European broadcasters who belonged to the European Broadcasting Union (EBU), including AVRO (Netherlands), Bayerischer Rundfunk (southern Germany), the BBC in Britain, CBC (Canada), RTB (Yugoslavia), RTT (Tunisia), PBS (US), RAI (Italy) and TRT (Turkey). The films were circulated to the fellow members for showing in their own national territory and were given translated voice-over soundtracks in each national language. The producer was Molly Cox, who worked on the BBC story-reading series *Jackanory* in 1965–1966 and later on *Why Don't You Switch Off Your Television Set and Go and Do Something Less Boring Instead* (1973), which featured film segments authored by children themselves. The director was Tim Byford, who worked on the staff of BBC's Children's Department, directing film segments about children's lives for the magazine programme *Blue Peter*.

In common with many British programmes, short runs of episodes were made, beginning with six films shown in 1971. In the first episode, James Currie from Melton Mowbray in Leicestershire swapped lives with Andrea Franchi from Assisi in Italy. In the following week, Nicola French from the village of Swanmore in Hampshire exchanged with Milica Zaric from a Serbian village in Yugoslavia. In the third episode, Keith Powell from Rawmarsh in Yorkshire swapped with Kamel Khalfallah from Dar Cha Bane in Tunisia, and on 24 February 1971, Campbell

Aiken from Aberdeen in Scotland exchanged lives with Jan Oosterbroek from Hoorn in Holland. In the episode from 3 March 1971, Jane Curtis from the village of Lavenham in Suffolk swapped with Stephanie Kranz from a Bavarian village in Germany. In the final episode of the first series, on 10 March 1971, Nicola Snook from Bath exchanged with Ginger Gonzales from Salt Lake City, Utah, in the US. The intention was to show the diversity of children's lives and the potential equivalences between them. So, for example, there were featured children who came from villages and swapped lives with village children from other countries. In the same way, children from major cities swapped with other urban children, and the ages of the children were similar in each case (not least because they were integrated into the school systems of each country). There was an important limitation on the recognition of the overseas childhoods being represented. Since in each programme it was a British child who travelled, and with whom the overseas child swapped, the overseas child could only be seen in relation to a known UK childhood that stays the same as the measure of comparison. *If You Were Me* was conceptually linked to the concept of town twinning, on which school exchange schemes and pen-friend relationships between children were often built. Twinning had been set up in 1947 after the Second World War to foster friendship and understanding between former enemies and to encourage trade and tourism. It was a high-profile means to create European identity by acknowledging and repudiating national conflicts, featuring twinning between cities devastated by war like Coventry (UK), Dresden (Germany) and Stalingrad (USSR), for example. Children's mobility and communication between countries was a concrete instance of this transnational idealism.

Within Britain, comparison programmes featuring children were not new, with the most celebrated example being the documentary series *7 Up* made by the commercial broadcaster Granada TV in 1964, initially for its current affairs series *World in Action*. Annual editions of the *Up* series followed the life stories of the same children, chosen from different social classes and geographical locations around the UK. But it was designed for viewing by adults as an analytical study of cultural difference and class privilege and was longitudinal – it is still being made some 50 years later. The EBU's infrastructure made *If You Were Me* possible. The EBU was formed in 1950 by 23 broadcasters across Europe and the Mediterranean, with further national members and associate members (some of them outside Europe, such as broadcasters from Canada, Japan, Mexico, Brazil, India and the US) subsequently joining from public and commercial sectors. The EBU's unstated ideology was that childhood was interesting to its multinational audience and comprehensible as a shared concept or currency that was exchangeable across borders. Like money, it was nationally distinctive, but the childhood of one country could be compared with that of another. In 1971, the year that *If*

You Were Me began, the Eurovision network broadcast *Children of the World*, hosted by US actor Danny Kaye, which presented segments representing children's lives in 45 countries, using 22 land stations and two satellites. The idea of uniting the world's audiences by means of transnational live broadcasting was not new and was celebrated by, for example, the programme *Our World* (1967) in which The Beatles performed "All You Need is Love". The ideal was inclusiveness despite diversity, and broadcasting could enable people to recognise their distinctiveness but also their common membership in a 'family of man'. The ideologies associated with childhood made it appear to be a common ground on which such a broadcast event could be based. As I have previously suggested (Bignell 2011, 181):

> The circulation of children's television across borders has drawn on transnational conceptions of what childhood is and what child audiences want and need. That circulation has not been prevented by national regulatory regimes or political boundaries like the Iron Curtain ... [and] the child audience has been constructed as a transnational entity that could be addressed and provided for by transnational programming.

Effects and Regulation

Adults consistently try to protect children from television, on the basis of defining childhood by its inherent value but also its transience and vulnerability. In the developed nations of the Western world, childhood is seen in two contrasting and contradictory ways. On one hand, children are regarded as innocent and naturally predisposed to be good. On the other hand, children have been regarded as irrational, immoral and in need of adult guidance, and this has justified regulation and censorship. Children watching television have been a focus of studies looking for evidence of (usually negative) effects for several decades (Lemish 2007, 69–100). In the 1950s and 1960s, researchers devised interview techniques or opportunities for play in which children could be monitored, to see whether the television they had viewed made them behave differently. Results were inconclusive, but this work legitimated campaigns for the regulation of children's television. The aim was to protect what were seen as vulnerable audiences from programmes that might turn children into anti-social adults. Binary oppositions between rational child and irrational child, active and passive, agent and victim have underlain much of the debate on both childhood and popular culture for more than a century. Parents, educators and regulators in both the UK and US have argued that programmes for children should have regard for the functions of television in education and child development. These responsibilities on the part of programme-makers and broadcasters have underpinned much of the discourse of British television production in the public service tradition. For example, the British BBC producer Roger Singleton-Turner (1994, 23) argues that the competencies and knowledge held by children and the adults who make children's television are different, and he claims that:

> The whole grammar of television needs to be learnt by each viewer. There is evidence that the language of film and television is learnt in a similar way to spoken language and that children of increasing maturity accept with understanding an increasing vocabulary of filmic conventions.

Therefore, narrative forms should be relatively linear and clear, to avoid the child creating "extraordinary constructions in his [sic] mind to explain what he has seen". A discursive model of child development is constructed as an evolutionary learning process that moves teleologically toward the normative adult viewer. The use of this developmental schema prescribes the audio-visual form of programmes, according to the 'stage' of development in which the child is assumed to be, with the simplest forms for the youngest audience. Relations between long shots and close ups should be signposted (to avoid confusion over the sizes of objects and people), time ellipses between shots should be rare in programmes for young children and cutting rates should be slower than for an adult audience. In essence, the form of children's programmes comes to resemble early cinema and repeats the 'evolution' of film from the static camera shooting theatrical boxed sets, with little cutting or change of frame size, to a contemporary style of rapid montage, fast cutting and 'unmotivated' use of pan or close up in programmes for older children.

David Buckingham (1996) cuts through this, adducing children's and parents' talk about television to focus on the 'positive' and 'negative' emotional responses to television. Buckingham discovers that both watching television and talking about television are important means for children to understand themselves and others and to perform their own identities to themselves and others. This dynamic interaction involves gaining and deploying knowledge of television codes and conventions, such as distinctions between genres, narrative forms and contextualisation of the programme text through knowledge about the production processes that gave rise to it. Children sometimes seek out disturbing programmes in order to test their own maturity in coping with troubling emotions. It is not simply pleasure that drives viewing preferences but also a desire to self-educate and confront challenging material. Television programmes can empower their audiences by requiring attention to the conventions of signification in the television medium. So a positive outcome of effects research, however misguided it may be, has been the teaching of 'media literacy' (also known simply as 'media education') in British schools, on the assumption that if children understood how television representations were constructed they would be better able to negotiate the meanings of television for themselves. Long ago, a major report for the government by Lord Newsom and the Central Advisory Council for Education (Newsom 1963, 155), which analysed the British state-funded school system and its curricula, explicitly called for "the study of film and television in their own right, as powerful forces in our culture and significant sources of language and ideas". Media literacy empowers child viewers to recognise the degree of modality (the closeness or distance of the fit between reality and representation) in the material they see on screen (Hodge and Tripp 1986, 100–31). Work on cognitive and emotional responses to television argues that watching and talking about television play a significant role in children's self-understanding in relation to others and to society. Arguments for media literacy accept that adult control over children's viewing can only ever be partial, so the wish to protect them is displaced into a wish to equip them with skills for self-defence. Watching television is pleasurable for children, but it is also an essential part of their integration into society as a whole.

The recognition that television and other mass communications media have shaped how childhood is experienced and thought about has led to pronouncements such Neil Postman's (1983) that television puts an end to childhood. Children are addressed similarly to adults, especially as consumers, Postman argued, and adults and children are offered opportunities for recreation and play in similar ways. While this thesis was presented as a critique that called for the preservation and protection of childhood, a related diagnosis of the importance of media culture by Buckingham (2000) views contemporary media culture as a vigorous arena for the realisation of child identities. Contemporary television and the associated media of computer games, films and toys offer a plethora of images and experiences that shape different, possible modes of childhood. For Buckingham, contemporary childhood is a performance in which the identity of the child is repeatedly staged for audiences such as siblings, friends and adults including parents and teachers. Television is thus an important resource for the making of childhood identity.

Childhood only makes sense in distinction to adulthood, and adults are responsible for broadcasting regulations and make decisions about what children should or should not see on television. Broadcasting in Britain is largely self-regulated on the basis of codes and guidelines drawn up and interpreted by the Office of Communications (Ofcom), a body appointed by the government to "further the interests of citizens in communication matters" and to "further the interests of consumers", which are of course potentially conflicting aims. The main channels have for a long time agreed on a 9.00 p.m. 'watershed', before which time programmes that could be offensive or disturbing to children will not be broadcast. Uncut films with a 15 age rating cannot be shown before 8.00 p.m. even on a dedicated film channel, and films with an 18 rating cannot be shown before 9.00 p.m. on any channel. Potential or actual upset to children is often cited as a ground for viewer complaints; for example, there was a controversy in 2010 when the pop stars Rihanna and Christina Aguilera performed sexualised dance routines during the final programme of *The X Factor* talent show. *The X Factor* is on the main channel ITV1, shown in the early evening and is watched by both adults and children (often viewing together in the same room), and this familial, domestic context made protests by adults on behalf of children likely. But Ofcom has less control over minority digital channels, where sexual content is much stronger, than it has over the dominant mass audience channels like ITV1. For example, Ofcom (2010) published the results of a formal investigation that found that the companies Bang Channels and Bang Media had breached the Broadcasting Code with their programmes *Early Bird* and *The Pad* in November 2010. In these programmes, broadcast in the early morning on a channel called Tease Me, young scantily clad women stroked themselves, adopted sexual body-positions and jiggled their breasts, among other things. The aim was to invite viewers to phone premium-rate chat lines, whose numbers were advertised via on-screen captions. Ofcom decided that the Tease Me programmes had caused offence because they could be seen by children due to the time of day when they were broadcast.

In 2007, the regulator decided (Ofcom 2007) that advertising 'junk food' during children's television programming might encourage children to consume too much fat, sugar and salt, following an investigation and consultation with interested groups. Ofcom calculated that banning these ads would reduce child obesity and save about £1 billion on medical treatment for overweight children. But the effect was that Britain's main commercial channel, ITV, withdrew from commissioning new children's programmes since the advertising ban meant it could not gain revenue from the companies that bought advertising time during children's programmes on the channel. ITV had previously spent about £30 million each year on new British children's programmes (M. Brown 2010), but instead commissioned factual entertainment and comedy for adults that would occupy the schedule slots vacated by children's television. Although programmes for children have been part of the British television landscape since the beginning of the medium, commercial pressures, competition among the large numbers of channels now available and wider political concerns about public health came together to threaten the genre. Ofcom had to compromise between the widely supported idea that children's programmes are beneficial and the economics of deregulated multi-channel television.

Audiences as Children

Protecting children from television is connected to assumptions about how other vulnerable groups can be adversely affected by television. Elites tend to consider mass audiences as 'them' in contrast to the more sophisticated 'us', and mass audiences have been regarded as childlike and unable to discriminate between programmes. In the 1960s, a liberal discourse on contemporary media gained currency by linking aims to expand audiences' intellectual horizons with a discourse that claimed childlike openness to experiment and the valuation of childhood as a mode of experience that liberated perception from the dry conventionality of 'adult' relationships with contemporary media. Marshall McLuhan ([1964] 1987), for example, argued that media users, especially television viewers, interacted with media in a way parallel to children's supposed creative and involved relation to the world around them. McLuhan's work proposed that electronic media like television surpassed the linear, rationalistic and literary heritage of Western civilisation by returning to an iconic, tribal and bardic mode, which he associated both with 'primitive' tribal societies and with Modernist works of art. Young people, McLuhan argued, were better equipped than adults to respond to television and other recent media forms as well as having the energy to bring about social change. Like some of the popular movements of the 1960s, which drew on Romantic conceptions of nature, childhood and organic social utopianism, this use of the figure of the child represents a call for the reinvigoration of technological culture by a paradoxical return to a pre-existing nature (Heywood et al. 2017). Broadly positive and negative theories of media draw on childhood in ways that largely reinforce conventional understandings of the child as different to adults and socially and culturally incomplete. For both pessimists and optimists, the figure of the child is a key component in understanding a Western metropolitan society perceived to be dominated in new and significant ways by mass media culture.

The media theorist John Hartley argues that broadcasters think about audiences in a way that is parallel to adults' attitudes to children. Hartley argues that "there's a struggle between what are presumed to be *paedocratic* audience practices on the one hand (governed *by* childlike qualities), and *pedagogic* discourses on the other (government *over* childish tendencies)" (1992, 17, emphasis in original). Although television viewers can be addressed in a range of ways, for example as citizens, as workers or as members of ethnic, gender or class groups, Hartley suggests that television is understood primarily as an entertainment medium and focuses on the delivery of pleasure to its audience. Despite the fact that there are some genres, such as news, that address the audience with information, and genres such as some children's television programmes that aim to educate the audience, the majority of programmes are either entertainment or use entertainment forms in order to attract viewers, retain them on a channel and encourage viewing of future programmes. Hartley claims that broadcasters

> appeal to the playful, imaginative, fantasy, irresponsible aspects of adult behaviour. They seek the common personal ground that unites diverse and often directly antagonistic groupings in a given population. What better, then, than a fictional version of everyone's supposed childlike tendencies which might be understood as predating such social groupings?
>
> (111)

The argument is that treating the audience as children is a strategy of control.

The other strand of John Hartley's argument is that television also aims to instruct television viewers, just as adults seek to instruct and train children. Some programmes have an explicit educational aim, but also the promotion of television programmes, trailers and reviews of programmes instructs the audience about what is available to watch and how to watch it. The regulation of television both within the industry and by official regulatory bodies can also be regarded as instructional. Institutions control and instruct the audience in the way that adults seek to control the behaviour of children. By discussing the television audience in this way, Hartley draws our attention to the contradictory status of the audience in television culture. On one hand, the audience is very valuable to broadcasters. It is the group that they address and the source of their income. Like the love that adults have for their children, broadcasters show care and interest in the audience. On the other hand, audiences can be hard to understand and difficult to communicate with, and it is difficult for broadcasters and regulators to gain control of viewers' attitudes and behaviour. Like children, audiences can be unruly and undisciplined. Broadcasters, regulators, commentators and parents draw on their anxiety about what children might see on television in order to frame ideological strategies that unconsciously depend on assumptions about the audience as a whole, both adults and children.

The original meaning of 'broadcasting' was the scattering of seed over the soil, a metaphor that has become the accepted term for the transmission of radio and television signals (Winston 1998, 77). Thus broadcasting as dissemination retains the connotations of fertility, growth, renewal and promise that it inherits from that agricultural language. At the same time, both broadcasting and dissemination signify the control of the process by a single agent, the indiscriminate nature of the distributive act, the necessary delay between casting the seed (or sending the signal) and its arrival at its destination and the impossibility of knowing whether the seed or message will take hold and lead to a desired result.

Like the concept of childhood, broadcasting as a concept holds together contrasting and mutually implicated notions, implying fertility but also uncertainty. At stake here is whether communicative address and interaction can establish a substantial relation between two figures, or whether it is evidence of an absence of relation. Jacqueline Rose (1984, 1) elaborated on this question in her landmark study of literature for children, in which she concluded:

> Children's literature is impossible, not in the sense that it cannot be written (that would be nonsense), but that it hangs on an impossibility of which it rarely ventures to speak. This is the impossible relation between adult and child.

This chapter argues a similar position about broadcasting for children. Non-communication, as much as communication, is inherent in the nature of broadcasting itself, where messages may not arrive, may not be understood or may fail to produce a desired effect. Contemporary interactive forms of children's media might promise greater benefit to children and fewer attempts to exercise power over their viewership, but they also imply greater investment in the communicative relation. Inasmuch as 'the child' is necessarily an 'other', he or she is always elsewhere.

References

BBC. 1971. *Radio Times*. London edition, January 30–February 5.
Bignell, Jonathan. 2011. "Television for Children: Problems of National Specificity and Globalisation." In *Children in Culture, Revisited: Further Approaches to Childhood*, edited by Karín Lesnik-Oberstein, 165–85. Basingstoke: Palgrave.
Brown, Ivor. 1951. "T.V. in the Englishman's Castle." In *BBC Year Book 1951*, 17–9. London: BBC.
Brown, Maggie. 2010. "Is Funding for Kid's TV just a Fantasy?" *The Guardian*, Media Section, June 14.
Buckingham, David. 1996. *Moving Images: Understanding Children's Emotional Responses to Television*. Manchester: Manchester University Press.
———. 2000. *After the Death of Childhood: Growing Up in the Age of Electronic Media*. Cambridge: Polity.
Hartley, Ian. 1983. *Goodnight Children ... Everywhere*. Scarborough: Midas.
Hartley, John. 1992. *Tele-ology: Studies in Television*. London: Routledge.
Heywood, Sophie et al. 2017. *The Children's '68*. Accessed 22 February 2017. https://children68.hypotheses.org.
Hodge, Bob, and David Tripp. 1986. *Children and Television: A Semiotic Approach*. Cambridge: Polity.
Jenkins, Henry. 2006. *Convergence Culture. Where Old and New Media Collide*. New York: New York University Press.

Lemish, Dafna. 2007. *Children and Television: A Global Perspective.* Oxford: Blackwell.
McLuhan, Marshall. 1987. *Understanding Media: The Extensions of Man.* London: Ark.
Newsom, John. 1963. *Half Our Future: A Report of the Central Advisory Council for Education.* London: HMSO.
Ofcom. 2007. *Television Advertising of Food and Drink Products to Children.* February 22. www.ofcom.org.uk/consultations-and-statements/category-2/foodads_new/statement.
———. 2010. *Breach Finding: Bang Channels Ltd.*, November 26. www.ofcom.org.uk/__data/assets/pdf_file/0023/72176/breach.pdf.
———. 2014. *Public Service Broadcasting Report, 2014: Children's PSB Summary.* London: Ofcom.
Oswell, David. 1995. "Watching with Mother in the Early 1950s." In *In Front of the Children: Screen Entertainment and Young Audiences*, edited by Cary Bazalgette and David Buckingham, 34–46. London: British Film Institute.
Postman, Neil. 1983. *The Disappearance of Childhood.* New York: Vintage.
Rose, Jacqueline. 1984. *The Case of Peter Pan, or, the Impossibility of Children's Fiction.* London: Macmillan.
Scannell, Paddy. 1990. "Public Service Broadcasting: The History of a Concept." In *Understanding Television*, edited by Andrew Goodwin and Garry Whannel, 11–29. London: Routledge.
Silverstone, Roger. 2006. *Television and Everyday Life.* London: Routledge.
Singleton-Turner, Roger. 1994. *Television and Children.* London: BBC.
Siune, Karen, and Olof Hulten. 1998. "Does Public Broadcasting Have a Future?" In *Media Policy: Convergence, Concentration, Commerce*, edited by Denis McQuail and Karen Siune, 23–37. London: Sage.
Turner, Graeme. 2009. "Television and Nation: Does this Matter Any More?" In *Television Studies After TV*, edited by Graeme Turner and Inna Tay, 54–64. London: Routledge.
Winston, Brian. 1998. *Media Technology and Society, A History: From the Telegraph to the Internet.* London: Routledge.

6 An Inconvenient Growth

Watching Child Actors, Growing Up, Sideways and Backwards in Contemporary British Film and Television

Karen Lury

This chapter has three linked aims. Its primary aim is to explore, through a discussion of contemporary British film and television texts, the apparently inevitable and neutral topic of growth, or growing, in childhood. Second, it addresses questions of agency and identity in relation to that growth and, third, it considers the question of the child's growing body and its interdependence with his or her closest kin, peers and environment.

I begin with a caveat: as writers such as Erica Burman and Kathryn Bond Stockton (Burman 1994; Bond Stockton 2009) have made clear, while in most instances, the growth of children (in terms of height and weight) is to be expected – children 'grow up' – the 'normalisation' of growth-as-development in childhood is deeply problematic. This is because it is established via a process of standardisation, frequently a quantification, that produces a homogenisation across the category of children. This may be in relation to the child's anticipated size at a particular life stage, the expression of sexual orientation and desire at an appropriate point in his or her development or in relation to the child's expected educational achievement at a specific biological age. What Burman and others have suggested is that such standardisation and the related normalisation of development are not sustainable in relation to the diversity of actual children at different stages in the life course. Indeed, as Bond Stockton (2009) has argued, there are benefits in thinking about how children might grow otherwise, or as she suggests, considering how children might grow 'sideways' as well as 'up'. This chapter accepts these challenges to the conventional understanding of growth within the normative model of child development.

The texts I focus on here provide instances in which the viewing audience is able to watch child actors 'grow' alongside their fictional characters in films and television series. I argue that in doing so, these films and programmes self-consciously allow for the difference of – and the differences between – children and enable viewers to glimpse a wider and more inclusive understanding of what it means to 'grow'. I provide a close analysis of Michael Winterbottom's 2012 film *Everyday* (also screened on television in episodic form on Channel 4 in the UK) and highlight key moments relating to the child actors and their performances from the BBC's long-running television sitcom *Outnumbered* (BBC, 2007–2014), thereby concentrating on the contemporary British context. The theoretical underpinning of my argument is indebted to work by Jonathan Herring and P.L. Chau (2007, 2014) who, from the perspective of medical ethics, have re-examined the status and integrity of the human body and conclude that "[n]o single model can capture the nuances of bodily life: that our bodies are ours; are in relationship with others; are in constant flux; and yet central to our identity of ourselves" (2007, 52). In other words, Herring and Chau argue that bodies should not be seen as wholly self-sealed containers but rather as complex and interdependent entities defined by their ongoing evolution, vulnerability and mutability. Their arguments help to make sense of the particular affect and resonance of the child actor's body and the representation of the child as character in the film and television programmes I discuss. Employing their arguments creates a space for a reflection on the significance of inter-generational relationships within childhood and the importance of care and caring as facilitating relations between individuals in families and externally within their wider communities.

Child performers on the stage and screen have long been seen as desirable, special or particularly appealing (Varty 2008). Writers, directors and audiences place a high value on the positive and possibly unique qualities that, seemingly, can only be achieved by the presence of a child actor and his or her body. This might include aspects such as the child actors' apparent spontaneity – read as 'naturalness' – which, in addition to the child's cuteness, littleness or higher-pitched voice, is frequently understood to add a particular charm to children's performances, a charm that is less easily achieved by other substitutes that do not grow, such as young-looking adult actors, dogs, other animals or individuals with short statures.

However, for the child actor, these cherished qualities are put at risk or are vulnerable to the changes that result of growing. While in most instances, for the child at least, growth seems inevitable and indeed desirable, these changes are likely to mean that the child actor will no longer appear to be the age of the character he or she is playing. In effect, the child actor may simply become 'too big' for the role and be unable to appear as little, cute, adorable, precocious or as apparently innocent as the role requires. Even if the character being played can and does age (as would be the case for many television soap opera children for example) another and related problem often emerges: what guarantee is there that the original infant or child actor (or more often actors) playing the 'cute baby' in the soap opera – or long-running sitcom – will satisfactorily develop into a gifted actor capable of playing a more adult role? The issue is, of course, one of temporality; the duration of filming, the biological age of the child actor and the developmental narrative of the child's character rarely proceed at the same pace.

The misalliance in terms of temporality between the actual child and the role as a film or television character is also complicated for what might seem to be the opposite reason: since children cannot satisfactorily appear to age (facial prosthetics can do little in the way of their smaller body size), it is very rare to see a young child play a character older than the child actor's own age. Indeed, one of the few examples in which the child actor does play a fictional character older than his actual age actually serves to underline my argument: in the film adaptation of *The Tin Drum* (Volker Schlöndorff, 1979) the child actor, David Bennent, who plays the role of the main protagonist Oskar Matzerath, was 11 at the time of production. Unusually, Bennent did continue to play the character as he ages within the film. However, this was feasible only because 'Oskar' is characterised precisely by his *refusal* to grow. Oskar is a stunted child, whose refusal or inability 'to grow up' is a symbolic and apparently pathological response to the terror and tyranny of the Nazi Germany in which he lives. Further evidence as to the discomfort provoked by seeing children play characters older than they appear to be can be seen by the way Bennent's continuance in the role later provoked huge controversy since his character (aged 16 in the context of the film) is involved in scenes of a sexual nature. Later legal action (in relation to the distribution of the film in the US) was taken against the filmmakers as it was alleged that Bennent must have performed acts of a sexual nature with his older co-stars. Ultimately, the case was disproven, as evidence from the older actors and from rushes demonstrated that the actual filming of these sequences had been carefully organised to prevent Bennent being involved in any actual acts that could have been deemed inappropriate for his age. Here, then, although a child actor does play a character older than his biological age, the fictional character's ageing – yet without the child actor actually growing in terms of his physical size – provokes a deliberate, uncanny and clearly uncomfortable effect for many viewers.

Conventionally, the most common way for the ageing of the child character in film and television to be managed – particularly if there are constraints in terms of the duration of filming – is to employ different actors to play the same character at different ages. One such example of this is the British film *Atonement* (Joe Wright, 2007) in which the same character, the protagonist Briony Tallis (who is 13 when the film begins), is played by three different actors: Saoirse Ronan (Briony at 13), Romola Garai (Briony at 18) and Vanessa Redgrave (the character's age is not specified but Redgrave was 77 at the time of production). Here, careful casting in relation to body type/appearance and the older actors' dedication to mimicking the voice and gestures of the youngest actor (Ronan) provides a convincing enough simulation.

Nonetheless, despite the difficulties in aligning the growth of child characters with the growth of child actors, there are some well-known films/film series in which the time of the characters and that of the child actors are in parallel; interestingly, the most obvious and recent example is British. In the eight *Harry Potter* films (film adaptations of the seven-book series by J.K. Rowling), which were in production between 2000 and 2010, we can witness Harry (Daniel Radcliffe), Hermione (Emma Watson) and Ron (Rupert Grint), alongside a number of returning child characters and cast, as they 'grow up'. In European cinema, another well-known example would be Jean-Pierre Léaud's performances as Antoine Doinel. Léaud has played Doinel from his earliest appearance as a child delinquent in *400 Blows* (Francois Truffaut, 1959) and reappeared as Doinel (at different stages of his life) in four other films over a 20-year period. Most recently, Richard Linklater's 2014 film, *Boyhood*, also filmed and employed one child actor, Ellar Coltrane, in his fictionalised portrayal of Mason Evans Jr. over an 11-year period (filming took place between 2002 and 2013). This unusual mode of production is similar to, although more sustained than, Winterbottom's filming of the child actors (the Kirk siblings) over a five-year period (between 2007 and 2012) during the making of *Everyday*.

What then is our response to watching children who do 'grow up' on screen? In most instances, we may be aware, primarily, of a change in size. As the child increases incrementally in size, there is almost a sense in which we are watching growth captured through a form of 'time lapse photography' – a filming technique most often used to depict changes in the natural world, such as climate or seasonal changes or the growth of plants. This formal association may imply that the representation of growth via film/photography is simply capturing a natural and inevitable process and that growth takes place without human intervention. This sense in which 'things' – plants, animals, children or icebergs – just 'grow' recalls the infamous character of the slave child Topsy from Harriet Beecher Stowe's 1852 novel *Uncle Tom's Cabin* and specifically Topsy's speculation, when asked about her origin, that she 'jus' grow'd'. In common use now, this notion that things, people or places 'jus' grow'd' more often means not just that we don't know where things have come from (Topsy's response is due to her ignorance as to her biological parents or family) but also that the objects, subjects or events in question – for example, children, cities or sometimes natural disasters – have simply 'grow'd and grow'd', uncontrollably, comically but generally in an alarming manner. Growth is therefore something that we may understand as natural but is also a process that frequently makes us fearful.

In the context of a chapter focusing on child performance and the child's body, Topsy's representation on stage and screen should be noted as having its own notorious history, with many early twentieth-century stage and screen portrayals of Topsy inappropriately enacted, not just by an adult – and therefore a performer that might be able to 'pass' as a child – but more specifically the role was generally portrayed by a *white* adult actor who did so in black face. The morphology of the comic but largely sympathetic child character of Topsy in the novel to her exploitation as a deeply racist caricature on stage, perhaps reflects an underlying concern about the 'freakish' quality of a character whose potential to disturb is amplified by the sense in which she is both a child (without origin) and also raced (African-American), who is also uncontrollably 'growing'. Her portrayal by an adult, white woman and in several instances an adult, white male actor (Frick, 2015) may have served to contain contemporary white adult audiences' anxieties about the unregulated potential of 'little, cute children' and 'docile slaves' who might 'grow up' and out of their control.[1]

The relationship between race and growth connects the fascination and the investment in the child's growth with a model for 'civilized' development, an association dependent on a more or less explicit adoption of 'recapitulation theory' – which suggests that 'ontology recapitulates phylogeny'. Topsy's irrational, uncivilised and unregulated ability to grow may be, supposedly, all the more ridiculous (or alarming) because she does not fit the implicitly racist model that is propagated in versions of this thesis. This presumption is that white civilisation should be recognised as the pinnacle of evolutionary progress and this necessarily situates the 'primitive races' as phases that must be passed through – or grown out of – in the process of development. As she is simultaneously black, a girl and a child, Topsy might be seen as a triply marginalised 'other' and a particularly disruptive figure in this context.

One interesting but problematic inversion of recapitulation theory as it relates to growth and development appears in Disney/Pixar's *Wall-E* (Andrew Stanton, 2008). In this animated fantasy, a little robot – Wall-E – is the last animate being left on earth. In the course of the story, Wall-E travels to a space ship on which he finds humans who have apparently been living there since they escaped from the devastating ecological impact of their actions on the earth. Yet the humans Wall-E now finds are helpless, baby-like figures, unable to walk or feed themselves. This disturbing evolution is recorded via a series of portraits that depict successive captains of the spaceship ballooning into infantile figures, similar in size and shape to the other humans now populating the ship (and the portraits, of course, operate as forms of time-lapse photography). Although these baby-ish adults are presented sympathetically and comically, their grotesque appearance implies a lurking sense of anxiety about the consequences of the mismanagement or unchecked potential of 'growth' and its relationship to evolution and civilisation.

Growth and growing are therefore seen as inherent to childhood and to development: to 'grow up' is seen as inevitable, anticipated and desirable, but the process of growth itself is, at the same time, alarming, comic and even grotesque. I now want to provide an analysis as to how these divergent perspectives on growth and growing in childhood are managed and exemplified in two contemporary British film and television texts.

Outnumbered

This successful British television sitcom was written and devised by Andy Hamilton and Guy Jenkins. The story focuses on a middle-class family: the father, Pete Brockman (Hugh Denis), and mother, Sue Brockman (Claire Skinner), are both working, and the extended family includes the mother's adult sister, Angela Morrison (played by Sue Bond), and their elderly father, Frank (David Ryall). At the start of the series, Frank is understood to be suffering from dementia, and in the 2016 Christmas special (BBC, 2016) he has died and the family is gathering to scatter his ashes. Pete and Sue live with their three children, two older boys, Jake (Tyger Drew-Honey), Ben (Daniel Roche) and their youngest child, a girl, Karen (Ramona Marquez), in the outer reaches of London. At the start of the series, the youngest child actor (Marquez) was five and the oldest (Drew-Honey) was 12. While the set up (a nuclear family living together in the suburbs) was entirely conventional for a television sitcom, the innovation in the series was tied to the performances of the child actors, whose speech and activity – at least in the earlier seasons of the show – was largely improvised. Jenkins and Hamilton provided a broad framework for each episode's plot and action but allowed the children to improvise their own response to certain situations and questions. This meant that the adult actors were often required to respond (retrospectively) to the child's behaviour. One early and relatively typical sequence is an extended scene in an episode from the first season in which Sue laboriously combs the (then blonde and curly) hair of Karen, during which they have a largely circuitous discussion about whether or not, from Karen's perspective, you could have a nit 'as a pet' and if not whether a giraffe might, or might not, be a suitable alternative (Figure 6.1).

The way in which the conversation is led and pursued by Karen/Marquez, along with its iterative and repetitive nature, in addition to its articulation through a variety of hesitations and pauses, creates an entirely naturalistic effect. Marquez-as-Karen's precocious 'little madam' appeal was perhaps a significant aspect of the series' early success, and Ramona Marquez's growth and development from the first season – where she was little, with blonde and curly hair – to her later appearance as a taller, gawky brunette with a fringe was much remarked on in the press and publicity for the series. Within the development of the series itself, it would seem that the infantile precociousness of 'Karen' as an articulate and opinionated five-year-old evolved so that in Marquez's

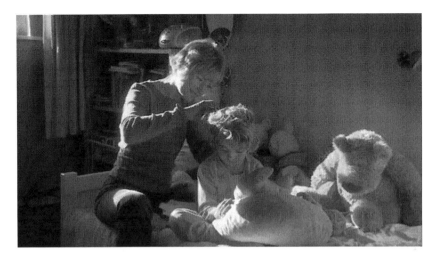

Figure 6.1 Sue (Claire Skinner) and Karen (Ramona Marquez) combing for nits, from *Outnumbered* (BBC, 2007–2014).

portrayal of the teenage 'Karen' her 'precociousness' and certainty appear as a more pathological and potentially disquieting performance of a 'superiority complex'. Karen's development from an adorable 'little madam' to a less than sympathetic (but still amusing) young woman suggests that while the writers could not bear to abandon the memory of the adorable but precocious little girl, they believed that her previous behaviour and demeanour would not be acceptable in an older female (in fact, it could only be a personality disorder).

Equally significant is the transformation of 'Ben', the middle son, who across the series grows from a small and rebellious seven-year-old to a huge young man, finally towering over his adult parents. Ben's 'remarkable' growth is incorporated into the development of his character, and there are several different instances in which he carries or picks up his parents (initially his mother and in the most recent episode his father as well) thereby emphasising the passing of time, as well as demonstrating the implicitly alarming and comic potential of children who 'outgrow' their parents. The slapstick comedy that is a key aspect of the smaller Ben's rebellious behaviour is managed in his later appearances by his reincarnation as a clumsy but largely benign (and apparently uncomplicated) 'giant'. At several points in the series – as he is growing up – Ben uses the phrase 'puny humans' (in relation to his parents and siblings) and in doing so refers directly to the recent movie adaptations of the Marvel comic's 'Hulk' character who also employs this phrase. Not coincidentally, the Hulk is another fictional figure whose key characteristic is a tendency for excessive and unregulated growth. In aligning himself with the Hulk, Roche-as-Ben deflects the unspoken anxiety that might be associated with his actual growth and consigns it safely to the realm of fantasy. These concerns arise because Roche's increasing size – and thus his potential for physical dominance – is problematic in relation to his characterisation of Ben as a (previously small) child with an unregulated appetite and a propensity for violence. The older and larger Ben's self-conscious and continued acknowledgement of himself as a 'monster' helps to deflate any concerns that might be associated with his relentless challenging of the established family hierarchy, although his potential to harm his family is tacitly acknowledged: in the Christmas special it emerges that Ben has managed to break his mother's toe by (accidentally) dropping a frozen turkey on it.

Despite the series' unusual centring and privileging of the child actors – in which their performance is facilitated through improvisation and their actual growth is managed and allowed within the continuing narrative, *Outnumbered* – and the title of the programme, of course, makes this explicit since there are three children as opposed to two adults – remains a show that portrays children as 'other' to the adult. The 'doubling' or alignment of the growth of the child actors with the fictional child characters is made to work to the programme's advantage but only at the expense of the actual development of the child characters becoming young adults' personalities. Within the series, growth and growing up are therefore presented, implicitly and explicitly, as comic, uncanny, fascinating and (a little bit) threatening. The more worrying aspects of growth and its potential for disruption are unsurprisingly, in the context of a mainstream television sitcom, carefully and playfully deflected. The potentially unsettling aspects of what 'growing up' means is, perhaps, necessarily obscured in what is generally a largely sentimental and comforting vision of family life.

However, it is worth noting that the series also incorporates what might be seen as the inverse to the conception of growth-as-development, where ageing is more often associated with decline rather than progression. A more complex and reflective interpretation of 'growing-as-ageing' is glimpsed in the character of the grandfather, Frank, whose increasing dementia across the run of the series facilitates some surprising instances in which the children's 'growing up' – their increasing size, physical competency and deeper understanding of the world in which they live – is met and aligned with the grandfather's perceptible 'growing down'. This process is made evident through Rydall's performance as Frank, demonstrating with comic pathos his increasing frailty, memory loss and unwillingness to abide by the conventions of adult behaviour.

Everyday

Everyday was originally transmitted in episodic form on Channel 4 in 2012 then later released in cinemas as a stand-alone film in 2013. Its director Michael Winterbottom is regarded as an innovative if sometimes controversial director responsible for films such as *9 Songs* (2004) and *The Killer Inside Me* (2010) as well as more populist (if still 'art house') works such as *A Cock and Bull Story* (2005) and *24 Hour Party People* (2002). *Everyday* was made over a five-year period and featured the adult actors John Simm and Shirley Henderson. Simm's character is imprisoned (his crime is unspecified but seems likely to be drugs related) and the story unfolds over the duration of his prison sentence, featuring visits to Simm in prison from his wife (played by Henderson) with their children. In addition, there are glimpses of their home life (at Christmas, at school, on the beach) and occasional sequences (for example, in a small country town) that feature Simm and the family together, presumably on day release, until his final return home. Simm and Henderson's fictional children are played by four actual siblings: Stephanie, Robert, Shaun and Katrina Kirk. The children's growth and physical changes recorded during the making of the film are an essential aspect of the story; indeed, they are what the film is 'about'. The significance of their growth is emphasised by the fact that it is the focus of a special DVD 'extra' – the 'kids montage' – that illustrates, through a process very similar to time-lapse photography, the changes captured in the children as they grow over the years.

The montage and many sequences in the film depict the children doing the same things: travelling; walking; riding in cars, buses and trains; eating breakfast, lunch, tea or being at school singing at Christmas or Harvest Festival; playing games and fighting in the playground or football field. By repeating these moments, walks and gestures, the passage of time is made more explicit. As the children grow, spoons and forks become smaller in their hands and mouths, and while there is some consistency in terms of their school uniform, their hair changes, their postures shift and their voices deepen. Early in the film, Shaun, the youngest boy, is woken up and we can see he is wearing a nappy; by the end of the film, he is a confident ten-year-old in long trousers. That the filmmakers were acutely sensitive to the 'time lapse' aspect of the project is evident from Winterbottom's own observations of the filming process:

> And it's strange, it's like having your own children – you don't notice them growing up, it's very incremental; time passing in the real world is very different to time passing in the fictional world, where you would cast a different actor for each stage of a boy growing up.
> (Barton 2012)

The time lapse is also marked by another formal repetition across the duration of the film's narrative. There is a recurring sequence in which Simm's character – sometimes in a different prison context – returns to his cell after a visit from the family and lies down on his bed, reaching with his hands to clasp behind his head and closing his eyes. This moment generally marks a shift to another (later) period of the story and therefore the children's lives so that the father's repeated 'book ending' of each visit makes explicit his fluctuating presence in his children's lives. This father's position therefore reflects the viewers' own limited access to the children and makes clear the 'lapse' between the incidences of filming the children as they grow up.

'Time-lapse' photography is very close to 'stop-motion' animation in its effect, although the former filming technique is designed to *capture* movement and the latter to *create* it. The significance of animation for my argument is its dependence on the 'in-between': this 'in-between' is the 'space' or unseen moment that occurs either between the images (from drawing to drawing in cel animation) or the unrecorded moments that allow for the physical manipulation of the model by the animator (the barely perceptible changes made, for instance, to the puppet's fingers, eyes or legs.) The 'in-between' is where change happens. It is therefore where the performance, the identity, the physical changes to the character and his or her identity are located. As a technique or process, animation, or 'to be animated', refers to both control and to a potential for excess or revolution. To be 'animated' has two distinct meanings: first, that you can be animated *by* someone else, as in a character that is drawn and manipulated, and this would suggest that animation is oppressive action – as in the expression of being someone else's 'puppet'. At the same time however, animation as a form is often unruly, establishing a world that may be plastic and mutable, inhabited by characters that use excessive gestures and express wild emotions and seemingly unlimited potential. Many animated characters are ruthless, often indestructible, and do not obey the rules of gravity or indeed size. In the recent film adaptations of the Marvel comic books, for instance, (e.g. *The Avengers* directed by Joss Whedon in 2012) while Dr. Banner – the Hulk's alter ego – is performed by a human actor (Mark Ruffalo), it is unsurprising that the Hulk himself is portrayed through animation (CGI). To suggest, therefore, that the Kirk children and their growth is 'animated' within the context of the film may indicate a possible ambiguity inherent to the representation of children 'growing up'. On the one hand, viewers may be conscious of and perhaps alarmed at their intimacy with the children's unchecked potential related to their growth – whether this is made visible through their changes in height, size and weight, via their minor rebellions or their excessive behaviour as they erupt into tears or burst into laughter. On the other hand, we may also tacitly intuit that we are also witness to the children's repression or manipulation by external forces through which they are being 'animated'. This may be in relation to their schooling or the repetition of adults who demand that they "sit straight", "give me a kiss" or "eat that".

Our intimacy with the children over a number of years and the naturalistic context of the film brings the audience very 'close' to them, emotionally and in terms of physical proximity. This closeness is emphasised through the large number of sequences and shots of the children that are in close-up in which the children's faces fill most of the film frame. This means that, as viewers, we are frequently very close to the bodies and, more specifically, to what is visible of the skin of the children as they grow. Skin takes on a particular significance here as it too exemplifies another contradiction in relation to our understanding of the human body and growth. Conventionally, we may believe that our skin and therefore the children's skin represents an impermeable surface, a container, something that is 'lived within' – a barrier to the outside world that must be, to use another concept from animation, 'stretched and squashed' or expanded like a rubber balloon to facilitate growth. However, as Steven Connor has noted, skin is not impermeable; it is rather

> a topology rather than a topography, a shape which does not present itself all at once to the eye, but emerges, like the gathering of a wave, or the piling of a cloud, through the passage of time, whose shape itself it comes to be.
>
> (2003, 37)

The human skin, he suggests, should be recognised as less like a membrane or barrier and more like a 'cosmos' since skin cells are constantly being shed, new ones established and the skin itself inhabited by hundreds and thousands of bacteria, thereby establishing it as an environment that is as much about exchange as protection. Skin is an organ through which we mingle with and encounter other bodies and other skins. *Everyday*, in its attention to the minutiae of the children's bodies as they grow and to the changes and fluctuations in their skin, is attentive to this deeper recognition of the characteristics of skin itself as well as its relationship to the body, to growth and identity. At numerous points in the film, priority – in terms of focus, inclusion, repetition – is given to the evidence of the skin: the shivering, blushing, erupting and scarring of the children's skin articulates how the children are feeling and growing more often than what the children say or do. For example, in a sequence in the headmistress's office, Robert and Shaun are reprimanded for fighting in the playground, and the deepening flush on both of the boys' cheeks expresses much more than what they actually verbalise. Similarly, in another, otherwise unremarkable sequence set on a beach, Shaun's shivering, or the visible trembling of his skin, not only expresses his personal and temporary discomfort on a cold English summer's day, but also evokes a powerful somatic

114 *Karen Lury*

Figure 6.2 Shivers, sunshine and skin – Shaun Kirk in *Everyday* (Michael Winterbottom, 2012).

memory for viewers through which they may recall their own childhood encounters with the sea (Figure 6.2).

This apparently coincidental recording of a very ordinary encounter between the child's body and environment is a 'memory of and by the skin'. Several other sequences also bring viewers close to a variety of small scars and bruises on the children's faces and knees, thereby paying close attention to the endless little events and encounters of childhood. In these moments, the camera's attention to the skin suggests an implicitly tactile mode of seeing that feels clinical, tender and intrusive.

However, our apparent access to the children as they grow is illusory and the result of a broken promise: while we are seemingly offered a narrative in which we will see the children grow up 'before our eyes', the trembling and flushing of their skin or the tracing and recording of their various scabs and grazes do not capture growth 'as it happens', that is within the apparent 'present tense' of the unfolding narrative; rather, they are its legacy – milestones – much like the successive pen marks made on a doorway by parents who wish to record the growth of their children.

Despite this broken promise, *Everyday*, like *Outnumbered*, does offer something more in its sensitivity to the interdependencies and inter-generational relationships that are essential to a more inclusive model of childhood and the uncertainty and contradictory emotions that are related to the growing and the growth of the child. In an early sequence, in which the two boys accompany their mother on a visit to their father in prison, Robert holds Shaun, who is sleeping, with his hand held fast against his little brother's chest (Figure 6.3).

Figure 6.3 "Our bodies are not in a straightforward sense, ours" – Robert and Shaun Kirk in *Everyday* (Michael Winterbottom, 2012).

Without Robert's intervention, Shaun would be likely to slump forward and fall off the seat of the bus in which they are all travelling. The very ordinary quality of this gesture, along with the mixture of resilience, boredom and the untranslatable in Robert's gaze at the camera at this moment, seems to me to capture the 'everything in the nothing' within the shifting relationship between the siblings as they grow up together. At this moment, we see Robert take care of his brother, holding him in place whilst travelling with him across space and time, taking responsibility for him whilst also acknowledging Shaun as a 'fellow traveller'. As Herring and Chau suggest: "Our bodies are not in a straight-forward sense, 'ours'. They are interdependent, interconnected and intermingling with others" (2007, 45). In this and other sequences, the children's growing up 'together' reflects an understanding that 'growth' is not achieved individually (it is not autonomous) but rather emerges through our relation to others and to the environment. As Herring and Chau further argue, "Our true sense of self and identity is not found in our bounded, owned body, but in the breaking, mixing and interaction of our bodies with others and the wider environment" (2014, 42).

Everyday articulates a more nuanced representation of growth and growing than many films that feature children, not just because the child actors grow up at the same time along with their characters but also because we are witness to a careful and naturalistic re-enactment of the ordinary relations and choreography of family life. In addition, while our attention is primarily drawn to the children, the father's character is also concerned with growth, or its repression or regression because as a prisoner he is explicitly subject to a system that effectively and deliberately infantilises him, aligning him, perhaps, with the adult babies in *Wall-E*. As a prisoner, the father is 'animated' by others within the system, whether guards or fellow inmates; his activities and behaviour are continually scrutinised, monitored and recorded and his bodily routines and walking routes circumscribed and managed. When inside he also wears childlike garments – uniforms of soft shirts and jeans or a grey sweatshirt and sweatpants – and he is helpless, watched over, touched, searched, bullied while being 'cared for', as he is given a bed to sleep on and regularly fed. While we may be tempted to read the film as suggesting that the real pathos is the fact that he is missing out on seeing his children as they 'grow up', his imprisonment also acts as an example and potentially a critique of the way in which different social institutions, be they prisons or families, determine in part the ability of everyone, whatever their age – to 'grow'.

All this suggests a rather bleak view of the childhood being represented and performed in the film since I am perhaps implying that the family is a prison and that childhood is something to be endured, as in 'doing time'. However, an alternative and more optimistic perspective is suggested by the ending of the film. In this sequence, there is a glimpse of a future for the family in which the inter-dependency of all its members is represented and made possible, where growth of all kinds – upwards, sideways, backwards – may be permissible. At this point in the narrative, the family is reunited and the father has apparently been released from prison permanently. The family makes a trip to the beach, a location familiar to us from an earlier sequence in the film. On the way, the family walks through a small area of woodland, and here the mother climbs a tree, a childish act that is further reinforced as she is then carried on the father's shoulders and, with her legs swinging, she seems, almost for the first time in the film, relaxed and playful. Appropriately and perhaps not coincidentally, the adult actor, Shirley Henderson, who plays the mother, is slight and has a rather childlike appearance as she wears little or no make-up and her hair is worn long and loose.[2] Here, then, the mother performs and is accepted as if she were physically and emotionally a child, and her regression, or her backwards growth, is not seen as problematic but playful. Yet her regressive act is also done with a purpose, since by doing so, she is allowing or asking the father to now take on the responsibility of care for the family. Previously forced by the father's incarceration into the position of a single parent, the mother was, as we have seen, solely responsible for her children and herself; now, simply by sitting on his shoulders, she makes it very clear that the father should now carry the responsibility and the 'burden of care'. The family then makes its way on to the beach and heads towards the sea. As they do so, they are positioned further and further away from the camera so that the height differences among the children and between the adults and children are increasingly indistinguishable; an equalising effect that is further amplified by the fact they are wearing very similar thick coats and hats. Therefore reiterated in this sequence are the non-verbal qualities – the bodily intimacy – of the family members as they are together, and we are therefore encouraged to see that their relationships as much as their individuality is important. Here, their bodies are interconnected, interdependent and the exchanges of touch and gesture, their breathing, warmth and proximity to one another acknowledges a complex topology that reflects a sense in which these are bodies that are growing together. In a sense, as a 'happy ending', it is possibly a too neat or utopian ending for an otherwise persuasively naturalistic film, but its setting on the beach, during which the tide and therefore the sea is out and barely visible on the horizon, suggests that this ending is also happening in a space that is 'in-between', a liminal place, suggesting that it is not so much an ending but an interlude and therefore not a definitive conclusion to the family's story.

What we see when we watch children grow on screen is an oscillating display of different points in time and space in which growing – happening within the in-between – is precisely what is not seen. The growth of the child, despite the filmmakers' best attempts – through improvisation, via close-ups, durational filming, animation and editing – is never satisfactorily topographical (map-able) or chronological (time-ordered). While the use of time-lapse photography, like the pen marks on the doorframe, may construct a fixed temporality and a sense of progression, it is also an illusion. While both *Outnumbered* and *Everyday* may present a chronology of sorts, there is also a sense in which, in different ways, the growing child these quite different texts capture is also recognised as an incoherent, temporally inconsistent and incredibly diverse figure, whose growth and growing is never autonomous. In these texts, the child's growth is not, as Topsy might have argued, something that 'jus' happens'. And while the child's growth may appear remarkable, graspable, *growing* is always 'in-between' and remains just out of sight.

By employing Herring and Chau's arguments, I have suggested that human growth, in children and adults, is actually a complex negotiation between the bodies we call our own, other bodies we encounter (both human and inhuman) and the environment. The greater visibility of the changes that emerge from the physical growth of the human body during childhood may be fascinating to both filmmakers and viewers, but what I hope my analysis of *Outnumbered* and *Everyday* reveals is that growing cannot be properly captured by either film or television because it is an iterative process that is (in)between the self and the world, an ongoing process that is experienced by everyone, whatever the biological age. That said, the incremental effect – or final legacy – of having examined the experience of witnessing child actors grow in parallel to their fictional characters may provide some inkling as to what it might be to grasp the contradictory responses we have to the 'growing child' and to the complexity – or mystery – of growth itself.

Notes

1 For a fascinating discussion of the Duncan sisters' twentieth-century stage and screen portrayals of Little Eva and Topsy, see Jocelyn Buckner, "The Angel and the Imp: The Duncan Sisters' Performances of Race and Gender," *Popular Entertainment Studies* 2.2 (2011): 55–72.
2 In fact, in a previous role, Henderson successfully 'passed' as a child, since she is best known for playing the recurring character 'Moaning Myrtle', the school-girl ghost from the *Harry Potter* films.

References

9 Songs. 2004. DVD. Directed by Michael Winterbottom. Sony Pictures Home Entertainment, 2012.
24 Hour Party People. 2002. DVD. Directed by Michael Winterbottom. 20th Century Fox, 2003.
400 Blows/Les Quatre Cents Coups. 1959. DVD. Directed by François Truffaut. Tartan Films, 2002.
A Cock and Bull Story. 2005. DVD. Directed by Michael Winterbottom. Lions Gate Home Ent. UK Ltd, 2007.
Atonement. 2007. DVD. Directed by Joe Wright. Universal Pictures UK, 2008.
Barton, Laura. 2012. "Silver Screen Siblings: The Child Stars of Michael Winterbottom's *Everyday*." *The Guardian*, October 15. Accessed 12 February 2016. www.theguardian.com/film/2012/oct/15/child-stars-michael-winterbottom-everyday.
Beecher-Stowe, Harriet. 1852. *Uncle Tom's Cabin: or, Life among the Lowly*. Boston, MA: John P. Dewett and Sons.
Bond Stockton, Kathryn. 2009. *The Queer Child, or Growing Sideways in the Twentieth Century*. Durham, NC: Duke University Press.
Boyhood. 2014. DVD. Directed by Richard Linklater. Universal Pictures, 2015.
Buckner, Jocelyn, 2011. "The Angel and the Imp: The Duncan Sisters' Performances of Race and Gender." *Popular Entertainment Studies* 2 (2): 55–72.
Burman, Erica. 1994. *Deconstructing Developmental Psychology*. London: Routledge.
Connor, Steven. 2003. *The Book of Skin*. London: Reaktion Books.
Everyday. 2012. DVD. Directed by Michael Winterbottom. Soda Pictures, 2013.
Frick, John W. 2015. *Uncle Tom's Cabin on the American Stage and Screen*. London: Palgrave Macmillan.
Harry Potter – The Complete Collection. 2011. DVD. Directed by Chris Columbus, Alfonso Cuarón, Mike Newell and David Yates. Warner Home Video.
Herring, Jonathan, and P.L. Chau. 2007. "My Body, Your Body, Our Bodies." *Medical Law Review* 15: 34–61.
———. 2014. "Interconnected, Inhabited and Insecure: Why Bodies Should Not Be Property." *Med Ethics* 40: 39–43.

Outnumbered Christmas Special 2016. DVD. Directed by Andy Hamilton and Guy Jenkin. BBC One.
Outnumbered – Complete Series 1–5. 2014. DVD. Directed by Andy Hamilton and Guy Jenkin. BBC/2 Entertain.
The Avengers. 2012. DVD. Directed by Joss Whedon. Touchstone Pictures, 2012.
The Killer Inside Me. 2010. DVD. Directed by Michael Winterbottom. Icon Home Entertainment, 2010.
The Tin Drum/Die Blechtrommel. 1979. DVD. Directed by Volker Schlöndorff. Arrow Academy, 2012.
Wall-E. 2008. DVD. Directed by Andrew Stanton. Walt Disney Studios, 2008.
Varty, Anne. 2008. *Children and Theatre in Victorian Britain: All Work and No Play*. London: Palgrave Macmillan.

7 Adults Looking at Children
Books, Bodies and Buying in Children's Book Covers[1]

Jessica Medhurst

The production of children's books with alternative covers for the adult market in the UK is a very recent phenomenon and is founded on ideas of appropriateness and commercialism, ideas that are also at stake in critical considerations of childhood. Twentieth-century novels such as *The Curious Incident of the Dog in the Night-Time* (Haddon 2003a) and the *His Dark Materials* trilogy (Pullman 1995–2000), as well as classics such as *Alice's Adventures in Wonderland* (Carroll 1866) and *Treasure Island* (Stevenson 1883), have been rejacketed for both child and adult markets, raising questions about what is child-like or child-appropriate in and about the texts.[2]

This chapter examines the 2014 cover for Penguin Modern Classic's *Charlie and the Chocolate Factory* (Dahl [1964] 2004) and its wider paratexts – including articles in *The Independent* (Denham 2014), *The New Yorker* (Talbot 2014) and *The Washington Post* (Kaplan 2014), and Penguin's original announcements and press release – in order to question what is at stake when ideas of childhood are marketed to adults in this way (Figure 7.1). In doing so, it takes a transdisciplinary and theoretical approach to addressing the cultural anxieties raised in the media coverage of the book jacket and suggests alternative feminist-informed constructivist readings of childhood and motherhood on the book's cover.

The current scholarship on rejacketing what are taken to be children's books for an adult market focuses on the performative element of being seen to read, an aspect that this chapter will challenge through its reconsideration of perspective and the gaze. Sandra L. Beckett, in *Crossover Fiction* (2008), locates the rejacketing trend as starting in the US in 1997 with the publishing house Knopf Group. She argues that the production of different book jackets for child and adult editions came about due to a perception that adults' books should and do look different to children's books and that an adult edition jacket must look acceptable to other adults. Citing the *Harry Potter* series as the standout occurrence of children's books being rejacketed for adults, she understands the change in cover as the publisher's response to the perception that adult readers would feel shame in being seen to read a children's book.

Adults Looking at Children 121

Figure 7.1 Front and back cover of *Charlie and the Chocolate Factory* (Penguin Classics, 2015 edition). Source: Cover photograph by Sofia Sanchez and Mauro Mongiello/Trunk Archive. Copyright © Penguin Books, 2014. Author photograph © Leonard McCombe/Time & Life Pictures/Getty Images. Text within the Work copyright © Roald Dahl Nominee Ltd, 1964. Introduction copyright © Sam Mendes, 2014. Reproduced by permission of Penguin Books Ltd.

Her construction of the result of this in the adult cover of *Harry Potter and the Philosopher's Stone* (Rowling [1997] 1998) is that it has "a more sober cover design so that adults feel comfortable reading it in public" (243). Similarly, Rachel Falconer, in *The Crossover Novel* (2008) quotes Jim White's column in *The Telegraph*, to explain *Wolf Brother*'s (Paver 2004) popularity with adult audiences as being in part due to the cover's "simple, cave-painting design set against a muted red-brown background, which insured that, as one journalist put it, the book 'could discretely be read on the train by adults on their way to work'" (17).

Alan Powers, in *Children's Book Covers* (2003), also argues that producing editions of the *Harry Potter* books "with an 'adult' cover meant that adults did not have to feel ashamed of being seen reading it" (132). The cover, then, relates not to reading but to the look of reading – to being seen to read. He points to book covers as part of a performance of reading that does not, itself, read since

> [t]he cover certainly plays a part in the process of physical engagement with a book, for while, almost by definition, one cannot look

at the cover while reading, it establishes the book as a physical object to be picked up, put down, and perhaps kept over time.

(7)

Reading, in these constructions by Beckett, Falconer and Powers is, therefore, about performance: it is witnessed by others, and there is a drive to maintain an appropriateness in the look of the reading matter, which is determined not by the claimed content of the book but by the book's cover; that is, by what it looks like to one who is not reading but is seeing the reading. These claims require a stability of looking that this chapter refutes. It questions a reader's ability to read on behalf of others or to be able to fix the meaning of a book jacket through its close readings of what constitutes looking on the Penguin cover of *Charlie and the Chocolate Factory*.

The claim to be able to read on behalf of others is also at stake in the controversy over *Doing It* (Burgess 2003), a book about a group of teenagers' sex lives, which was originally published by children's publisher Andersen Press. The hardback version the front cover was a black background with the author's name in white at the top and the title on an unopened condom packet in the bottom right hand corner. In a review in *The Guardian*, fiction author Anne Fine (2003) asked "[w]hat are three separate children's publishers thinking of, peddling this grubby book, which demeans both young women and young men?" Despite its removal from children's lists and reissue as an adult title, Fine constructs the damage as already and irrevocably done:

> And, make no mistake, the publishers may slap a warning and a picture of a condom on the front and substitute a grown-up penguin for a puffin, but it was the children's publisher Andersen Press that commissioned this novel. It is Random House Children's Books who have it in their catalogue beside Emma Chichester Clark's *Up in Heaven* and Ken Brown's *What's the Time, Grandma Wolf?* (ages 4 and up). And the people who are putting most into this book are Penguin Children's Books, who were thrilled to win the paperback auction.
>
> (ibid.)

The difference between what constitutes a children's book and what constitutes an adult's book is such that, in this claim, shifting the book to an adult market does not make up for the damage done by originally marketing it for children.

The online newspaper coverage of the rejacketing of *Charlie and the Chocolate Factory* for the Penguin Modern Classics list focused largely on online reaction to an image of the cover, prompted by the response on Facebook to Penguin's two posts about the cover, by Penguin's follow-up blog post, and by Joanne Harris's two tweets about this. These articles, tweets and Facebook posts will be analysed in this chapter in order to think through the implications of the claims made about the child, the book and the cover, principally what the female sexualised child is understood to be in the cover of *Charlie and the Chocolate Factory* and the threat posed to it by perverted and negligent gazes.

Much of the criticism the cover received appealed to the inappropriateness of the cover, both in terms of its supposed role as representative of content and in terms of its construction of childhood. This chapter therefore addresses these two charges, specifically the appeals to other texts as evidence for the cover's inappropriateness and the construction of uncanniness and sexuality in readings of the cover. It will address the unstable boundaries of the text the critiques work to fix and will interrogate these ideas of looking and appropriateness, all of which, I will argue, are repeated in the mainstream media responses to Penguin Modern Classic's *Charlie and the Chocolate Factory* jacket. Rather than attempting to ascertain a 'correct' notion of childhood in the cover, it will read how these responses construct childhood and what the implications are for our claims about the child and children's literature. It will make the case that the newspaper and social media responses to the cover ironically repeat the shameful performance of looking that these critics read and that are implicated in the problems of seeing that their insistence on a stable, photographed, sexualised child (and a priorly innocent one) require. In concluding, the chapter will turn to what is not read by these critiques – the back cover – not in an attempt to complete a reading of the covers but in order to think through what is at stake in this absence and to argue that the critiques' investments in a gaze that can access the child wholly and without supplement is repeated in the notions of the commodification and commerciality of the text that I read on the back cover.

Inappropriate Representation

The Penguin Modern Classics front cover of *Charlie and the Chocolate Factory* was initially released as an image on the company's Facebook page on 6 August 2014, with the title and author redacted. Penguin invited Facebook users to "guess which tasty tale this cover belongs to", adding "[w]e could give you a clue [...] but that would be worth more than a golden ticket". Amongst the first 20 comments, received within 20 minutes of the question being posted, there were nine suggestions of *Charlie and the Chocolate Factory*, four of *Lolita* (Nabokov 1955) and two of *Valley of the Dolls* (Susann 1966), as well as one apiece for *Goldilocks and the Three Bears*, *A Moveable Feast* (Hemingway 1964), *The Godfather* (Puzo 1969), *The Stepford Wives* (Levin 1972), "Stepford Children" (1987) and "Barbie". These responses include novels characterised by manipulation of women and engagement with childhood and adolescence, as well as one, *The Moveable Feast*, that, the respondent commented, "doesn't go with golden ticket or doll". Respondents, then, not only responded to the wordless cover but also to the text that framed it as a competition. In this, the cover is produced as subject to a deferral to and in language that is supposedly removed by the redaction of the title and author. These suggested texts, then, were produced not only as a result of the cover but also of the Facebook post, an idea that is not engaged with in the media reports on the responses to the cover.

This appeal to other texts was picked up by Jess Denham in her article for *The Independent*, using it as evidence for the response of readers: "authors and readers have been left shocked, with many suggesting the image would be more appropriate for Vladimir Nabokov's *Lolita*, about a literature professor obsessed with a 12-year-old girl". *Lolita* here is singled out as the shocking association, suggesting a privileging of this kind of inappropriateness. Joanne Faulkner (2010), among others, argues that 'Lolita' no longer only refers to the Nabokov novel but that it "is currently shorthand for an unwitting sexual precocity of young girls in search of adult approval" (11). Graham Vickers (2008) claims, that "Dolores Haze, alias Lolita, was reduced to a logotype for salable images of child abuse in progress" (163) and Alyssa Harad (2003) argues, in her feminist return to the novel, film and iconography of *Lolita*, that

> 'Lolita' has grown into a vague and generally applicable brand name, the way 'Xerox' has come to mean 'copy' or 'Kleenex' to mean tissue. Now any underage girl whose sexiness is a compound of childish prettiness and erotic potential and who appeals to, or is attached to, older men, can be a Lolita.
>
> (86)

Whilst these three claims agree that the meaning of 'Lolita' has become othered and extended, this meaning is multiple and unstable – at once commodified abuse, sexual precocity and brand. So, whilst Denham's focus on *Lolita* may in one sense be taken as an appeal to a textual child sexuality, what constitutes that sexuality is contested.

It is not only the instability of meaning that is implicated in Denham's privileging of *Lolita*: Erica Burman (2008), discussing Carolyn Steedman's construction of the use of "Mignon" as "the word for little girls you fancy" (1995, 38), takes issue with this move, finding in it a "double dynamic of identification and projection (including of erotic investments), structured by the current dominant meanings accorded our embodied histories, that renders the status of the child so problematic" (131). As this chapter will continue to explore, the media responses to the Penguin Modern Classics cover repetitively claim to secure its meaning, erotic and otherwise. This entails, as Burman argues here, an insistence on an "identification" of the child and a "projection" of meaning onto it – a projection that is not addressed or critiqued in the claims – that produces these readings of the child on the cover as, to my argument, contested.

In asking for suggestions of books that the cover "belongs to", the Penguin Facebook post produced the cover within a context of other texts, suggesting that a cover may appropriately "belong[...]" to multiple or differing books, depending on the reader. This is a claim refuted by Margaret Talbot in her article "Meant for Kids", published in *The New Yorker* (2014). She suggests the possibility of a link between the cover and characters from *Charlie and the Chocolate Factory,* which she immediately refutes: "And if the Stepford daughter on the cover is meant to remind us of Veruca Salt or Violet Beauregarde, she doesn't: those badly behaved squirts are bubbling over with rude life". For Talbot, there is the possibility of an intention to "remind us of Veruca Salt or Violet Beauregarde", characters in *Charlie and the Chocolate Factory,* but this remembrance does not occur. That is, she claims access to a possible artistic intention but also to the certain knowledge that, if this was indeed intended, it has failed. The intention is both present and absent in her reading: invoked as a possibility in order to be rejected as unsuccessful. Reading another way, then, and regardless of intention, the 'Stepford daughter' *has* "remind[ed] us of Veruca Salt or Violet Beauregarde" in that Talbot has produced them as potential candidates for the figure on the cover.

Talbot's claim is also framed by an appeal to another text – *The Stepford Wives* – in her construction of "the Stepford daughter on the cover". She constructs the cover as somehow more appropriate to Levin's novel – as the descendent of or heir to it in her relation of the daughter to the wife but without an exploration of what is "Stepford" about the "daughter on the cover". The deferral is an appeal to a shared knowledge of what constitutes "Stepford" (which is not dependent on the idea of wife). Talbot constructs an assumed familiarity with another literary text – a kind of literacy upon which this understanding of the cover's misunderstanding of the text is premised.

The idea of appropriateness, and the relationship between the cover and what the book is taken to be about, is also constructed in Penguin Books' short blog post on the now-closed penguinblog.co.uk, published on 6 August 2014, the same day the cover was announced on Facebook. In explaining their choice of cover they write that:

> The new image for *Charlie and the Chocolate Factory* looks at the children at the centre of the story, and highlights the way Roald Dahl's writing manages to embrace both the light and the dark aspects of life, ready for Charlie's debut amongst the adult titles in the Penguin Modern Classics series.

This construction produces *Charlie and the Chocolate Factory* as in part a "story" and puts "children at the centre" of that story. Outside of the story is the "image", which "look[s] at the children" who are "at the centre of the story" and "highlights" another aspect of *Charlie and the Chocolate Factory*: "Roald Dahl's writing". In producing a relationship between "the image" of the cover and what is between the covers ("the centre"), the blog post produces *Charlie and the Chocolate Factory* in terms of distinctions of child, writing and authorship.

Whilst the cover is positioned as non-central to this – as peripheral – it bears a relation to these ideas since its function is to "look[...]" at the story. For this rationale of the cover, then, the cover looks – and what it looks at is structural and "children". This look is, here, objective and rational but also selective since the cover can look at these children and highlight the writing that constitutes them. Beckett, reading the adult and child market covers for the first book in the *Harry Potter* series, also appeals to the peripherality that I have been reading: "The only differences between the adult and children's editions, with the exception of the price (adults were expected to pay more), are of a paratextual nature" (243). She constructs "paratextual" differences as insubstantial or of little importance: the text of *Harry Potter and the Philosopher's Stone* is the same across the two editions.

This is in contrast to Talbot's understanding of the relationship between the cover and children as inappropriately disassociated, yet it relies upon the same assumptions. Both Talbot and Penguin claim that a book jacket should be representative of a book; what constitutes a book and its cover can be stably distinguished. They produce *Charlie and the Chocolate Factory* as other than its cover, although the cover ought to (or does) represent it. The cover is blindly taken by both texts as representative regardless of whether it is felt to be successful. They also both assume that the cover represents children (one well, one badly). The child is conflated with text in this, and this assumption of child representation is the basis for concerns about, as Joanne Harris understood it in her tweets on the launch, the "inappropriately sexualised" nature of the cover and what it says about adult–child relations.

"Inappropriately Sexualised"

On 7 August 2014, the day after the cover was announced, fiction author Joanne Harris (@Joannechocolat) posted two comments on Twitter: "Seriously, Penguin Books. Why not just get Rolf Harris to design the next one?" and "I'm not sure why adults need a different cover anyway, but who was it who decided that 'adult' means 'inappropriately sexualised'?" Harris produced the cover as akin to being designed by Rolf Harris, a well-known artist and broadcaster who the previous month had been sentenced to five years and nine months in prison for 12 counts of indecent assault, 11 of them against a minor (Sweeney 2014). This constructs the intention of the cover's designer as key to an understanding of the cover and that intention as comparative to that of a convicted paedophile. Yet there is also an instability in this charge: in a move that is often repeated on the Twitter platform, the "one" that Harris is condemning is oblique – she does not link to the cover in any way. As I read with Talbot's "Stepford daughter", there is a sense here that the cover is certainly known about or already being discussed. That is, a certain literacy or knowledge is being appealed to. In this way, her claim about the cover is framed in terms of its obvious rightness: her constructed reader must know from the two sentences what the "one" and "different cover" are and therefore the two sentences must be an appropriate or correct claim about them but also unstable in this certainty.

Harris raises the question that Beckett answers as to "why adults need a different cover anyway", but dismisses it to take issue with what it means to have an "adult" cover, which, to her reading, is, erroneously, "inappropriately sexualised". Whilst Penguin is responsible for the cover in the first tweet, Harris frames the second in terms of an attempt to assign responsibility or blame. For her, the cover should not be sexualised – there is something about it that is sexual and should not be. In line with Talbot's relation of the cover to Veruca Salt and Violet Beauregarde, Harris claims access to an intended effect and this effect's failure. The cover, for her, fails to appeal to the non-paedophilic adult.

The idea of the cover as "inappropriately sexualised" was picked up by a number of mainstream media outlets, including Anita Singh in the title of her *Telegraph* article, "Charlie and the Chocolate Factory Cover Condemned as 'Creepy', 'Grotesque' and 'Inappropriately Sexualised'" (2014). As with Harris, Singh does not question the sexualisation: she repeats Harris's claim without a consideration of what might be inappropriate about the sexualisation or what might constitute appropriate sexualisation. The questions that my readings of these claims to an obvious sexualised child raise are what constitutes a sexualised child and by whom (and for whom) she is sexualised. As the next section will argue, the articles I discuss understand the child as passively supplemented in this role and as working to maintain an innocence that is produced as prior and permanent.

The Made-Up Doll-Like Child

In addressing the question of sexualisation, the girl is produced as a covered innocent – sexualisation has been added to her, but there remains an accessible girl who is innocent to this and is distinguishable from these accoutrements. Jess Denham, in *The Independent*, understands the book as having been "given a 'creepy' new cover by *Penguin*, featuring a young doll-like girl in full make-up", and Margaret Talbot's *New Yorker* article constructs the photograph as "of a glass-eyed, heavily made-up little girl". For Talbot, the make-up is "heavy", producing its weight as its defining characteristic, and this weight is something that is accessible to Talbot's look at the cover. The "girl" is understood as having been supplemented with "make-up", an addition that is constructed in terms of its substance. Denham's construction of it as "full" produces the addition as at its maximum, suggesting that no more make-up could be added to the "young doll-like girl". That is, the make-up cannot be supplemented and the girl cannot be supplemented in terms of her made-up-ness. Her availability is such that her potential, in this respect, is also known.

Denham's claim to a fullness of make-up is understood as part of her construction of the girl as uncanny – as part of a "'creepy' new cover" and the girl as "doll-like". Whilst, for Denham, the status of the subject is unquestionably also "girl", she is a particular kind of "girl", one characterised in terms of the way in which she is not-girl. Her humanness is put into question by her "doll-like" quality, not because this erases the "girl" but rather because it qualifies her and contributes to the creepiness of the cover. For both Denham and Talbot, there is a concrete materiality to the make-up that elides the photograph in which they are reading the make-up: their claims are to the real of the scene of photography rather than to an interpretation of the text.

Denham situates the cover as "mark[ing] the 50th anniversary of the classic children's book" and as something that "has been given" to *Charlie and the Chocolate Factory* "by Penguin", claiming that they hold responsibility for this decision and the cover's meaning. This positions her understanding of the girl in terms of publishing, appealing to the commercial aspect of the cover and the company that sells it. This commerciality and use is in contrast to the way in which Denham claims access to what she critiques: "The girl is seen on the front [of the cover] wearing a pink bow in her long blonde curls, dressed up in feathers, mascara and bright lipstick". For Denham here, "girl" is stably available to be seen, and that seeing is universal: "[t]he girl is seen" irrespective of who is looking. Denham elides perspective and produces instead an unavoidable sight – one that is visible to anyone who is seeing, thus claiming an authority both of her own reading and of the cover she constructs. There is no deviance in looking in this: any such charge is located firmly in the intention of the creator of the cover, even in the very move in which this is problematised.

Like Talbot, Sarah Kaplan, in *The Washington Post* (2014), constructs make-up in terms of its heaviness: she reads the cover as showing "[a]n image of a doll-like little girl decked out in heavy make-up and a feather boa á la JonBenét Ramsey – no Willy Wonka, no Charlie, and certainly no chocolate". In this, then, the weight of the make-up is in contrast to the lack of "Willy Wonka, […] Charlie, and […] chocolate", replaced instead with "a doll-like little girl decked out" in the style of a murdered child, JonBenét Ramsey. This is a victim who the same newspaper previously constructed as photographed "wearing lipstick, makeup and elaborately coiffed hair" (Schudel 2006) and Kaplan, in a later article, described as having an "immaculate doll-like appearance, seemingly designed for magazine covers" (2015). The construction of the girl as a made-up doll here becomes an appeal to that appearance as linked to victimhood and death. The girl is again othered, but here she is, in addition to being inhuman-like and supplemented, also related to death – not her own but another, equitable, girl's. The uncanniness of the girl on the cover is one that is invested in both an appeal to real death and in gothic tropes seen as inappropriate to *Charlie and the Chocolate Factory* (understood as separate to the cover) and as inappropriate to what constitutes a live human "girl".

A concern for what is appropriate for the child is by no means a novel approach in children's literature criticism. From F. J. Harvey Darton's *Children's Books in England: Five Centuries of Social Life* (1932) to Peter Hunt's claim that children's literature criticism should be concerned with "how real readers read – not students, or critics, or others who deliberately read in a deviant way" (1991, 4) and from banned books lists to scholarly book reviews, much of what is written about children's literature is concerned with uniting the right child with the right book. As Karín Lesnik-Oberstein has argued in her introduction to *Children's Literature: New Approaches* (2004), this is a trend that continues even in some sectors of criticism that understand themselves as constructivist. In addition to arguing that "[t]here is, after all, no conclusive evidence of which critic predicts better than which other critic which children will like which book and why" (2004, 19) she also, reading David Rudd's *Enid Blyton and the Mystery of Children's Literature* (2000), constructs children's literary criticism as frequently positioning itself on a premise it claims to reject, "on an adult definition of the child as 'other' to itself, and an appropriation of that child for the sake not of the child, but of the adult who needs to see the child in that way" (18). This claim, which I read as aligned with Burman's "double dynamic of identification and projection", can also be read in the anxieties around reading the girl on the cover as inappropriately sexualised, heavily made up and doll-like. These constructions all maintain an innocent child, that is, the non-doll-like-ness of the girl, beneath the make-up and beyond the deviant gaze.

What is bypassed in this return to the well-worn trope of Romantic childhood innocence is any idea of perspective.[3] As I read with Denham, the photograph is simply "seen", a necessary claim in an assertion that a book or characteristic is or is not appropriate for the child. The child must be wholly accessible and spoken on behalf of, as must the text. This is problematised, as Jacqueline Rose ([1986] 2006) argues, by feminist critiques of visual culture:

> [...] we know that women are meant to *look* perfect, presenting a seamless image to the world so that man, in that confrontation with difference, can avoid any apprehension of lack. The position

of woman as fantasy therefore depends on a particular economy of vision [...] Perhaps this is also why only a project which comes via feminism can demand so unequivocally of the image that it renounces all pretentions to a narcissistic perfection of form.

(232, emphasis in original)

Rose argues that a feminist intervention can destabilise the insistence that women "*look* perfect", bypassing substance or perspective in order to efface "any apprehension of lack". I read a move to avoid lack in the fullness and heaviness of the girl's make-up and in the repeated understanding of her as "girl" and like a doll (to compensate for any attributes that are read as not appropriate to the girl) just as I read it in Kaplan's construction of the lack of Wonka, Charlie and chocolate in which she constructs what ought, by her argument, to be present, constructing an alternative cover to the rejected imperfect girl. The girl must "*look* perfect" not only because she is female but also, returning to Burman and Lesnik-Oberstein, because she is a child.

The Unseeing Mother and Child

As I have been arguing, the availability of a look is at stake in the media coverage of the jacket and, as this section will explore, it is also the reason for the reading of the second figure on the cover as 'mother', a similarity that is understood here as uncanny. That is, the child is understood in terms of the way she looks (albeit in her transgression of the critics' understanding of child) and, as I will argue in this section, by her own lack of seeing, conditions that she has in common with the second figure. The demand for the woman who looks perfect can be read in contrast to claims in the media responses to the cover of the construction of the woman who looks imperfectly: both the girl and the figure they take to be her mother are produced as not looking or as having an objectless look. Denham, for example, constructs the girl as "star[ing] blankly ahead while sitting on her mother's knee". Whilst we have a look *at* the girl (albeit a passive one, since "she is seen"), the girl is denied a look back at us. She does not see our look at her, or the dubious look Joanne Harris attributed to Penguin, because her stare is blank. It is a look that is prolonged and focused, but it is also impotent and without object. The girl is denied the scopophilia that Denham and Harris have access to (but do not align their readings with), not because the girl has no desire but because she has no look. This denial further denies the girl, in Freudian terms, the inevitable reversal of voyeurism: exhibitionism. That is, if the girl does not engage in a pleasure of looking, she also cannot engage in a pleasure of showing herself, in the knowledge of being looked at; thus she can remain, for Denham, innocent in terms of an absence of sexuality, since sexuality is constituted by the look.[4]

Denham reads the other figure as a mother who is physically supporting the child – as the seat on which she sits – but this sitting is also the seat of a blank stare. The child is physically close to the mother but emotionally distant, staring not at the mother but at nothing. The mother cannot protect from the blankness of her stare or the inappropriateness of the deviant looking; rather, the frame of the front cover denies this mother any look at all since she is without an upper head. She is, in this sense, both lobotomised and without eyes with which to see either her daughter or the inappropriate looks at her. There is no safe maternal look (an absence I am reading from Denham's investment in seeing, her construction of mother and the frame of the photograph) with which our looking can be either sanctioned or disbarred.

On Denham's terms, the mother's not-seeing is a repetition of her daughter's, who "stares blankly ahead", but with different implications: the girl's blank stare protects her insisted-upon innocence, and the mother's blank stare implicates her in the deviant look at her daughter. Neither subject, as Denham constructs the photograph, sees us looking at them, in contrast to her claim to a complete access to the photograph that both sees in full and sees beyond the frame of the photograph in her understanding of "mother": for her claims, nothing can escape her gaze. This position has greater access to the child than her mother, and yet this seer does not adopt a surrogate nurturing maternal position: it sees the possibility of perversion, the inappropriateness of the child and the culpability of the mother in this.

This claim to an all-access gaze is repeated in Talbot and Kaplan's constructions of the cover in their certainty of what they are looking at and what this means, a move that I have also read in Beckett, Falconer and Powers's constructions of adult covers and the performance of reading. In Denham, Talbot and Kaplan's accounts, for example, this permits a reading of "mother" in the photograph that, I will argue, is founded on a reading of inappropriate similarity and an appeal to a genetic-centric idea of motherhood. Rather than reading the "mother" as physically supporting the child as Denham does, Talbot understands the mother as behind her daughter: "Behind her sits a mother figure, stiff and coiffed, casting an ominous shadow". The differing readings of the physical relation between the mother and daughter contrast Talbot and Denham's uninterrogated construction of their familial relationship. What for Denham is a photograph of the girl "sitting on her mother's knee", for Talbot is a photograph of a girl whose mother sits behind her. These differing accounts of where the mother and daughter are in relation to each other suggest an inability to differentiate between them: their boundaries are not distinct so that "on" and "behind" may both be read in the same photograph in spite of the critics' certainty that they may be distinguished as mother and child.

Talbot produces the mother and daughter in the same terms as each other, relating this to what she constructs as the provenance of the photograph:

> The image is a photograph, taken from a French fashion shoot, of a glassy-eyed, heavily made-up little girl. Behind her sits a mother figure, stiff and coiffed, casting an ominous shadow. The girl, with her long, perfectly waved platinum-blond hair and her pink feather boa [...].

Both mother and daughter are understood in terms of their hair and grooming, prefaced by their construction as, previously, part of a "French fashion shoot". For Talbot's construction, that provenance is maintained in the reappropriation of the photograph for the cover of *Charlie and the Chocolate Factory,* and it produces a similarity between the mother and the daughter. The understanding of a mother-daughter relation is, then, premised on a similarity of supplement as well as on not looking: it is the way in which the two have been styled, resulting in a visual similarity, which they themselves do not see and is the foundation for this understanding of relatedness.

In one sense, then, the daughter, in her position as the younger in the relationship, doubles the mother; she is the mother in miniature – styled, made-up and looking without object. The uncanny daughter, who is in one sense too much like the mother and in another not like her but like a doll, troubles the mother–daughter relationship constructed by both Denham and Talbot. In Talbot's account, however, the daughter is not the only double of the mother as the "mother figure" "cast[s] an ominous shadow" from her seat behind the daughter, further troubling this relationship. The reading of a shadow cast from the mother, along with the daughter cast *as* the mother, introduces a third excessive figure into this couple. The mother–daughter relationship cannot be contained in the photograph: it repeats itself and produces an excess. The child is like and unlike her mother, as is the shadow; but that does not produce the child *as* the shadow, rather it constructs another mother–child relationship in which the shadow and the child are both mother and child.

By positioning the mother as "[b]ehind her", Talbot produces the child's not-seeing, this time of, as she understands it, her own mother. The mother who is not seen but who is, as was the case with Denham, seen by Talbot is also attributed a further not-seeing, which is repeated in her daughter: that of the shadow she casts. The mother, who is duplicated in the daughter, is also unseeingly duplicated by the shadow. This positions the child as in some way similar to the shadow in their relation to the mother: they are both from her but not her, uncanny repetitions that articulate the lack of the mother, that are not seen by the mother and do not, themselves, see and that reaffirm the claim to an all-seeing constitutive gaze that produces them.

The Back Cover

Although the critiques I have been reading in this chapter are all invested in the accessibility of the cover to their sight, they do not read the back cover, coming, as they do, before the release of the paperback (Figure 7.1). That is, the cover they have been reading is the image of the front cover released by Penguin rather than a cover on a book. This conflation of the digital image on a website and a cover of a printed book effaces any difference in these mediums. This chapter concludes with a reading of the back cover, not because this will somehow complete the readings I have been analysing here or to suggest that they are lacking in some finitely supplemental way but to consider the ideas of looking and appropriateness in terms of the claims made about the child and *Charlie and the Chocolate Factory* on the back cover.

As I read in the Penguin Facebook post's invitation to "guess which tasty tale this cover belongs to" and in constructions of *Lolita*, the back cover also appeals to other texts, positioning *Charlie and the Chocolate Factory* in terms of two collections of short stories by Roald Dahl, *Someone Like You* and *Over to You*. These are positioned above the barcode, the edition's identifier, which distinguishes it from other versions of *Charlie and the Chocolate Factory*, other books, and other products at the point of sale. These books, then, are positioned as proximate to a construction of the text as a tradeable commodity in relation to other commodities.

The book is produced as part of a system of commerce and of adaptation. Sam Mendes, director of the West End musical of *Charlie and the Chocolate Factory* (2013), is cited as having written "a new introduction to the text", and Tim Burton, director of the 2005 film adaptation, is quoted: "I responded to it because it respected the fact that children can be adults". What "it" is, is thrown into question by the notion of adaptation, as I have previously read in the Penguin blog's construction of a "story" that has children at its centre.

According to Burton, "children can be adults", however, which in one sense is in opposition to Lesnik-Oberstein's understanding of children's literature criticism's repeated positioning of the "child as 'other' to [adult]". However, Burton repeats the appropriation of the child for the purposes of the adult that Lesnik-Oberstein (2004, 18) argues since children remain children, even in their "be[ing] adults" and since this is framed in terms of his own response. Burton has access to the children of the "it" to which he is responding just as Denham, Talbot and Kaplan have claimed in their readings of the cover. This is despite *their* understanding of the front cover as inappropriate, whilst on Burton's terms it precisely *is* appropriate in its claims to produce the child as adult.

That is not to say, however, that Penguin Modern Classics has, after all, got the cover right; rather, my claim here is that even when critics are arguing against each other – either preserving the childness of the child or constructing its adultness – what unites the critiques is their claimed access to what is child. Whether a child is a "young doll-like girl in full make-up" in a photograph or multiple children in an "it" or a story, the child is always and must be available.

This position of absolute access then, in what I have been reading here, is applied to the ideas read as to do with the child: what constitutes "overly sexualised" becomes obvious, the construction of "mother" is invested in the same notions of availability to sight and the construction of the cover of the text is produced as apparently without lack. This necessitates a repetition of what is critiqued: an ironic repetition of the possession of the child that is the anxiety to which the articles and social media posts here construct themselves as responding. In all this, it is the gaze of the child that is denied. As this chapter has argued, what constitutes child cannot be fixed by these critics' readings or by my own, in spite of the texts' agreement that a child is that which is seen to not see. This blindness of the child enables their negotiation of her constructed sexuality, positioning her as innocent in it and allowing a denial of it as their own construction. Their investment in the gaze seems to permit a possession of the child even as they signal her vulnerability to this gaze, but it ironically returns the perverted look in this denial.

Notes

1 My work on this article first appeared in a blog post for the Feminist and Women's Studies Association (Sage 2014) and then as a paper at the *Transformations of Childhood in Contemporary Britain* symposium sponsored by the Centre for Interdisciplinary Research in Bielefeld, Germany. I am very grateful to the commentators and attendees for their generous and helpful insights, which have helped shape this chapter.
2 Haddon's novel was published simultaneously by Jonathan Cape and by children's publisher David Fickling (Falconer 2008, 96); Scholastic, who published the Pullman trilogy, released adult editions of the novels in several jackets, including the black and white Lantern Slides covers, illustrated by John Lawrance in 2007. Both *Alice's Adventures in Wonderland* and *Treasure Island* have been rejacketed for adult markets as part of the Penguin Classics (2008 and 2000) and Oxford World Classics (2009 and 2011) series among others.
3 For more on this idea in twentieth-century British and American visual culture see Anne Higonnet's *Pictures of Innocence* (1998).
4 My understanding of scopophilia and exhibitionism as related opposites is taken from Freud ([1915] 1957).

References

Beckett, Sandra L. 2008. *Crossover Fiction: Global and Historical Perspectives*. New York: Routledge.
Burgess, Melvin. 2003. *Doing It*. London: Andersen Press.
Burman, Erica. 2008. *Developments: Child, Image, Nation*. Hove: Routledge.
Carroll, Lewis. (1866) 1992. *Alice's Adventures in Wonderland*. Ware: Wordsworth Editions.

Dahl, Roald. (1964) 2004. *Charlie and the Chocolate Factory*. London: Penguin.
Darton, F. J. Harvey. (1932) 2011. *Children's Books in England: Five Centuries of Social Life*. Cambridge: Cambridge University Press.
Denham, Jess. 2014. "New Roald Dahl's *Charlie and the Chocolate Factory* Book Cover Sees Joanne Harris Ask: 'Why Not Get Rolf Harris to Design One?'" *The Independent*, August 8. Accessed 12 September 2016. www.independent.co.uk/arts-entertainment/books/news/joanne-harris-hits-out-at-new-charlie-and-the-chocolate-factory-book-cover-why-not-just-get-rolf-9656367.html.
Falconer, Rachel. 2008. *The Crossover Novel: Contemporary Children's Fiction and Its Adult Readership*. New York: Routledge.
Faulkner, Joanne. 2010. *The Importance of Being Innocent: Why We Worry About Children*. Cambridge: Cambridge University Press.
Fine, Anne. 2003. "Filth, Which Ever Way You Look at It." *The Guardian*, March 29. Accessed 12 September, 2016. www.theguardian.com/books/2003/mar/29/featuresreviews.guardianreview24.
Freud, Sigmund. (1915) 1957. "Instincts and Vicissitudes". In *On the History of the Psycho-Analytic Movement, Papers on Metapsychology and Other Works*, translated by James Strachey, 109–40. London: Hogarth Press.
Haddon, Mark. 2003a. *The Curious Incident of the Dog in the Night-Time*. London: David Fickling.
———. 2003b. *The Curious Incident of the Dog in the Night-Time*. London: Jonathan Cape.
Harad, Alyssa. 2003. "Reviving Lolita; or Because Junior High Is Still Hell." In *Catching a Wave: Reclaiming Feminism in the 21st Century*, edited by Rory Dicker, and Alison Piepmeier, 81–100. Lebanon, NH: Northeastern University Press.
Harris, Joanne. Twitter Post. August 7, 2014, 12:14 PM. https://twitter.com/Joannechocolat/status/497339944852271104.
———. Twitter Post. August 7, 2014, 12:19 PM. https://twitter.com/Joannechocolat/status/497341343619100672.
Hemingway, Ernest. 1964. *A Moveable Feast*. New York: Bantam.
Higonnet, Anne. 1998. *Pictures of Innocence: The History and Crisis of Ideal Childhood*. London: Thames and Hudson.
Hunt, Peter. 1991. *Criticism, Theory and Children's Literature*. Oxford: Wiley Blackwell.
Kaplan, Sarah. 2014. "What Divisive 'Charlie and the Chocolate Factory' Cover Says about Books and Readers." *Washington Post*, August 15. Accessed 12 September 2016. www.washingtonpost.com/lifestyle/style/what-divisive-charlie-and-the-chocolate-factory-cover-says-about-books-and-readers/2014/08/15/23163b8a-219a-11e4-86ca-6f03cbd15c1a_story.html.
———. 2015. "Ex-Police Chief Inadvertently Reveals Misgivings about JonBenet Ramsey Investigation." *Washington Post*, February 26. Accessed 23 October 2016. www.washingtonpost.com/news/morning-mix/wp/2015/02/26/ex-police-chief-inadvertently-reveals-misgivings-about-jonbenet-ramsey-investigation/.
Lesnik-Oberstein, Karín. 2004. "Introduction. Children's Literature: New Approaches." In *Children's Literature: New Approaches*. Basingstoke: Palgrave Macmillan.
Levin, Ira. (1972) 2011. *Stepford Wives*. London: Corsair.
Nabokov, Vladimir. (1955) 2000. *Lolita*. London: Penguin Books.

Paver, Michelle. 2004. *Wolf Brother*. London: Orion Children's Books.
Penguin. 2014. "Exclusive: 'Charlie and the Chocolate Factory' as a Penguin Modern Classic." *Penguin Blog*, August 6. Accessed 23 October 2016. https://web.archive.org/web/20140812223330/http://penguinblog.co.uk/2014/08/06/exclusive-charlie-and-the-chocolate-factory-as-a-penguin-modern-classic.
Penguin's Facebook page. Accessed 6 August 2016. www.facebook.com/penguinbooks/posts/10154417129150371:0 and www.facebook.com/penguinbooks/posts/10154417763395371:0.
Powers, Alan. 2003. *Children's Book Covers: Great Book Jacket Cover Design*. London: Octopus.
Pullman, Philip. 1995–2000. *His Dark Materials*. 3 vols. London: Scholastic.
Puzo, Mario. 1969. *The Godfather*. New York: Putnam.
Rose, Jacqueline. (1986) 2006. *Sexuality and the Field of Vision*. London: Verso.
Rowling, Joanne K. (1997) 1998. *Harry Potter and the Philosopher's Stone*. London: Bloomsbury.
Rudd, David. 2000. *Enid Blyton and the Mystery of Children's Literature*. Basingstoke: Palgrave.
Sage [Medhurst], Jessica. 2014. "Penguin's New Cover for *Charlie and the Chocolate Factory*: Securing the Image, Securing the Female Child." *The Feminist and Women's Studies Association Blog*, August 9. Accessed 12 September 2016. http://fwsablog.org.uk/2014/08/09/penguins-new-cover-for-charlie-and-the-chocolate-factory-securing-the-image-securing-the-female-child/.
Schudel, Matt. 2006. "Obituary: Patsy Ramsey, 49; Mother of Slain Child Beauty Queen." *Washington Post*, June 25. Accessed 23 October 2016. www.washingtonpost.com/wp-dyn/content/article/2006/06/24/AR2006062400776.html.
Steedman, Carolyn. 1995. *Strange Dislocations: Childhood and the Idea of Human Interiority*. Cambridge: Harvard University Press.
Stevenson, Robert Louis (1883) 1999. *Treasure Island*. London: Penguin.
Susann, Jacqueline. 1966. *Valley of the Dolls*. New York: Bernhard Geiss Associates.
Sweeney, Mr Justice. 2014. "R v Rolf Harris. Sentencing Remarks." July 4. Accessed 23 October 2016. www.judiciary.gov.uk/wp-content/uploads/2014/07/sentencing-remarks-mr-j-sweeney-r-v-harris1.pdf.
Talbot, Margaret. 2014. "Meant for Kids." *New Yorker*, August 29. Accessed 12 September 2016. www.newyorker.com/culture/cultural-comment/meant-for-kids.
Vickers, Graham. 2008. *Chasing Lolita: How Popular Culture Corrupted Nabokov's Little Girl All Over Again*. Chicago: Chicago Review Press.
White, Jim. 2004. "Sign Here to Book Your Money-Back Guarantee." *The Telegraph*, October 4. Accessed 12 September 2016. www.telegraph.co.uk/comment/columnists/jimwhite/3611619/Sign-here-to-book-your-money-back-guarantee.html.

8 Reflections on British and American Images of and for Children

Ellen Handler Spitz

Introduction

The distinguished British art historian Ernst Gombrich (1987) writes to applaud his colleague Francis Haskell for asking what historians can learn from visual evidence, that is, from studying images created in and/or circulating in a given period under review. A similar question is implied by Philippe Ariès in his *Centuries of Childhood* ([1960] 1962), an influential albeit controversial study of childhood that relies on examples drawn from paintings, illuminated manuscripts and other visual sources to make arguments about the way children were seen and, mostly, not seen, in centuries prior to the late Renaissance and claims, on the basis of this evidence, that childhood is a modern idea. Borrowing Haskell's question, and cognizant of some of the pitfalls into which Ariès stumbled, particularly his over-reliance on a paucity of examples, the selection of which occasionally seems random, we might nevertheless ask what can be learned about evolving concepts of childhood by studying visual artefacts designed for children or made with children in mind. Can imagery and artefacts fashioned expressly for children or that depict children teach us how children have been conceived by adults and about nuanced alterations in these conceptions over time? This essay is an attempt in that direction. It draws unapologetically, however, on an idiosyncratic sample and ends inconclusively by showing that the interpretive possibilities opened by images cannot be authentically delimited. Nevertheless, while reflections based on selected examples cannot supply resolution, they may possess the power to inspire a richer engagement with notions of childhood and shed light on the ways children have been and continue to be manipulated by adults. Among examples cited in this chapter are selected British and American picture books and British and American exhibitions, all dating with minor exceptions to the years between the 1960s and the present.

I

In our globalised twenty-first century, what is occurring in the Anglophone cultural world of childhood in Britain chimes to some extent with what is occurring correspondingly in the US. As the introduction of this collection shows, contemporary childhood is shaped by various complex developments, including neoliberal politics, the pluralisation of family practices and technological advances. Among other differences, one with obvious historical significance and that, at least some have claimed, carries profound psychological sequellae, may be the enduring legacy of World War II: to wit its presence in the UK and its relative absence in the US and the fact that American children have historically never, except during a few years around 1865, when our Civil War ended, endured the ravages of a homeland war: no bombings, no air raids, no destruction of homes, cities or countryside. Yet, decades afterwards, according to British scholar Professor Mathew Thomson (2013) in *Lost Freedom*, the aftermath of those horrors perdures in the cultural lives of British children. Thomson traces some of homeland war's enduring effects on British childhood and argues, as reflected in his title, that significant sequellae concern the virtual disappearance of children's freedoms to roam, wander, explore and play openly out of doors. Certainly, additional causes of these lost freedoms may be adduced, such as the spread of high-speed road networks and technological advances that provide appealing indoor activities for children. The contemporary discourse of child protection, which Nigel Parton elaborates on in his chapter in this volume, certainly plays an important role in this context. All these factors are discernible in the US as well, and, moreover, with the rise of global terrorism and its attendant fears, this particular gap between the two principal Anglophone nations is narrowing. On the American scene, restrictions on children's freedom to roam outdoors stem largely from rampant urban sprawl, from ex-urban and suburban development of former woodlands and from concomitant accelerating traffic congestion (Goodenough 2010).

What Thomson points out is ever shocking to me, as a foreigner in England: a reminder of the bombings and civilian deaths and the fact that, although British cities that fell victim to massive destruction have long since been rebuilt, there remain undetonated bombs, shells and air raid shelters that continue to be unearthed as new construction sites are opened. To the contrary, while American children continue to be bereaved by war and some grow up fatherless or with fathers permanently impaired by foreign wars, their everyday worlds have not been demolished by a foreign power. Consequently, after the 2001 terrorist attacks in New York City and Washington, D.C., there was a rush by United States educators, mental health workers and publishers to find appropriate means for addressing these frightening events with children. Unlike their counterparts in the UK, they had no prior comparable knowledge upon which to call.

It may be valuable, apropos, to revisit a notable picture book that was produced a decade after the events of 2001, by the prominent children's book author/artist Don Brown: *America Is Under Attack*. This book received considerable attention when it first appeared, possibly because it represented an actual attempt to bring the event to children pictorially or perhaps because of its creator's cachet. Nevertheless, when examined, it seems dubious and problematic. Why, first off, is it ominously titled in the present tense, as though the event were ongoing, had never been processed and should elicit from children, many of whom were not born when it occurred, the shock and terror it provoked at the time? We would be hard-pressed to find children's books in the UK that adopt a similar conceit. Why are its pages filled with alarming pictures, including billowing black smoke and terrified people with distorted faces? Why is the narrative burdened with numerical statistics (the numbered floors of the towers, the precise times of the impacts, the exact death tallies)? It is very likely that such numbers are unintelligible to young children and, if so, then they are surely irrelevant while nevertheless instigating a kind of ungrounded anxiety. By way of contrast, let's consider Nobel-prize-winning physicist Richard Feynman's delightful memoir, *Surely You're Joking, Mr. Feynman* (1985), wherein he describes his father's mode of explaining the height of a brontosaurus to him when he was a child. Feynman's father recited no statistics. Instead, he led his son upstairs, with no fanfare, to a second story window of their modest house and told him that the beast's head – if the creature were still alive – would come up to just about that height. This empathic child-centred mode of explanation made a lifelong impression on the future scientist. My point here is that the American author-artist Don Brown, while apparently recycling his own adult trauma in his 'children's' book, may have failed to create an object of meaning and value for his contemporary young audience. One wonders whether this has to do with the uniqueness of the event in comparison with others' very different experiences in the UK or whether a more-present sense of history actually engenders a greater capacity for proportion and distance.

A contrasting children's book relating to the same events ("9/11"), appeared very soon after they took place. Mordicai Gerstein's *The Man Who Walked Between the Towers* (2003) depicts the yet-to-be demolished twin towers directly and facilitates mourning for them by celebrating a daring aerialist, Philippe Petit, who walked between the lofty structures on a tightrope as they were being completed. One boon of this book is that it gives children born afterwards a clear picture of what the towers looked like while reminding those who continue to miss them of their erstwhile visual dominance over the cityscape. In the years before 9/11, children riding by rail would routinely press their noses against grubby windowpanes on the right side of northbound trains and, when they spied the towers, pull their parents' sleeves with excited voices: "Look! It's New York! We're almost there." Gerstein addresses life, art and cultural symbol, rather than fear; his book functions to preserve a semblance of what has been lost. Interviewed after winning the coveted Caldecott medal for it, Gerstein said he pored over books on Rembrandt when he was a boy and then made his own pictures.

II

Turning now from children's books to exhibitions related to childhood, let us consider a significant exhibition of 2005, titled "Only Make Believe: Ways of Playing", which was conceived and curated by the distinguished British mythographer Dame Marina Warner and mounted at Compton-Verney in Warwickshire (Warner 2005). Can this show of images of children as well as images for children tell us anything about British childhood in its time? First off, let us consider Zbigniew Libera's 1996 installation piece titled *Lego Concentration Camp Set*, included in the show. This work, when first displayed in the 1990s, proved so highly controversial that the Lego Company in Denmark tried unsuccessfully, in court, to suppress it. An American venue, however, curiously and bravely displayed it three years prior to the Compton-Burney show. This was the Jewish Museum of New York City, where, in the context of a complex, highly contested exhibition called "Mirroring Evil: Nazi Imagery/Recent Art," Libera's work was shown. Indeed, the museum purchased the piece. "Mirroring Evil" was a courageous albeit flawed attempt to get beyond what was perceived then as the museum's one-sidedly exclusive attention to victims of Nazi sadism by approaching the art of World War II from perpetrators' and bystanders' perspectives. In Libera's piece, Lego pieces are pictured on their ersatz box. (Typically, when sold, small building pieces of the toy and diminutive figures inside the box are depicted as being capable of assemblage into particular, illustrated constructions). In this case, the pieces can be 'used' by children to form a miniature Nazi concentration camp, replete with crematorium, guards and smoke tower. When challenged to explain himself, the artist defended his work by claiming that his intention was to expose and highlight the destructive elements in many of the toys we give unwittingly to children. For some viewers, however, the horror of the choice pre-empted any didactic agenda (Spitz 2001).

"Only Make Believe" also featured the mysterious cut-paper silhouettes for *The Adventures of Prince Achmed* of 1923–1925, by Berlin artist Lotte Reiniger, whose fanciful, shape-shifting take-off on *The Thousand and One Nights* form an exquisite dreamlike shadow film. Taken from what is possibly the earliest surviving animated film, Reiniger's gossamer confection was painstakingly made by hand, its forms inspired by finger puppets, embroidery and lace. Inventing her own techniques of intricate scissor work, cutting out characters of astonishingly delicate beauty, who, in their evanescent world, sway, prance, bow and embrace while enacting stories of intrigue, romance and suspense,

Reiniger channels as her villain a wicked enchanter known as the African Magician, a well-known maleficent from *Aladdin and the Magic Lamp*, a tale frequently made known to children.

Also included at Compton-Verney were recent paintings by the artist Paula Rego. Among them was one from 1995 that portrays Snow White writhing in agony after having tasted the poisoned apple. Another in the show, from 2003, is called *War*. It features mangled figures that seem taken from the pantheon of children's book illustrations: clothed, broken, distorted rabbits, a central figure with bloodied face, the entire canvas suffused with pity, chaos and supplication. What then can be deduced from such imagery and from this exhibit vis-à-vis contemporary views of childhood in Britain in its time? Would it be right to say that wide-eyed innocence plays little or no role? That the innocence imputed to children in Victorian or Edwardian England has vanished in the wake of all the violence of the twentieth century? Both Libera and Rego seem keen on pointing out its effects on childhood. Regarded as such, the Compton-Verney show evokes the illusory child as an unstable nexus of magic, violence and the uncanny. One struggles to grasp how such a construct reflects its epoch; yet, in subtle ways, it surely must: the child as vulnerable to and participatory in all its turbulence. Yet, reading against the grain might also reveal a hidden current of nostalgia for an idealised childhood absent from it. To my mind, none of this can be easily separated from war and its aftermath, for war unhinges us like nothing else from the rational.

More recently in New York, the Museum of Modern Art mounted its own major exhibit, "The Century of the Child: Growing by Design, 1900–2000" in 2012, which contained rooms of photographs, toys, film clips, clothing, picture books, furniture and other artefacts (Kinchin and O'Connor 2012). In their zeal to showcase the ingenuity of adult design, however, MoMA curators bypassed all meaningful engagement with actual children. The historical and media-based themed galleries reflected the curators' own professional interests in Modernist style rather than any serious inquiry into the ways in which the objects on display actually may have served to organise children's own experience of their surroundings.[1]

From this, we may conclude, as per the Don Brown book mentioned above and "Only Make Believe", that even when children are the apparent subject of cultural productions, whether intended for them or about them, they themselves are often appropriated, objectified or even bypassed. Interestingly, "The Century of the Child" also included the work of Lotte Reiniger. Her film played silently in a gallery labelled "Avant Garde Play Time". To stand spellbound watching the silhouettes unfurl their sinister plots and metamorphoses in ever-swirling motion until Prince Achmed is at last reunited with his slender fairy Peri Banou, was, perhaps for many spectators, to recapture a childhood in which magic is real and flying demons more true than anything attached to solid earth.

III

Returning now to illustrated books made by adults for children, we have reason, perhaps, to assume that such books presuppose at least a nebulous notion of what children are and to what they ought be exposed. In 1962, the distinguished UK illustrator Brian Wildsmith produced an alphabet primer that won the Kate Greenaway Medal. It was republished in the US, where it garnered appreciation because of its opulent colour and fanciful animal pictures that seem to leap out of its pages and spark imagination. The assumption here seems to be that children learn best when they are aesthetically engaged and their creativity tapped, an assumption quite novel in the genre of English language alphabet primers and hornbooks, which, as we know them, date back at least to Shakespeare's time (Tuer 1896).

The primer, an early genre of book made expressly for children, must instruct youth. That is its unchallenged goal, and its format is strictly prescribed: it juxtaposes a picture with the first letter of its name in a predetermined sequence and serves generally as a model of language acquisition based on the priority of noun or name. It is also worthwhile to note that, as such, it features (and fosters) an imitative, static model of learning, i.e. text over image, locked into non-reversible, hierarchical order. The listener is conceived as an unformed child (*tabula rasa*) who, ignorant of her ABCs, must subordinate herself to the speaker, a knowledgeable, literate adult. Each primer observes this template. This is so even in the work of contemporary conceptual artists, such as Michael Craig-Martin of Goldsmith's, University of London, where, in his *Alphabet* piece of 2013, however, he challenges viewers to find their own links between letter and picture, links that are not immediately obvious. 'A,' for example, is illustrated by an open, angled umbrella suggesting perhaps the notion 'Against the rain'; while 'C' shows a knife encouraging the idea of 'Cut' (Alan Cristea Gallery 2016).

Another contemporary artist, Michele Beck of New York, splits screened images of herself perched uncomfortably on a stool in a riveting performance piece of 1995, called *Alphabet*, where she painfully repeats the pronunciation of each letter and thus shows how a child may inwardly rebel against this imposition of rote learning – an imposition that, for some youngsters, renders the project of learning to read nightmarish.

Brian Wildsmith (1962) subverts the given paradigm. He retains the expectable sequence; yet, his bright pictures of wild animals leap out of the page to haunt young minds and spark fantasy. On his website, Wildsmith writes: "I believe children appreciate details as well as color.

I want to help young people wonder at the world and to become close observers of the beauty and harmony in nature." Unashamedly, Wildsmith strives to stimulate the imagination of his child readers, extract their aesthetic responses and – by means of saturated colour, innovative design, scale and gesture – carry them far beyond the fixedness of the formatted primer. Nouns in his books give rise to verbs and adjectives, pictures give birth to stories and staid primers blossom into works of art. His implicit concept of childhood seems to include notions of agency: the child as cultivating a burgeoning mental world, much in keeping with the developmental theories of Jerome Bruner and, before him, Jean Piaget. Like the colourist Eric Carle, an American counterpart, Wildsmith makes images that are models of inspiration rather than indoctrination. Medium matters here, for paint and brushes generate pictures that feature masses of colour not outlines. Paint and brushes breach borders, a feature with metaphoric significance. Children are given tacit license, in other words, not just to fill in lines as conceived by someone else.

Wildsmith's project works, of course, because of the intrinsic power of images (Freedberg 1989). Vivid pictures simply overpower words, just as strong emotions like hate, anger or erotic passion tend to knock reason out of the ring. Wildsmith wants children to engage with his exuberant artistry, but for a moment, let's turn back to the nineteenth century, where we find an innocent-looking undated English "Home Primer". When we open it, we discover – among others – a troubling page for the letter 'V'. It reads: "V is for vulture, fierce, wicked, and old. He'll do anything vile that will bring him in gold." These words mention only the name of a bird, but birds – even vultures – do not perform vile deeds for gold. Indeed, the image implies a great deal more. The vulture on the page, replete with hooked nose and fur-trimmed overcoat, channels a host of anti-Semitic caricatures, which go back not only to the infamous Julius Streicher of Nüremberg and his odious *Der Stürmer* picture books of the 1930s but also to *Le petit journal,* with its horrific grotesques of Jews during the Dreyfus affair in 1890s France. The vulture is not only an avian species but an image clandestinely perpetuating religious prejudice in a book aimed shamelessly at young children, who are – because of their lack of experience and sophistication – particularly vulnerable to being subliminally corrupted outside the bounds of written language. Like clever publicity and advertising, these images work subconsciously. Given to children, they fall outside the awareness of adults who buy and read the books that contain them.

IV

It is a hard call with an artist like Anthony Browne to know how much ambiguity is intentional. Browne is one of the most renowned British illustrator-authors. He was Children's Laureate from 2009 to 2011 and he won the Hans Christian Andersen Award. He has produced dozens of works. Browne has spoken of what he calls "the tantalizing gap between the pictures and the words" (Walker Books), a salubrious gap, which leaves room for imagination. Beyond that idea, however, his concept of childhood seems complex and open, as I hope to demonstrate by a close reading of his book, *Willy the Wimp,* published in 1984 and republished with huge success in the US. My discussion of his book segues into matters of race, gender and sexuality, where concepts of childhood have been gradually transforming in recent decades.[2]

Stereotypes of gender seem to grip with a particular tenacity. A *Huffington Post* article claims that only 7 per cent of UK engineers are women because of a widespread notion that engineering is a man's job (Elson 2014). Even when denied, images of sweet, innocent girls and naughty, rugged boys persist as spectral norms. Despite real shifts that include the acceptance of women into numerous roles and institutions that formerly excluded them, girls in many cultures worldwide are made to feel they must conform to a stereotype of passivity and quell natural feelings of occasional anger, vociferousness and aggression; boys, by contrast, are made to feel shame at signs of gentleness. *Willy the Wimp* explores the latter theme.

The book's title page is broken through by a fist, indicating that aggression will be a major motif. To emphasise the link between aggression and gender, we might note that "willy" is British slang for penis. Browne's protagonist, a pale, stoop-shouldered young chimpanzee, dressed in an argyle vest, polka dot tie, striped pants and well-shined laced shoes, is introduced to us with the words: "Willy wouldn't hurt a fly".[3] Indeed, he is so polite and reticent that he does not even shoo away an annoying insect buzzing near his face; he avoids stepping on bugs when he walks, and he apologises even when someone inconsiderately knocks into him. From the start, his quality of gentleness and his abhorrence of cruelty are caricatured by pictorial exaggeration and made to seem foolish. Children are encouraged to laugh at Willy while simultaneously identifying with him as an anti-hero type whose reactions mirror feelings experienced by many little boys as well as girls. Laughing at Willy may therefore, for some children (girls as well as boys), entail a tacit repudiation of aspects of themselves. It is important, moreover, to see the phenomenon as equally significant for both genders, since it is through cultural products like this that young people internalise and thus perpetuate stereotypes of masculinity.

When a large gorilla jostles him on the street, Willy apologises, although what happened was clearly not his fault. We laugh automatically, but the words "I'm sorry" are, in fact, often difficult for young children to say and mean because they signify an acceptance of responsibility and regret that betoken a high level of maturity and moral evolution. To acknowledge one's own wrongdoing signals a major developmental achievement. Casting blame is a more primitive position that attempts to maintain the ego intact. Frequently, small children, so as to preserve a core image of themselves as 'good' and to avoid rebuke and the risk of temporary loss of love, tend to project 'badness' outward. (Typical childish retorts to accusations of wrongdoing are: "I didn't do it" or "It wasn't me"). To be able to say the words "I'm sorry" and mean them is an indication that a child has attained the level of self-awareness that accepts the co-existence of 'bad' and 'good' impulses within the self as well as the recognition of his or her own capacity to do harm, which must be curbed rather than denied.[4] Surely, this is a fundamental desideratum for a moral life and a hallmark of mature adulthood in psychological terms. To burlesque the notion of apology and exploit it for comedic purposes seems ill-conceived in a children's book.

What does this choice, then, say about its author's and admirers' views of childhood and of objects made for children? Shall we understand that amusement is the paramount goal? Could one argue contrariwise that the blatant absurdity of the situation allows children to laugh superficially while processing the imagery unconsciously on deeper levels? Such questions remain moot because, on the final page of the book, Willy's apology to a telephone pole once again places his "I'm sorry" in a nonsensical context. The book comes full circle.

At night under stars and a full moon, a black cityscape serves as backdrop, and Willy is harassed by a "suburban gorilla gang", whose members call him a wimp. The biggest attacking gorilla has Willy's neck in a vise-like grip while another restrains his hands. Through imagery alone, not words, gender themes now slide into racial ones. The gang of dark-skinned tough guys aggresses against a 'sissy' fairer-skinned lad. The attacking gorillas are not only dressed differently so as to denote their lower class, they have sepia-toned, nearly black skin. Although these differences fall outside the purview of verbal language, children surely perceive them. One wonders: do coded messages like this sink in even more deeply if they are *not* verbalised? It could be argued that the visual differences (between Willy and the gorilla gang) are ironically intended. If so, I would suggest that sophisticated visual irony is often opaque to young children. More about this anon.

Back home after the attack, the little chimp Willy sinks into a pink armchair. Why pink? The traditional gender implications are clear: pink is code feminine; blue, code masculine. More than the physical assault, what rankles is the humiliation of being called a wimp. Willy's sense of shame over this 'name' reveals the strong element of denial in that centuries-old English nursery rhyme: "Sticks and stones can break my bones, but names will never harm me". Actually, of course, names hurt aplenty. Nestled in the pink armchair, Willy holds a comic book with an end-cover that channels Superman as Supergorilla. This pictorial detail is easily overlooked. However, it is emblematic of the book as a whole.

Flexing his biceps in a menacing gesture and about to zoom off, Supergorilla's blue, red and gold suit brings to mind Superman's alter-ego, the mild-mannered Clark Kent. Totally unremarked by the words, this small image symbolically encapsulates the book's central theme, namely: the ambiguous relations between masculine strength and tenderness, between boldness and reticence, between what is on the outside and what is within.

Willy spies an ad in the comic book. Adjacent to the drawing of a brawny, grinning gorilla, bold black letters read: "DON'T BE A WIMP! MAIL THIS NOW!" He sends away for a promised instruction manual, and over the next 12 pages, the self-deprecatory little chimpanzee makes heroic efforts to refashion himself to conform to the perennial masculine gender ideal. He jogs daily and adheres to a diet of bananas. He takes up weight lifting, works out in a body-building club; he learns how to fight. We watch him grow larger, stronger, darker and hairier. Finally, when "Willy looked in the mirror," Browne writes, "He liked what he saw." What, however, does Willy see?

Pale yellow daffodils adorn the wallpaper that surrounds this great new macho Willy. Why? Might they betoken a feminine element that cannot be expunged? Meanwhile, his former self, shy and stoop-shouldered, persists in the form of a black-and-white photograph that rests unobtrusively on the bureau next to his large mirror. Do these visual details subvert or expand the meaning of the accompanying text? Within the range of Willy's gaze is not merely the tough new gorilla-self he has forged but also his former chimpanzee-self and the flowers. Or is he blind to these reminders, so that the details work only on child-readers, subliminally, as a form of visual persuasion? At the centre of the image, our gaze meets Willy's fire-red jockey briefs – a visual allusion to the bold red headgear of the bullies and a sign that his nickname still holds.

Suddenly we have an uncanny repeat of the gorillas' attack on Willy. Now the place of the helpless, victimised boy is taken by a girl! Instead of Willy, it is Millie who is being held in a vise-like grip by the gorilla gang leader, who also grabs her purse. The visual equation is unmistakable: "Wimp equals Girl." On the following page, Millie has been left on the ground by the gorillas, who are running away. We notice Willy's looming shadow in the foreground and presume it is he who has sent them fleeing. By being able to scare, Willy has changed from a wimp into a hero. Big, strong and alarming now, he attracts the girl, and, on the next page, we see Millie covering his face with lipstick kisses in gratitude for her rescue.

Willy marches cockily down the street, smiling to himself that he is now truly a hero, no longer a wimp. On the final pages of the book, however, he bumps into a telephone pole. Instantly, he shrinks back to his original size. His last words are addressed to the pole: "Oh, I'm sorry!" he says. Adults laugh at this ending, but the young children with whom

I have shared the book are more confused than amused. As in the examples above, one wonders to whom such a cultural product is actually addressed. One wonders, moreover, at its immense popularity.

If Haskell is right and historians have much to learn from a careful consideration of images circulating in a culture, what can be discovered about transformations of childhood in Britain from this slender book? Does Willy change? Does he change on the outside but not on the inside? In the end, he is portrayed as ridiculous, and we laugh at him and pity him. The book seems to record adult ambivalence about age-old masculine stereotypes but perhaps without sufficient consideration for the reactions of the young audience itself, the very children who are trying to find out who they are, what they want, who they are expected to be and how to grow up in this fast-changing world.

Browne's book, it seems to me, records a cultural moment – very much ongoing as this chapter is being written – in which conventional images of masculinity are being challenged by society (British and American) so that what to teach children has become less clear than in the past, the past which we, of course, can know only at a distance and which we tend to simplify and even idealise. Riddled with ambiguity, Browne's children's book pulls away from any clear, simple, direct message and thus betrays, perhaps, a change in the perception of childhood in our times. Children now are more than ever a proving ground for competing ideologies and values, and I claim this on the basis of unprecedented worldwide population displacements, the reality of diverse cultural groups co-existing in close interactive proximity and the increased awareness in modern times of childhood as a distinct phase of life. No matter how one analyses Browne's book, however, its quasi-ironic macho ideology and its blatant yet unacknowledged racial stereotyping cannot be gainsaid. It would be evasive to assert, for example, as I have heard, that some chimpanzees do truly have lighter skins than gorillas. In point of fact, the common chimpanzee is jet black.

The book's gentle irony – which is why adults (rarely children, in my research) laugh spontaneously – is a mode of apprehension that is available to sophisticated grownups, who come to cultural experiences with attitudes formed over a lifetime; irony is considerably less available to most young children, whose values and beliefs are still in the process of formation and who therefore often tend, first off, to process words and ideas concretely. As James Thurber unforgettably demonstrated ([1945] 1953), irony is readily misunderstood by children, who take it straightforwardly and feel puzzled by it. Consider the expression, for example: "her father just doesn't know how to put his foot down".

Browne's book is a classic example of the ambiguities that swirl around our concepts of childhood. The age-old tenet apparently persists: To be successful, men require prodigious physical strength and a frightening demeanour. Relentless war and mass destruction have taught us to distrust this shibboleth at our peril; yet, do we? Browne's tiny "Supergorilla" hints that outside and inside may indeed differ in the psyches of boys and young men but co-exist as legitimate aspects of masculinity. Must they? As I have tried to show, the picture book complicates this notion by mixing it with other themes: racial difference, gender confusion and morality that require unravelling. On a page where Willy is doing aerobics, one little boy to whom I was reading pointed quite matter-of-factly and said: "Look! Now Willy is a girl".

With its salient and subtle confusions, a children's book mirrors its cultural moment but through a trick glass. Riddling and ambiguous, it exposes cultural drift. Browne's character appeals, and Browne himself clearly loves Willy while poking fun at him, which is itself characteristic of age-old adult attitudes to childhood, a stage of life ridiculed – like old age – as a way of putting it at a distance from us when it seems to edge too uncomfortably close. Parenthetically, a marvellous and unsurpassed pictorial rendering of these extremes of viewing childhood can be found in Pieter Brueghel's 1560 masterpiece, *Children's Games*, in the painting collection of the Kunsthistorisches Museum in Vienna.[5] Deceptive simplicity and arch humour belie a bewildering kaleidoscope of blended themes, as confusing to adults as to children, so that Browne's book may truly be considered a vision of childhood in uneasy transformation.

I want, however, to return to that fist on its title page. This fist takes us back to Gombrich and Haskell: punching through the paper, it makes me ask myself whether a picture book itself, complex artefact that it is, doesn't pose a defiant challenge to all who try confidently to decode it. As a coda, let me briefly juxtapose *Willy the Wimp* with a beloved 1936 American classic by Munro Leaf and Robert Lawson, called *The Story of Ferdinand*, which also deals with gentleness in boys. The differences are legion, but what I think matters most is that Ferdinand, the shy little bull calf who absolutely refuses to fight in the bull ring in Madrid, is sent back eventually to his pasture, where he sits under his favourite cork tree and smells the flowers. Children are not encouraged to laugh at him. The book resolves into superficial clarity. Unlike *Willy the Wimp*, it is designedly not left open-ended and unresolved. It ends with the definitive words: "He was happy". However, what the child encountering this picture book sees via the final illustration is the price Ferdinand pays for his deviance from the norm, for his refusal, in other words, to enact the expected masculine aggressivity. That price is solitude, isolation, serenity, but even, perhaps, a denied morbid loneliness. Ferdinand is shown in dark silhouette, faraway, under the tree all by himself. The word "happy" may not, in other words, be read by some children as borne out by its accompanying illustration. Or, at very least, the accompanying illustration may subtly undermine the positive verbal ending.

Has our increasing pluralism and diversity, both in the UK and the US, exceeded the level of comfort for some, such that hypocrisy crops up as a coping strategy? If so, it may be that *Willy the Wimp* – in parallel with the Compton-Verney show – can be seen as a continuation of what has gone before rather than a break with the past. The comparison of these two books, *Willy* and *Ferdinand*, however, thematically twinned as engaged with issues of gender identity and masculinity, yet separated by an ocean and a half-century, point to my conclusion that, along with other examples adduced in this chapter, while Haskell and Gombrich are surely right to claim images as constituting primary data for the understanding of a culture, a 'correct' interpretation of images cannot be taken for granted, certainly not in the field of childhood studies. We confidently label and fix their 'meanings' only at our peril, for they betoken far more than meets the eye. As an aside, with regard to childhood and irony, Ferdinand the bull is shown sitting under a cork tree, which bears actual wine bottle corks on its branches. This is done, of course, in knowing acknowledgement of the literal-mindedness of its child readers. Irony is not expected of them here, to which, the present author gives a smile of grateful affirmation. She ends her essay in a da capo gesture returning to Richard Feynman's wonderfully imaginative father and his lesson on the height of an extinct species. While no right way can be found, those of us interested in children's cultural and aesthetic lives do well to play the jongleur, keeping coloured balls of meaning in the air as we think and write about and for and read to and play with the children in our lives, learning also, whenever possible, directly from them.

Notes

1 For further analysis, see Spitz 2012.
2 The following discussion borrows from and builds upon my earlier work, *Inside Picture Books*, 1999.
3 Note to the reader: picture books are, by convention, unpaginated; hence, the lack of page references in my discussions above and below of picture books.
4 For a fuller exposition of the developmental ideas drawn upon in this paragraph, consult the oeuvre of the renowned child analyst, Melanie Klein (1882–1960), who explicates them throughout her works.
5 For analysis, see Snow 1997.

References

Alan Cristea Gallery. 2016. "Michael Craig-Martin." Accessed 24 February 2017. www.alancristea.com/collection-84-357-Alphabet.
Ariès, Philippe. (1960) 1962. *Centuries of Childhood*, translated by Robert Baldrick. New York: Vintage Books.
Brown, Don. 2011. *America Is Under Attack*. New York: Macmillan.
Browne, Anthony. (1984) 2005. *Willy the Wimp*. London: Walker.
Elson, Dawn. 2014. "How Do We Inspire More Girls to Be Engineers and First Women of the Future." *The Huffington Post*, February 17. Accessed 18 April

2016. www.huffingtonpost.co.uk/dawn-elson/female-engineers_b_4800128.html.

Feynman, Richard P. 1985. *Surely You're Joking, Mr. Feynman: Adventures of a Curious Character.* New York: Viking.

Freedberg, David. 1989. *The Power of Images.* Chicago: University of Chicago Press.

Gerstein, Mordicai. 2003. *The Man Who Walked Between the Towers.* New York: Macmillan.

Goodenough, Elizabeth, ed. 2010. *Where Do Children Play? A Study Guide to the Film.* Ann Arbor: University of Michigan Press.

Gombrich, Ernst Hans Josef. 1987. "Review of *Past and Present in Art and Taste: Selected Essays.*" In *New York Review of Books*, edited by Francis Haskell. June 25, 25–7.

Kinchin, Juliet, and Aidan O'Connor, eds. 2012. *Century of the Child: Growing by Design, 1900–2000.* New York: MoMa.

Leaf, Munro, and Robert Lawson. 1936. *The Story of Ferdinand.* New York: Viking Press.

Snow, Edward. 1997. *Inside Bruegel: The Play of Images in Children's Games.* New York: North Point Press.

Spitz, Ellen Handler. 1999. *Inside Picture Books.* New Haven, CT and London: Yale University Press.

———. 2001. "Childhood, Art, and Evil." In *Mirroring Evil: Nazi Images/Contemporary Art*, edited by Norman Kleeblatt, 39–52. New Brunswick, NJ: Rutgers University Press.

———. 2012. "MoMA and Child: The Century of the Child at the Museum of Modern Art." *Artcritical*, September 24. www.artcritical.com/2012/09/24/century-of-the-child/.

Thomson, Mathew. 2013. *Lost Freedom.* Oxford: Oxford University Press.

Thurber, James. (1945) 1953. *The Thurber Carnival.* Harmondsworth: Penguin.

Tuer, Andrew White. 1896. *A History of the Horn-Book.* vols. 1 & 2. London: Leadenhall Press.

Walker Books. "Anthony Brown." Accessed 21 March 2017. www.walker.co.uk/contributors/Anthony-Browne-1481.aspx.

Warner, Marina. 2005. *Only Make Believe: Ways of Playing.* Warwickshire: Compton Verney House Trust.

Wildsmith, Brian. 1962. *Brian Wildsmith's ABC.* Oxford: Oxford University Press.

———. "Brian Wildsmith: FAQS." Accessed 21 March 2017. www.brianwildsmith.com/bw.FAQS.html.

Section III
Historical and Social Dimensions of Childhood in Contemporary Britain

9 Childcare for the Under-Fives in Post-1945 England
Contemporary Reflections on Past Childhoods

Angela Davis

Introduction

How to care for the under-fives has been a problematic issue in Britain over the past 70 years. Pre-school childcare has repeatedly been on and off the political agenda as concerns about promoting children's wellbeing, the stability of the family unit and the country's economic performance were raised and re-evaluated. At the governmental level, tension has existed between the desire to expand free early years' care and education and concerns over how they will be funded. The responsibility for early years' provision was and remains divided between government agencies of health, education, social services and communities; this has meant that while improved childcare provision has been a commonly held aspiration, no one has been obligated to provide it. Consequently, while it has long been recognised that investing in the early years will be good for children, families and the country as a whole, agreeing who will finance these services has proved difficult.

The health and welfare of children in the twentieth century have received increased consideration in the discipline of history over the last 30 years. Infant welfare in the first decades of the century has received considerable attention (for example, Lewis 1980; Marland 1993; Peretz 1992; Smith 1995), but this has broadened to examine subjects such as school health services (for example, Harris 1995; Welshman 1988), and wartime evacuation (for example, Welshman 2010) and child welfare (for example, Hendrick 2003; Stewart 2013). More recently, there has been work on parenthood (Davis 2012; King 2015; Pooley 2013) and important contributions to the history of post-war childhood, psychology and social policy (Shapira 2013; Thomson 2013). However, the existing scholarship has not primarily focused on children between the stages of babyhood and attending school. The central concern of this chapter is the lives of children under five in Britain during the second half of the twentieth century. It explores the experiences of children who were looked after outside of the family on a daily basis in different forms of care, including day nurseries, nursery schools and classes, playgroups and childminders.

Furthermore, while the interplay between policy and the provision of care for pre-school children has received some attention (Blackstone 1971; Randall 2000; Riley 1983), these accounts have focused on the debates about children's welfare rather than the children themselves. As Hugh Cunningham has argued, "A history of childhood can easily become a history of what adults have done to children" (2006, 16). Through oral history, this chapter extends the existing historical debate by uncovering the experiences of those who attended childcare. This chapter is based on 20 oral history interviews with adults who had attended childcare.[1] The interviewees were found through advertisements in the publications of childcare organisations, such as the Preschool Learning Alliance, through local nursery schools (to find parents who had attended the same schools as their children who currently attended) and snowballing, where interviewees passed on the details of other potential interviewees. They were chosen to include people who had attended different forms of care and who did so at different moments during the second half of the twentieth century. The interviews were conducted between 2010 and 2013 under the Conservative-led coalition government, which was combining traditional Conservative values promoting the private family unit, and Liberal Democrat initiatives to promote gender equality. Early years' services formed an important part of the 2010–2015 coalition government's family policy with the coalition agreement supporting the provision of free nursery care and the launch of a free nursery scheme for disadvantaged two-year-olds funded through an Early Intervention Grant. Childcare was therefore a topical issue at the time the interviews were conducted, and present debates influenced the ways in which interviewees reflected on their experiences.

For historians, the term 'contemporary' usually describes the period from approximately 1945 to the present, although, as Michael Kandiah (2017) has shown, the definition has varied from country to country, from group to group and, even within countries, from time to time. For example, Kandiah notes that historians of the British welfare state have found it more useful to go back to the earlier part of the twentieth century, or even the nineteenth century, as longer-term analyses can provide better explanations for most developments of the recent past (2017). This chapter will demonstrate how childcare decisions made during and immediately after the war shaped the provision of childcare up to today. Historians have also demonstrated the value of bringing a historical perspective and methodological approach to analysing the recent past. An oral history approach offers particular benefits as it enables an engagement with recent events but seen through a wider historical trajectory. Many of the interviewees whose testimonies are discussed in this chapter were parents (or sometimes grandparents) of young children themselves and were reflecting upon their own experiences of childcare when they were children through their present perspective. They also described how their experiences as children determined their attitudes toward childcare for their own children. In this way, we can see how contemporary childhoods are shaped by the past, and how our understanding of the past is seen through the lens of present experiences.

Conducting oral histories of childhood raises many interpretive challenges, though. As with all interviews, an analysis needs to take into account the tension between self and public representation, the dynamics between interviewee and interviewer, the function of memory and the playing out of the past–present relationship in interview narratives (Wright and McLeod 2012, 16–7). In addition, as Jay Mechling has shown, oral history interviews with adults about their childhood experiences raise some particular methodological concerns. An adult reflecting today upon her (in this case) childhood, "will be perceiving and interpreting that childhood through her adult, learned categories – from adult notions of propriety to the special vocabularies of popularized psychology" (Mechling 1987, 580–1). Memories will also be influenced by the powerful cultural narratives of childhood given widespread expression in popular culture, for example, as the best of days of your life or the days of innocence and simple times (Wright and McLeod 2012, 15). Personal autobiographical memory is therefore functionally and structurally related to cultural myths and social narratives (Nelson 2003, 125). In her interviews with people who grew up in 1950s Australia, Carla Pascoe found that her respondents recollected their post-war childhoods as safe and free in contrast to the dangers and pressures surrounding the contemporary experience of growing up (2009, 231). Men and women construct their narratives of childhood in the context of these cultural representations (specific to their generation) and in relation to the experiences of others, such as their children and grandchildren (Wright and McLeod 2012, 15).

However, whilst it is important to be aware of the multiple strands of experience – public/private and past/present, etc. – within oral history narratives, the benefits of oral history outweigh the limitations. The work of oral historians (Dawson 1994; Passerini 1987; Portelli 1991; Thomson 1994) has demonstrated that oral history is a particularly suitable methodology for the study of subjective experience, and this chapter seeks to explore the subjective thoughts and feelings of people who attended childcare. It will take a chronological look at the developments in the provision of childcare for the under-fives in post-1945 Britain whilst reflecting upon individual children's experiences of these changes. It will pay particular attention to their recollections of their relationships with carers, their relationships with other children and their attitudes toward the structures and environment of their childcare setting.

Wartime and Post-War Experiences

There was a dramatic increase in the number of children cared for by state-provided childcare services during the Second World War. From approximately 100 day nurseries and 118 nursery schools on the eve of the war, the figures leaped by 1944 to 1,450 full-time nurseries, 109 part-time nurseries, and 784 nursery classes (Randall 2000, 34). The wartime expansion initially began as an endeavour to provide nurseries for evacuated children, but labour-supply considerations really drove the dramatic growth (Summerfield 1984, 74). Even so, Vicky Randall argues that the Ministry of Health, still responsible for day nurseries, would have been prepared to rely on widespread informal child-minding arrangements to deal with the needs of married women workers. She argues that demand from the women themselves, relayed via employers, together with pressure from organised labour persuaded the government, in the form of the Ministry of Labour, of the need for expanded nursery provision (Randall 1995, 333). As well as this conflict between the Ministries of Health and Labour, personnel within the Ministry of Labour were also divided on the subject, as Penny Summerfield has shown, demonstrating the controversial nature of state-provided nursery care for women workers (1984, 67–8).

After the war, central government halved its grant for day nurseries to local authorities; responsibility for the nurseries was handed over to these local authorities and buildings that had been requisitioned for nursery use were returned to their previous uses. Responsibility for childcare at the level of the national government remained divided between the Ministries of Education and Health. The Ministry of Health was responsible through local authorities (although control passed to social service rather than health departments on 1 January 1971) for state-provided child day care. Despite the dramatic expansion of provision seen during the war, Randall has demonstrated that the Ministry of Health made it clear in 1948 that day nursery places were intended only for children in special need (1996, 176–7). This change from day nurseries being seen as a resource for working mothers to a social service for vulnerable children represented a policy reversal. Until April 1946, nursery places were available only for the children of working mothers (Mayall and Petrie 1983, 17–8). Local authorities also had to make do with diminishing resources. In consequence, local authority day nursery places fell markedly from 71,500 in 1944 to 21,140 in 1969 (Melhuish 2006, 45).

Economic reasons were the principal driver behind the desire to cut back the wartime provision, but the reorganisation also took place within the context of growing concern about the effects of day care attendance on children's wellbeing. Already before the war, there were concerns raised about the desirability of removing children from the care of their mothers in the home. In 1933, the Hadow Report into Infant and Nursery Schools was published. It recommended that the compulsory school starting age should remain at five and that children aged between three and five (although not below three) should continue to be admitted on a voluntary basis. The report stressed the importance of the years from birth to five in the child's physical and mental development but asserted that where conditions were good the best place for a child below the age of five was at home (Board of Education 1933, 174–82, 187). During the war, anxieties about the children's physical and emotional health in day nurseries remained present. The Medical Women's Federation led calls about risks to children's physical health. In 1944–1945, they carried out an investigation into the effect of life in wartime day nurseries on the physical health of children under five, concluding in a 1946 article for the *British Medical Journal* that the evidence "does not indicate a beneficial effect of nursery life for the younger children – rather the reverse" (Day Nurseries Committee of the Medical Women's Federation 1946, 220).

While concerns about the effects of attending nurseries on children's psychological health became more pronounced after the war than during it, there was already unease. In an article published in *The Lancet* in October 1946, a public health doctor, Hilda Menzies, concluded that day nurseries were unsuitable for the under-twos because, "it is obvious from their behaviour that these children do suffer an emotional upset on admission to a nursery" (1946, 501). Furthermore, the experience of wartime evacuation, with the separation of children from their families, had led psychologists such as John Bowlby and Donald Winnicott to stress the importance of young children being cared for at home by their mothers. Such views about the dangers of nursery attendance to children's wellbeing, and the lack of any real health benefits, were widespread by the early 1950s (Davis 2015, 101).

Only two of the interviewees had attended day nurseries during the war or in the years immediately after, and both said that they had traumatic experiences. Gaynor was born in London in 1945 and went to a day nursery there in the late 1940s as her mother was the family's sole earner. Gaynor recalled that she "absolutely hated it, cried all the time." She added that she "had a very bad experience at school as well" and that it was "as a result of nursery". When asked what it was that she hated about it, she replied, "Parents weren't allowed in the door, for example [...]. It was just frightening all the time, nothing felt secure and I didn't have any support from home because my mother was out at work" (Gaynor, 18). The negative experience Gaynor had at the nursery was exacerbated by her family background. Her mother had to return to work to support the family because her father was ill with tuberculosis and subsequently died when Gaynor was six. Fiona, who was born in 1941 and grew up in Sanderstead near Croydon, attended a day nursery at the end of the war when her mother had a new baby. Her father was away in the forces at this time. She said,

> [W]e were sent off to day nursery, which we weren't supposed to be at because it was supposed to be for working mothers. And we

were there for about a fortnight I think and we picked up whooping cough, and so we were terribly ill. And I can remember that quite vividly too.

(Fiona, 1)

It is interesting that Fiona remembered attending the nursery, but it was associated in her mind with ill health, reflecting some of the contemporary concerns of critics of day nurseries.

It is difficult to know whether Gaynor's and Fiona's critical accounts of the day nurseries they attended were the result of their own experiences or whether they were influenced by the negative contemporary discourse surrounding them. Nonetheless, it is noteworthy that they both said they have strong recollections of attending. Whether it was their own individual recollection, part of the family memory passed down to them or a wider cultural memory of day nurseries, the episode had acquired significance and had become an important part of their narrative of childhood. The way they remembered their experience was also influential on their later lives as their perceived negative experience contributed to their own decision to stay at home when their children were young.

As well as day nurseries, nursery schools or classes also existed for the under-fives. During the last years of the war, plans were made for post-war reconstruction of the social services, which included large-scale nursery provision. A 1943 white paper, *Educational Reconstruction*, stated that the self-contained nursery school was the "most suitable type of provision" for children under five and should be provided as a universal service because "even when children come from good homes they can derive much benefit, both educational and physical, from attendance". The report also argued that nursery schools could be used as childcare, stating that they "are of great value to mothers who go out to work" (Board of Education 1943, 8). However, these proposals were not translated into post-war policy. While the Ministry of Education was concerned to the extent that the 1944 Education Act required local education authorities to provide nursery schools or classes for children under five, no guidance was given on how universal this provision should be (Whitbread 1972, 105).

Consequently, the provision of nursery education remained very limited due to other demands on local education budgets. From the late 1950s, most local education authorities introduced part-time provision. Part-time places (in the form of morning or afternoon sessions) were seen as a solution to the restraints on nursery schools and classes in light of the shortage of resources. In 1960, a Ministry of Education Circular (8/60) told local authorities that for reasons of economy the number of under-fives in school should be kept to the 1957 level (Statham et al. 1990, 1). Instead, the circular recommended to authorities that they change some of the existing full-time provision to part time to allow a greater number of children some pre-school education (Blackstone 1971, 66–7). To fill the gap in state provision, private nursery schools were also opened and several interviewees attended these.

The interviewees who attended nursery schools were generally more positive than their counterparts who had been at day nurseries. Their views reflected their belief that their parents had sent them to nursery school for their own educational benefit. While they often compared their nursery schools unfavourably with those of their children's or grandchildren's generation, they intimated that the shortages of the war years and immediate aftermath had restricted their schools' ability to provide more. Martha was born in 1945 in Taunton in Somerset; she attended a Froebel-inspired private nursery school in the late 1940s. While the school's philosophy was to meet the needs of the child, the shortages of the post-war period meant these aims could not be realised. She explained that the teachers "were very good, but they had no equipment really". Describing the nursery, she said it was a

> lovely building, it had been built in the twenties and on that [...] sort of German model with a lot of windows and everything child height. It was a beautiful building, but it hadn't been equipped since 1939 at the latest.
>
> (Martha, 4)

For example, the children had to "draw on little bits of thin paper" and the plasticine "was a sort of chocolate brown with a lot of hair in it" (ibid.).

Lynne, who was born and brought up in Wales, also went to a small private nursery school in the late 1940s, at the age of three. She experienced a more formal approach. The children

> always did sums in the morning, we didn't have a play time officially, this was curious, we never went outside, we sat and had this little bottle of milk that everybody had for a while then and we sort of read and wrote and did sums.
>
> (Lynn, 2)

While there was variation between nursery schools there was not a substantial difference between the private and state sectors as, recalling her reception class at a state-school primary in Newbury, Berkshire, in the mid-1950s, Lucy also explained that the day was much more rigid and routine-based than would be the case for children of the same age at school later in the century:

> We were definitely sitting in groups so there would be eight of us at a table, because I can actually remember having to move the chairs

when we did any formal work to face the teacher. I can remember the mornings being very structured with what would have been literacy and maths, I remember the alphabet being strung in very large pictures and letters across the front and every morning we would go "a" for apple, I can see her with her stick pointing. And we'd go through every letter ... it was never any different, it was exactly the same every day so it was quite formal.

(Lucy, 3)

It is likely that, as for the adults who had been to day nurseries, the accounts of the nursery school attenders were also influenced by both contemporary and later discourses about nursery education. Their later contact with ideas about child-centred approaches to learning, often through their own children, led them to contrast the structures and environment of their nurseries with the less formal approach they thought had subsequently developed. Their accounts were also influenced by memories of wartime and post-war shortages in contrast to the increased resources and opportunities they thought were available to later generations. Unlike the day nursery attenders, however, their own experiences of nursery had not led them to reject nursery education, and these interviewees chose to send their own children to nursery schools. It is likely that as, both at the time and subsequently, nursery education was looked upon more favourably than day care and as being a positive benefit for children, they were also more positive in their recollections.

The 1960s–1990s: Changes and Continuities

The numbers of women in paid employment was growing in the post-war decades. Between 1955 and 1975, the percentage of working-age women in the labour force rose from 45.9 to 55.1 and then to 66.6 by 1995 (Walsh and Wrigley 2001, 2). However, state-provided early years' care did not grow to meet this demand. By the late 1970s, the day nursery service had become an extremely limited form of provision, intended to prevent children from being harmed by inadequate homes or parents and to avoid the last resort of residential care, including children from difficult family backgrounds, one-parent households and some disabled children (Mayall and Petrie 1983, 29–30). In the absence of a universal system of state-provided care, women turned to private providers of childcare. This care could either take the form of private nurseries, for parents who could afford them, or the cheaper alternative of childminders. These decades also saw the playgroup movement spring up as a reaction to the lack of nursery education. The Pre-school Playgroups Association, which had been founded in 1961 to provide "Do-it-yourself Nurseries" in direct response to Circular 8/60 and the limit on state nursery places it imposed, rapidly expanded during the 1960s and 1970s. By the early 1980s, it exceeded 17,700 members (Mathivet 2011, 41–3). At that point, more children attended playgroups than any other single type of provision for the under-fives (Osborn, Butler and Morris 1984, 109).

It was against this background of growing demand for early years' care and education that three successive government reports discussed aspects of provision for the under-fives. Randall notes that the Plowden Report (1967), into primary education in England, advocated nursery education on demand, though on a part-time basis; the Seebohm Report (1968), on social services, argued for some expansion of local authority day nursery places and better coordination of under-fives' services; and the Finer Report (1974), on one-parent families, stressed the day care needs of the growing contingent of one-parent families. Partly in response to these recommendations, a programme of limited expansion was planned. Most famously, a 1972 Department of Education White Paper, under the auspices of then Minister, Margaret Thatcher, announced that nursery education would be expanded to cater for all three- and four-year-olds by 1982; local authorities were also set targets for increased day nursery provision by the Department of Health and Social Security (Randall 1996, 177). These targets were never met and were among the first casualties of the cuts and restraints in public spending that were in place by the mid-1970s.

Demand upon and concern about the existing services continued to grow. In response, in 1976, the Department of Health and Social Security and the Department of Education and Science organised a conference that was held at Sunningdale, entitled "Low Cost Day Care Provision for the Under-Fives". Then Minister of State, Dr David Owen, introduced the conference and explained why it had been called. He set it in the context of "restraint in social expenditure" and concern for the under-fives. He concluded his address by stating a possible solution to the dilemma: "We could improve the provision for 0–5s substantially by spreading the low-cost best practice which already exists proven and documented on the ground". Most of the conference members argued that this "low-cost best practice" was to be found among childminders and playgroups (cited in Mayall and Petrie 1983, 24–5).

The striking picture that emerged from the conference, therefore, was that the state could not be expected to provide care or indeed education for under-fives and that families would have to rely on private solutions to their childcare needs. Indeed, during the Thatcher and Major governments that followed, childcare policy was limited to the regulation of provision. For example, the 1988 Children Bill required local authorities to review day care provision in their areas, and the 1989 Children Act obliged local authorities to register and inspect childcare services. However, during this period the number of local authority day nurseries actually fell with the real growth being in private and voluntary nurseries and childminding (Gregg, Gutiérrez-Domènech and Waldfogel 2003,

4–5). The parents of most pre-school children in the latter decades of the twentieth century were still expected to make their own arrangements for their care.

However, while levels of provision were either static or in decline, there were important changes in the practices of early years' care. One notable development was the introduction of child-centred learning. Already in 1933, the Hadow Report had recommended that children's lessons should be closely related to their practical interests and that they should be surrounded with objects and materials that would afford scope for experiment and exploration (Board of Education 1933, 179). However, Nanette Whitbread believes that it took until the 1950s before this child-centred approach became the norm (1972, 125), and many teachers thought it was not until the 1960s that there was widespread change (Davis 2015, 133). By the 1960s, teacher training did lay a greater focus on child development, and teachers who trained in the 1960s were more likely to be aware of theories of attachment (Cass 1971, 10–8, 33).

Interviewees who attended nursery schools in the 1970s and 1980s described notably more child-centred environments than did the previous generation. For example, Trudi Ashmall, who was born in Abingdon in 1971, went to the town's newly opened Dunmore Nursery. She described it as

> lovely because it was a nursery that was on two levels. It had lots of places you could go, not the one classroom. Feet painting out in the front bit where all the water and messy play happened. They used to run rolls of computer paper and we would step in a tray at one end and just walk up it, very messy.
>
> (Ashmall 2002, 24)

The influence of new teaching methods and an emphasis of learning through play were clear. Rob, who was born in 1981 in Leamington Spa and attended Warwick Nursery School during the mid-1980s, remembered playing was an important part of the school day, and his favourite activity had been playing outside on bikes and cars (Rob, 1). While Trudi Ashmall and Rob focused on the environment in their accounts of their nursery school, other interviewees focused more on the relationships they had with the other children. The opportunity to play with other children was often commented upon. Reflecting upon his experience at a playgroup in the late 1970s, Jon, who was born in 1976 and grew up in London, talked about the opportunity to socialise with other children as having been a benefit of attendance and something he wanted to repeat with his own children (Jon, 1–2).

However, not all schools or teachers followed a child-centred approach. Some of the interviewees who attended nursery schools in the latter decades of the century recalled they could still be strict places rather than child-centred environments. Bianca was born in Leamington Spa in 1976 and went to nursery in Warwick the late 1970s. She remembered "putting my hands in the paint and getting shouted at and marched over to the sink to wash it off and told to use a paintbrush" (Bianca, 1). Justine and Cerys, who were born in 1981, both went to a nursery attached to a private school in Camberley in the mid-1980s. Justine remembered it as being "very formal compared to what the nurseries are like today, because we actually sat and did tasks even from little". She later added,

> I remember playing a little bit in the first year because they had this Wendy house thing, but you're only allowed [at] certain times to go and play in there and ... by the time we got to reception, I don't remember any playing when you were there.
> (Justine, 1–2, 11)

Similarly, Cerys said, "It was like school". Developing this theme, she continued, "I don't remember doing even anything particularly messy. ... I just remember it all being quite, formal" (Cerys, 3).

There were also changes in day nursery practice. There was a move away from the nurseries' main aim being the promotion of physical health. The National Nurseries Examination Board (NNEB) for England and Wales, which was established in 1945, had been closely connected with and subordinate to the relevant bodies for professional training in medical nursing (Baldock 2011, 49). However, in 1964, the National Society of Children's Nurseries launched an investigation into the status of nursery nurse training and recommended that the curriculum give more focus to children's general development, rather than simply health. Subsequently, more nursery nurses were trained in nursery schools and classes (Parry and Archer 1974, 49–50). In 1977, the NNEB became fully independent from the Royal Society for Health. In addition, research conducted during the war, particularly that of Anna Freud in her wartime nurseries, came to influence the routines and structures of day nurseries. The family grouping system, based around the figure of the substitute mother, whereby each child had an assigned carer, was adopted into nursery practice (Sayers 1992, 172–3).

Perhaps resulting from these changes, Margot, who attended a day nursery in Romford in the mid-1960s, found her experience of the nursery to be very different from those interviewees who had attended a generation before. She had attended the day nursery from a few weeks old in 1964 when her mother, a teacher, returned to work. Teachers had been added to the priority groups for local authority day nursery places in the mid-1960s to try to alleviate the shortage of teachers at this time. Margot described it as being a positive experience for her: "[M]y memories are of a confident time, being happy, and feeling safe". Margot thought that encountering a range of children had been beneficial in later life, because she "always found it easy to mix with people in general and especially with people from different backgrounds [and] nationalities". She also felt she established a relationship with her carers, particularly "matron" who "smiled a lot", adding that she still had "fond memories of her and can still recall her face". As well as enabling the children to form an attachment to their carer, family grouping allowed children to form bonds with the other children in the group. Margot remembered the relationships she established with other children as being important to her: "I remember hugging my friends and holding hands with other children". She continued,

> I very much liked playing with other children. I remember forming some good friendships and had 'favourite' children I liked to play with. I can also remember pestering my parents to go visit one of my best friends outside of nursery.
>
> (Margot, 1–2)

Change over time is not the only possible explanation for Margot's more positive experience of day nursery care, however. Local differences and individual staff could influence the environment and atmosphere within a day nursery. Margot's own background could also have played a significant part. She was not a priority case for admission; she did not have poor home conditions or only one parent at home (due to family breakdown or ill health), which were the common reasons for day nursery attendance at this time. Margot's mother chose to continue her work as a teacher alongside her father who was also employed. In addition, Margot could have been of a personality that suited nursery care. Whatever the reasons behind her more positive experience, it led her to send her own children to a day nursery (attached to a university), each from a few months old, when she returned to work after they were born in the early 2000s. She explained, "I wanted my two children to mix with a wide variety of other children – both are very sociable and mix reasonably easily with others". She also said that she particularly wanted her children to attend a nursery, rather than another form of care:

> I also felt confident in placing them within a nursery environment as I had confidence in the staff and their ability to care for and nurture them. I also liked the fact that there were multiple staff rather than just a single person as in the case of a childminder.
>
> (Margot, 2)

Margot's experiences also contrasted with those of Kathy, who was born in London in 1976 and attended the Thomas Coram Children's Centre in Camden from the age of two when her mother returned to work. The Coram Centre was an early combined nursery centre, which was founded in 1974 through the collaboration of the Thomas Coram Foundation, the London Borough of Camden and the Area Health Authority. Combined nursery centres were themselves a development in childcare services, whereby early education was integrated with full day care and other children's services on the same premises. Kathy was ambivalent about her experience at the centre. She said,

> I did play with other kids and some of it was nice and some of it not so nice. I remember it being a time of finding out what other kids were capable of and what their intentions were and I think I was quite pliable and manipulatable [sic].

Indeed, she had been left with mixed feelings about sending her own children to nursery:

> It makes me nervous to think of my kids going to nursery when they are three because of the other kids. Kids can be cruel and difficult but I do know that it is also of the utmost importance for them to be socialised.
> (Kathy, 10–11)

Kathy's older brother, Tom, had a different experience. While agreeing with Kathy that there were some "very unpleasant characters", he had "generally enjoyed playing with [the] other children". When asked how he thought going to nursery had affected him in later life, he answered:

> I certainly felt that it was important for my own son to go to nursery as soon as possible, at three, in order to start socialising with other children and start to gain a small degree of independence from us.
> (Tom, 2)

The contrasting accounts of Kathy and Tom indicate how early years' care was experienced at an individual level. Despite attending the same institute and coming from the same family, they remembered their time in in the nursery in divergent ways. Moreover, their different recollections shaped their attitudes toward childcare as parents and their belief in whether it would be beneficial for their own children.

For those interviewees who had been cared for by childminders, the one-to-one relationship they had with them was the main theme of their accounts. David, who was born in 1969 and grew up in Camden, was looked after by a childminder, Agatha, when his mother, Lillian, a teacher, returned to work. He developed a close relationship with his childminder's family: "I remember being extremely fond of Agatha – her husband and their daughter. I felt very safe and cared for". He also thought they were influential: "I'm sure they helped instil my moral outlook" (David, 1). Jade was born in 1986 in Birmingham. Her mother, a social worker, returned to work when she was a toddler, and she was looked after by a childminder with whom she had remained close until her death. Jade said, "[S]he was more like a grandma to us really because obviously she was paid, but it was kind of more a family relationship". Discussing whether she would like to replicate her childhood by using a childminder when she had her own children, Jade said she would, adding, "I think having someone like [my childminder] to have that role across your childhood is amazing" (Jade, 3, 5).

However, once again indicating the deeply personal nature of children's experiences of childcare, David's brother Ben, who was born in 1971, reflected differently upon his experiences. Ben also thought Agatha was an "[e]xtremely warm person", adding that he "absolutely loved her. That's how I felt at the time, and still do". Like David, Ben thought she had been an important figure in his childhood: "I think she taught me basic common sense, manners and to be a good listener, which is what she was" (Ben, 1). However, it was the absence of a peer group, which he thought that he had missed out because of the one-on-one nature of the relationship, which was the strongest theme in his account. He recalled being "lonely because I was on my own there". He felt this had affected him throughout his later life, stating, "I've always felt like an outsider due to being on my own". He, therefore, concluded, "I think that definitely childminding if it's just the kid on his or her own needs more intellectual engagement" (Ben, 1–2). While some adults' recollections of childcare concentrated on the physical environment, for many the emotional environment and the feelings attached to their early years' experiences were focal points of their stories. These were clearly memories that resonated deeply and had influenced their adult lives.

Conclusions

This analysis of oral history interviews with adults who had attended pre-school childcare has demonstrated the differing ways in which people experienced early years' care in Britain during the second half of the twentieth century. While their experiences were highly subjective, they do reveal something about changing practices, for example, in respect to increased emphasis on child-centred learning and a move from promoting physical health to a broader understanding of encouraging healthy child development. Yet their accounts most strongly demonstrate that childcare was experienced at the individual level. Even siblings who were cared for by the same person or place at the same time told very different accounts. This multiplicity of perspectives in part reflected the many childhood and later life experiences of individuals that were unrelated to their early years' care. This chapter also demonstrated how interviewees were engaged in a dialogue between their childhood selves and their present adult selves, who were often parents. While they indicated that their own childhood experiences influenced the decisions they made as parents, witnessing the experiences of the younger generation also influenced how they now told their stories of attending pre-school care.

Note

1 To preserve the anonymity of the interviewees, pseudonyms have been used. The interviewees will be referred to in the text by their pseudonyms with page numbers referring to the transcript of their interview. Recordings and transcriptions are held by the author.

References

Ashmall, Trudi. 2002. Abingdon Oral History Project (OT 529, TS 197), (held at the Oxfordshire History Centre).
Baldock, Peter. 2011. *Developing Early Childhood Services: Past, Present and Future*. Maidenhead: McGraw Hill/Open University Press.
Blackstone, Tessa. 1971. *A Fair Start: The Provision of Pre-School Education*. London: Allen Lane.
Board of Education. 1933. *Report of the Consultative Committee on Infant and Nursery Schools*. London: HMSO.
———. 1943. *Educational Reconstruction*. London: HMSO.
Cass, Joan. 1971. *The Significance of Children's Play*. London: B. T. Batsford.
Cunningham, Hugh. 2006. *The Invention of Childhood*. London: BBC.
Davis, Angela. 2012. *Modern Motherhood: Women and Family in England c. 1945–2000*. Manchester: Manchester University Press.
———. 2015. *Pre-School Childcare, 1939–2010: Theory Practice and Experience*. Manchester: Manchester University Press.
Dawson, Graham. 1994. *Soldier Heroes: British Adventure, Empire and the Imagining of Masculinities*. London: Routledge.
Day Nurseries Committee of the Medical Women's Federation in conjunction with W. J. Martin. 1946. "The Health of Children in Wartime Day Nurseries: A Report of an Investigation by the Day Nurseries Committee of the Medical Women's Federation." *The British Medical Journal* 4467: 217–21.
Gregg, Paul, Maria Gutiérrez-Domènech, and Jane Waldfogel. 2003. *The Employment of Married Mothers in Great Britain: 1974–2000*. London: Centre for Economic Performance, London School of Economics and Political Science.
Harris, Bernard. 1995. *The Health of the School Child: A History of the School Medical Service in England and Wales*. Buckingham: Open University Press.
Hendrick, Harry. 2003. *Child Welfare: Historical Dimensions, Contemporary Debate*. Bristol: The Polity Press.
Kandiah, Michael D. 2017. "Contemporary History." *Making History: The Changing Face of the Profession in England*. Accessed 18 February 2017. www.history.ac.uk/makinghistory/resources/articles/contemporary_history.html#resources.

King, Laura. 2015. *Family Men: Fatherhood and Masculinity in Britain, 1914–1960*. Oxford: Oxford University Press.

Lewis, Jane. 1980. *The Politics of Motherhood: Child and Maternal Welfare in England, 1900–1939*. London: Croom Helm.

Marland, Hilary. 1993. "A Pioneer in Infant Welfare: The Huddersfield Scheme: 1903–1920." *Social History of Medicine* 6: 25–50.

Mathivet, Stephanie. 2011. *Changing Lives, Changing Life: The Pedagogical Perspective of the Pre-School Learning Alliance*. London: Pre-School Learning Alliance.

Mayall, Berry, and Pat Petrie. 1983. *Childminding and Day Nurseries: What Kind of Care?* London: Heinemann Educational Books for the Institute of Education, University of London.

Mechling, Jay. 1987. "Oral Evidence and the History of American Children's Lives." *The Journal of American History* 74: 579–86.

Melhuish, Edward. 2006. "Policy and Research on Pre-School Care and Education in the UK." In *Early Childhood Care and Education: International Perspectives*, edited by Edward Melhuish and Konstantinos Petrogiannis, 43–64. Abingdon: Routledge.

Menzies, Hilda F. 1946. "Children in Day Nurseries with Special Reference to the Child under Two Years Old." *The Lancet* 248: 499–501.

Nelson, Katherine. 2003. "Self and Social Function: Individual Autobiographical Memory and Collective Narrative." *Memory* 11: 125–36.

Osborn, Albert Francis, Neville R. Butler, and Anthony Charles Morris. 1984. *The Social Life of Britain's Five-Year-Olds*. London: Routledge and Kegan Paul.

Parry, Marianne, and Hilda Archer. 1974. *Pre-School Education*. London: Macmillan.

Pascoe, Carla. 2009. "Be Home By Dark: Childhood Freedoms and Adult Fears in 1950s Victoria." *Australian Historical Studies* 40: 215–31.

Passerini, Luisa. 1987. *Fascism in Popular Memory: The Cultural Experience of the Turin Working Class*. Cambridge: Cambridge University Press.

Peretz, Elizabeth. 1992. "Maternal and Child Welfare in England and Wales Between the Wars: A Comparative Regional Study." PhD diss., Middlesex University.

Pooley, Sian. 2013. "Parenthood, Child-Rearing and Fertility in England, 1850–1914." *History of the Family* 18: 83–106.

Portelli, Alessandro. 1991. *The Death of Luigi Trastulli and Other Stories: Form and Meaning in Oral History*. Albany: State University of New York Press.

Randall, Vicky. 1995. "The Irresponsible State? The Politics of Child Daycare Provision in Britain." *British Journal of Political Science* 25: 327–48.

———. 1996. "The Politics of Childcare Policy." *Parliamentary Affairs* 49: 176–90.

———. 2000. *The Politics of Child Daycare in Britain*. Oxford: Oxford University Press.

Riley, Denise. 1983. *War in the Nursery: Theories of Child and Mother*. London: Virago.

Sayers, Janet. 1992. *Mothering Psychoanalysis: Helene Deutsch, Karen Horney, Anna Freud and Melanie Klein*. Harmondsworth: Penguin.

Shapira, Michal. 2013. *The War Inside: Psychoanalysis, Total War, and the Making of the Democratic Self in Postwar Britain*. Cambridge: Cambridge University Press.

Smith, Graham. 1995. "Protest Is Better for Infants: Motherhood, Health and Welfare in a Women's Town, c.1911–1931." *Oral History* 23: 63–70.

Statham, June, Eva Lloyd, Peter Moss, Edward Melhuish, and Charlie Owen. 1990. *Playgroups in a Changing World*. London: HMSO.

Stewart, John. 2013. *Child Guidance in Britain, 1918–1955: The Dangerous Age of Childhood*. London: Pickering and Chatto.

Summerfield, Penny. 1984. *Women Workers in the Second World War*. Beckenham: Croom Helm.

Thomson, Alistair. 1994. *Anzac Memories: Living with the Legend*. Oxford: Oxford University Press.

Thomson, Mathew. 2013. *Lost Freedom: The Landscape of the Child and the British Post-War Settlement*. Oxford: Oxford University Press.

Walsh, Maggie, and Chris Wrigley. 2001. "Womanpower: The Transformation of the Labour Force in the UK and USA since 1945." *ReFRESH* 30: 1–4.

Welshman, John. 1988. "The School Medical Service in England and Wales, 1907–1939." PhD diss., University of Oxford.

———. 2010. *Churchill's Children: The Evacuee Experience in Wartime Britain*. Oxford: Oxford University Press.

Whitbread, Nanette. 1972. *The Evolution of the Nursery-Infant School: A History of Infant and Nursery Education in Britain, 1800–1970*. London: Routledge and Kegan Paul.

Wright, Katie, and Julie McLeod. 2012. "Public Memories and Private Meanings: Representing the 'Happy Childhood' Narrative in Oral Histories of Adolescence and Schooling in Australia, 1930s-1950s." *Oral History Forum d'histoire orale* 32: 1–19.

10 Contingent Connections
Between German and British Childhoods – Marion Daltrop

Erica Burman

This chapter arises from personal-political associations, which in turn recapitulate methodological – including reflexive and ethical – questions posed by the study of childhood generally and British childhoods in particular. Based on her own autobiographical account and supplemented by analysis of interviews from friends and colleagues, I retrace and reflect on the life and contributions of someone who encountered and then lived a particular British childhood. A German Jewish refugee from Bielefeld, Germany, Marion Daltrop devoted her working life to engaging with difficult and disadvantaged children in Manchester, as well as being an activist and artist. She was 'saved' because she was a child, coming to Britain on the Kindertransport in 1939. Her engagements and activism, and the affection she continues to inspire, testify to the possibilities, as well as complexities, of cross-generational and transnational solidarities. But beyond this, they also fruitfully demonstrate the arbitrary conditions for access to and, notwithstanding these, transformations of British childhood, alongside how specific personal-political investments are always at play in the study of, and responses to, children and childhoods.

Rationale

As the introduction to this book suggests, although 'contemporary' seems to lay claim to a timescale, it deictically references its own context: it is relational. Hence, 'contemporary Britain' is only accidentally, arbitrarily whatever it is now, but references *the time at the site and moment of its enunciation*. Beyond this, it serves as a trace of how – through reflections or mobilisations – this past is narrated to assemble the sense of our selves-in-the-world now: our identifications, subjectivities, relationships, affinities and commitments. It also suggests something of what people do with their childhood experiences. That is, how they transform their own childhoods into relational resources that impact upon and can transform the lives of other children and childhoods. So the contemporary is inevitably situated, reflexive, even recursive, rather than a specific moment in a unidirectional timeline moving ever on.

I dwell on this point because the same reflections apply to qualifying a childhood with a specific national context. What claims to specificity and generality are relevant to the descriptor 'Contemporary Britain'? This is not to say that obviously linguistic specificities and social policy responses to what might be common Eurozone conditions and worldwide political pressures (neoliberalism, modernisation and so on) are not significant. Rather, I want to caution against the methodological nationalism of naturalising the (British) state as a separate, coherent entity (Chernilo 2008). Childhoods and children within Britain are of course diverse, as are British children, by age, class, gender, culture, religion, (dis)ability, sexuality, region and much more. My purpose here is to point to contingent, even arbitrary, connections that come to make a big difference. In this case, they mediate a specific as well as general story of recent British-German history, including the Nazi genocide of Jews, as reminded by the recent death of one who while not a victim of the worst Nazi atrocities (since she escaped) lived to consider and rework its impacts, both individually and more generally.

This chapter is also about me, as well as about here and now. To make this point is merely to recognise the inevitably situated, relational orientation we have to children and childhoods. Notwithstanding the ways categories such as 'children' and 'childhood' *appear* to stand alone, and thereby facilitate many of the political problems surrounding the recourse to discourses of saving children including removing community affiliations and cultural-political conditions, and facilitating a spurious globalisation of childhood (Boyden 1997; Burman 1996; Penn 2011), they always operate within other networks of relationships: child-adult; childhood remembered, desired, regretted, aspired to – whether describing one's own or another's.

An Introduction to Marion Daltrop (1926–2014)[1]

Marion Daltrop was born in Bielefeld in 1926 and came to Britain on what was said to be the last Kindertransport out of Germany in 1939.[2] Between the invitation to contribute to this volume and its realisation, Marion died and various occasions of collective remembrance, reflection and storytelling took place (at her funeral and burial of her ashes some two weeks later on what would have been her 88th birthday). My account here is informed by five interviewees who counted themselves as Marion's friends and adoptive family, as well as written comments and emails with former colleagues.

Marion was a child in Britain, a refugee, a German Jewish refugee. In the UK she was fostered and attended various boarding schools where she learnt English and trained first as a nursery nurse and later as a psychiatric social worker.[3] In other words, from being a child (as we all have been), she became someone who worked with children in Glasgow,

Hull and Manchester. 'Lily'[4] recalls she did her social work training in Glasgow. She came to Manchester in the mid-1970s and joined the Manchester School Psychological and Child Guidance Service, working alongside educational psychologists, child psychiatrists, specialist tutors and social workers. She worked there until her retirement (aged 60) in the mid-1980s when she returned to Germany for eight or nine years, to Bielefeld, to care for her mother.[5] Marion then returned to Manchester where she lived until the final two years of her life, when she needed more intensive care and moved to a nursing home in London near where her two nephews – the sons of her brother, with whom she had come to Britain on the Kindertransport – lived. So Marion's was a life literally lived between Germany and Britain, attesting to their complex relations and the dangers of an abstracting focus on one of them, crossing between these countries physically and emotionally, in ways that are of course both profoundly personal and political.

Yet I write this more than to provide a technical account of how a displaced and probably traumatised (as we would now say) young person became a highly accomplished professional working with children and young people, indeed apparently succeeding in this where no others could.[6] I write also to document the work and life of an activist whose engagements and commitments not only transformed the lives of others, but also resist easy classification or demarcation – whether in terms of professional or other role or chronological notions of age. As well as being an inspiring and principled advocate for and support to children and families, Marion was an artist, a poet, a peace campaigner, was passionate about environmental conservation, as well as sustaining many families and supporting many, many children and parent–child relationships.

Saying this not only adds to the picture of Marion, but also makes a specific political and methodological point about how histories are told and who is authorised to tell them. Documenting Marion's many contributions and impacts on people's lives complements other more celebrated émigré and refugee psychologists, psychoanalysts and psychotherapists who have made great impacts on British children's lives, such as Anna Freud. This focus on Marion is also a way of challenging the ways histories conventionally belong to families alone and are often held by them. So while Marion's family members (that is, who survived the death camps)[7] cherish her memory, my account of her is gathered across broader sources of those whose lives were deeply affected by and facilitated by Marion's support, affective ties that lie outside heteronormative or patriarchal familial discourses of memory-making and narration, and so risk being erased or forgotten. While other research in this vein has emphasised the redefinition of the domestic space and of intimacy (Roseneil and Budgeon 2004), here I also highlight connections with political activism and professional engagements.

Marion and Me: Here and Now

I first met Marion in the context of feminist anti-nuclear activism in the mid-1980s. We were in the same local Greenham Women's Support Group.[8] Indeed, despite already being retired, quite deaf and bent over with severe osteoporosis, she stayed at Greenham many times, as well as participating in other peace camps at military installations including Capenhurst and (the US military intelligence base at) Menwith Hill (Campbell 1983).

Principally, though, I engaged with Marion through her photos. She was a fixture at every community fair, selling her cards and pictures – mounted and framed with homemade glue produced by grating and boiling up conkers. Marion was never without her camera.[9] Her pictures of nature estranged, doubled and crossed, anticipated much digital manipulation but were composed by photocopying and so mirror imaging her photos and using reverse negatives, cutting them up and sticking them together to reveal patterns and shapes – that some people find alarming – shapes that arguably were already there but needed her particular eye to become something else (Figure 10.1). Some of these pictures and shapes she named – indeed my partner used one of them that she called 'Case Conference' as the cover to his book *Critical Discursive Psychology* (Parker 2002).

Figure 10.1 One of Marion Daltrop's creative pieces. Source: Reproduced with permission from the Marion Daltrop estate.

I knew little about Marion except that she was a former colleague of my sister-in-law who is an educational psychologist. I knew her as also a peace and community campaigner, and I bought and sent many of her cards and pictures to friends and colleagues all over the world (the proceeds of which she donated to various campaigns, including as holiday money for poor families who had no spending money other than their DSS [social security] allowance). It was only after she had moved from Manchester that I discovered when and how she had come to Britain.

Histories

Now that the introductions are over, like all histories of the present, we start by going backwards. Childhood is told later. We begin at the end, with some disciplinary and methodological considerations.

Disciplines

This analysis draws on a range of disciplinary perspectives, from social theory to psychoanalysis. What this account is *not*, however, is a *psycho*biography. Rather, this is a reading of available accounts, which happen also to include some by Marion herself. I draw on these texts to assemble a story that is personal but also institutional and cultural-historical, indeed transnationally so. In this sense, this chapter could be situated not only within psychological or educational – or indeed childhood – studies, as within the relatively new discipline of psychosocial studies emerging within Britain. This discipline explicitly aims to connect and explicate subjectivities in relation to social conditions and interpersonal and institutional relations (Frosh 2003, 2010). It also includes consideration of the disciplines that Marion was associated with through her work as a psychiatric social worker, and I return later to discern specific theoretical/disciplinary influences in her own accounts. However, this is also a cultural geography and history of particular events, debates, commitments and activities in which she participated.

History, Memory and Secrets

Marion died before I was able to know much of what I now know about her. Death can bring idealisation and hagiography, but all stories are told for a purpose, and while history is usually written by its winners (Benjamin [1955] 1973), Marion's stories and the stories about Marion – while distinctively individual – also tell of networks, contexts and relationships. Significantly, far from producing neat narrative trajectories, the stories generate more questions, since they do not all align and indeed some open up whole new vistas. One of Marion's supervisees, who later also became an acquaintance, had no idea that she was a poet; her social sciences Open University tutor, who became one of her closest friends, did not know she had undertaken Open University courses (indeed 'Lily' had thought it was a whole degree) in poetry.[10] Although 'Lily' is fairly certain that Marion undertook her psychiatric social work training in Glasgow, even her former colleagues could not recall this.

There are many relationships, then, but many occlusions and partial and multiple truths. Memory is not only about who knows what and how (or what social psychologists term memorial 'rights' (Harré 1994)), but also how knowledge and awareness are mediated by everyday practices. This includes, as Marie Louise Seeberg, Irene Levin and Claudia Lenz (2013) discuss in their book, *The Holocaust as Active Memory*, normalised assumptions about what is talked about in the course of particular routines or practices and correlatively what is overlooked within social practices of memorialisation and forgetting. The methodological consequence of this, as Seeberg et al. (2013, 6) emphasise, is the need for empirical research "[...] which works not only by following the timeline of events but also through tracing the related processes in its contemporary environment".

Equally, the timeline and places where Marion lived remains unclear, with a patchwork of different cities and connections emerging from the accounts of the people I have talked with. As if personifying a Lacanian analysis of the metonymy of desire, even her name shifts from place to place, making searches more difficult, eluding the tracing of continuities. In Germany and to her family she was 'Marianne', in Britain 'Marian' and in Manchester she became 'Marion': a multiple subject, resisting legibility, but marking out her own shifting identities on the move.

Like many immigrants, she was indeed mobile: moving for work, to take up interesting posts or courses, perhaps, but even earlier to take up live-in positions as a nanny looking after professional people's children. (As Brigitte Decker points out, refugee children were considered temporary residents and were directed toward practical occupations to avoid competition with British nationals for jobs, so it was only later that Marion gained higher qualifications.) Here we have an insight into the links between the trajectory of a post-war refugee and the British upper-middle class. I was told that Marion had done childcare at the household of W.H. Auden, during which time Dylan Thomas and his wife came to stay when on hard times; yet another account (from a former colleague) suggested she had worked for A.J.P. Taylor, looking after his children. 'Sarah' was confident that she also looked after the children of Dr Charles Hill, the 'radio doctor' whose broadcasts from the 1940s and 1950s always ended with "make sure the bowels are well open". Marion lived in Hull, in Glasgow (where she might have worked in child guidance or even in the clinic set up by R.D. Laing, although by then he was no longer working there), as well as (perhaps) in London. She eventually considered Manchester her home, as indicated by her desire to have her funeral and remains scattered there. Immediately after the war, she worked in the British Army overseas in Germany in orphanages. This was also a way of being close to her parents, who had survived but were weak and frail. After retiring, she also spent some years going back to Bielefeld to care for her mother.

Professional Practices

Alongside her participation in major political events, Marion's working life spanned major transformations in British society. Her early employer, the BBC radio doctor,[11] was an active consultant to the discussions that gave rise to the National Health Service. In Hull, she worked in an inpatient child psychiatric unit at a hospital. At that time Psychiatric Social Work was the high status end of social work, even then requiring graduate status and specialist training (which would now be called Mental Health Social Work and would likely involve more knowledge of the law and a less therapeutic approach). When she came to Manchester in the mid-1970s, Marion joined a multidisciplinary child guidance service, administratively situated at the centre of the working-class African-Caribbean community and close to what was to become a key site of Britain's so-called 'race riots' of 1981. By the time she retired in the mid-1980s, perhaps 1986, to return to Bielefeld to care for her mother, fashions and funding had changed and multidisciplinary working was abandoned in favour of separate professional provision. Child psychiatric social workers were moved into Social Services, where it was assumed by the local authority that the needs of children and families previously referred to Child Guidance would be met.

I have been told many accounts of Marion's work and role in this multidisciplinary team, and its preconditions and possibilities in relation to current restrictions and remits merit reflection. The team was able to offer family therapy; it certainly considered itself to provide therapeutic interventions, rather than only assessments. Marion's approach, appearance and methods were certainly unorthodox, but her former colleagues emphasised repeatedly her 'gift' for working with the most difficult children. I was told these included children who would now be labelled ADHD, and were even then called schizophrenic and psychotic and were sometimes criminalised. Indeed, at a gathering for Marion in June 2014,[12] I heard about how she corresponded with one young man for a long time, even when in later years he was in prison. Along with her generosity and her unstinting care (which extended to working all hours if necessary) was a principled and unwavering commitment to supporting children and countering abuse. This was no sentimental approach to children; indeed, her former manager mentioned at her funeral how she was the first person in their service to work with anatomically correct dolls, which in fact she had crocheted to help children who had been sexually abused to be able to talk about their experiences.

Marion's Pedagogies of Childhood

Marion's distinctive personality and practices can be discerned as informed by specific pedagogical approaches, highlighting the theories of childhood, development, learning and change she subscribed to, as well as illustrating the broader point that individuals engage with, interact with, play their part in changing and are shaped by the structural conditions they inhabit. Seven aspects of her personal philosophy and pedagogy can be inferred.

First, people told me how she was prepared to "go the extra mile" ('Hilary'), to make learning and training enjoyable. 'Hilary' describes herself as scarcely more than a child at the time she was supervised by Marion on a one-month pre-professional training placement, which inspired her to go on to train as a psychiatric social worker. Marion took the time to organise particular training experiences for 'Hilary', once she was satisfied that 'Hilary' was capable of working on her own: "Her reaction to me built my self esteem & confidence – she trusted me to visit her ex-clients, and she appeared to like me & enjoy our conversations" ('Hilary', post-interview email). She worked in enabling rather than regulatory ways, specifically organising encounters for her that would be enjoyable as well as professionally educative.

Second, she treated everyone as capable of learning and engagement, mobilising not only a strategy of enlistment, but also of personal engagement. Jane Graham (in her funeral address) recalled how on one occasion when they were driving together down to the women's peace camp at Greenham Common, the minibus broke down. When the police came to the roadside, Marion managed to get them not only to transport them all to the camp but also to bring all the firewood they had in the back of their van. Jane said how surprised Greenham women were to see them arriving in a police van and a police officer helping to unload the logs.

Third, a recurring theme in people's accounts of Marion was her capacity to wait, rather than impose. One of Marion's nephews (who now works as a child psychotherapist) spoke at her funeral of how she first engaged with his (then) infant daughter by waiting for the infant to engage with her. Marion's capacity to wait and listen included her tolerance for hearing about abuse, a matter that is now often silenced through fear and discomfort on the part of professionals (Warner 2000). This child-centred approach was not casual or indulgent. She was quite able to challenge and maintain clear boundaries in working with young people. For example, after retirement when Marion became involved in supporting several mothers having to cope on their own, 'Lily' recalls:

> One time when Marion was looking after x [her daughter] [when 'Lily' was away], x refused to go to school saying 'I'm not going to school to learn crap'. But Marion said, 'You don't go to school to learn crap, you go to school to learn to put up with crap'. X didn't have an answer to that, so she went.
>
> ('Lily', interview)

This is indeed an interesting theory of what schooling is for, which can be read alongside Marion's accounts of her own schooling (discussed later). Far from only 'empowering the child', Marion's support helped restore clear structures of generational authority and responsibility within the household, working to relieve the troubled young person of her sense of over-responsibility and to enable a stressed mother to have the confidence and skills to assert her role: "The main thing she did first was to help me get back in the position of being the adult in the relationship" ('Lily', interview).

So although both friends and colleagues talked of Marion's unorthodox practices ('Adam' said, "she broke every rule in the book"), this is far from implying she was unprincipled and unethical in her practice. Even when retired, when she decided to support a mother in her relationships with her children (one of whom was particularly difficult) at a time of significant physical illness in this woman's life, Marion was very clear about how she could not offer professional support and was not in supervision. 'Lily' appreciated not only Marion's engagement at a time of such great difficulty, but also her capacity to reflect with her afterwards. From this, a major, mutual mother–daughter relationship began that continued for the rest of Marion's life.

Fourth, as well as the ways she worked with children, one gets an impression of someone who was quite prepared to be unusual or to stand out to maintain her principled stance to do her job. A former Manchester colleague recalled Marion's appearing to accompany a group of young people on a seaside trip wearing a large red man's shirt. When asked why she was wearing this, she said: "To be seen from the sea, of course!" As her colleague said in wonder: "She had thought it all through" ('Sophie'). She also equipped these children with whistles in case they got into difficulties and carried a large stock of food.

Fifth is the question of reflexivity, of positioning. Marion was well aware of her own difference, even if the accent remained a stubborn marker that frustrated her. Unlike so many psychological professionals today, she understood her difference as helping her work. 'Hilary' (post-interview email):

> I remember discussing her unique take on life and she replied 'Well miss x [surname] if you are a tree where do you hide?', ME: 'In a forest i suppose' and her response was 'well I am here in a mental hospital!'.

Indeed, not only was she aware of her distinctiveness, it was also a tool in her repertoire. To draw on 'Hilary's' account again:

> It was almost as if she had a special gift. When I knew her she dressed oddly. She used to turn up for work wearing, they looked like children's sandals, and she never did anything in the way of hair or makeup. So there was almost an innocence about her.
>
> (interview)

Her being prepared to stand out and not conform was also a source of inspiration to others: "My meeting Marion in Hull was my first introduction to a professional woman in a work context. She showed me that not being totally conventional should not be a hindrance to my career" ('Hilary', post interview email).[13]

Sixth, one very clear and longstanding influence in her life was the philosophy of Lao Tzu. Hence, Rose Snow arranged for an extract from this to be read at her funeral as it was said she had encountered his ideas early on and that they continued to inspire her. This celebrates the three "'possessions' of 'being a simpleton': 'To care/To be fair/To be humble'" (Stanza 67). Marion's humility, as well as care, was commented upon by those who knew her:

> She facilitated a healing in me that was remarkable. I knew it at the time, but at this point now looking back I realise how remarkable it was. And she was so humble ... her facilitation, her acceptance and her love.
>
> ('Lily', interview)

Even her giving was pedagogical. As 'Hilary' recalls:

> One very Marion-ish conversation I remember. It was a hot summer day, at lunchtime, she bought me an ice cream. I offered to pay and she said – In her wonderful Dr Freud accent – 'Right Miss [name]' – as we were Miss [name] and Miss Daltrop in those days – 'You do not pay for your ice cream, but when you are qualified and have your own students, you will buy them an ice cream, so things get passed on.'

Finally, there is the question of conviction. When I asked former colleagues for examples or descriptions of Marion's practice, these were characterised by a sense of her utter conviction (as well as eccentricity).[14] Yet this sense of certainty is belied by some of her own writing. Her poem "Anniversary", which reviews periods of her life from childhood onwards, focuses on the anniversary of leaving Bielefeld on the Kindertransport (on 2 February 1939) (which Jane Graham read at the funeral). Far from being triumphal or celebratory of success or survival (the first line begins: "February 2nd seems to be a date for celebration"), the theme of this poem is failure – the failure as a child to be able to protect or even make a hot drink for her mother while they waited in fear lest their house was attacked, the failure to pass as British because of her accent, the failure to succeed at loving without hope of reciprocity.[15] This powerful poem ends by highlighting the capacity to try again in the context of failure as one key quality learnt in childhood:

> Now, self-image tarnished, faded & impaired,
> Not quite belonging, failing in the final test,
> Craven, - yet still capable of one success.
> A skill that in my childhood I acquired:
>
> To absorb my failure after each event,
> To shrug my shoulders, the day's routine survive;
> To clear my memory of all embarrassment
> And with glorious day dreams fill my life.
>
> Until the next time I am tried?
> (Marion Daltrop, "Anniversary", final section, punctuation and layout as in the original)

Beyond this, thinking institutionally rather than only personally, the examples above include many that would now not be possible within social work practice, not only in terms of giving gifts, visits, keeping in contact with former clients or not keeping to conventional time boundaries and session limits but rather of the limits imposed by professional practices of child protection. There is food for thought here on how current child protection practice in Britain neglects and sometimes (arguably, often, as recent revelations suggest) abuses children further (Piper and Stronach 2008; and Parton in this volume). Marion would not let codes of professional practice limit her commitment and involvement. She had obvious contempt for bureaucracy and power-mongering as one of her poems, "The Director Designate's Song", reproduced in a booklet of her funeral, indicates.[16] Her colleagues told many stories of how she appeared to sleep through staff meetings only to awake at the end when she would deliver a piercing and withering verdict on all that had been discussed.[17] As one close friend said: "The first thing she said to me in a meeting with her was 'You have a touching faith in professionals'" ('Lily', interview).

Alternatives

As already indicated, this story is not only personal but also institutional and geopolitical. Marion was clearly politically engaged before she came to Manchester, aged over 50, since 'Hilary' who had met her in Hull reported that it was the first time she'd met a mature person who shared her "[...] interests in politics, poverty and world peace, someone who was on the left" (interview). Nevertheless, Marion came to live in Manchester in the 1970s and made it her home. As well as arguably being the birthplace of capitalism (as the cradle for the infrastructure of the Industrial Revolution and its factories), Manchester also has a long radical history, from the Chartists to the Suffragettes and beyond, which Marion joined. 'Sarah' said: "She made herself and her philosophy of life fit every situation. She was involved in everything". Historically and geographically specific practices, networks and relationships are woven into her life and work. 'Sarah' again: "She lived in the moment - her fundamental philosophy was showing love and concern".

To take a single but telling example, she met one of her closest friends in later life at a Local Exchange Trading Scheme (LETS) event, where they first talked to arrange a barter: the exchange was vegetables for child guidance. While alternative currency and exchange systems were being generated across the UK and elsewhere in this period, Manchester was the largest LETS (with its made-up currency, bobbins, reflecting its industrial heritage) and one of the longest standing. In his doctoral research, Peter North (2007) focused on Manchester LETS to differentiate specific alignments and tensions within the diverse anti-capitalist, green, alternative, pro-poor and even protocapitalist models animating involvement in the scheme. He designated these tendencies as 'the resisters', 'the alternatives' and 'utopians'. My guess is that Marion – who is acknowledged in the Preface to his book – counted among the 'alternatives', although probably her approach would defy categorisation. She was a lifelong member of the Green Party and, as already mentioned, involved in the women's anti-nuclear and peace camp movements.[18] Her commitment was not confined to local or national concerns (of getting US cruise missiles out of British military bases, for example). She was involved in the various Pacific Rim/nuclear testing women's mobilisations taking place in that period. 'Adam' also noted that she generously supported the Vegan Organic Network (a charity that promotes farming without killing farm animals) from its inauguration in 1996. Some of her photos appear in the Network's magazine. A card was also designed with a series of her photos commemorating her Kindertransport journey and her work for peace.[19]

She is also described as having been a strong trade unionist, as documented by her photos of Greenham women supporting the miners' strike of the 1980s, which was a key political milestone in the struggle against Thatcherism and against the erosion of workers' rights and rights to work (Figure 10.2).

She was a passionate conservationist and recycler, and she found beauty and inspiration in nature. According to 'Sarah', some of her

Figure 10.2 One of Marion's Daltrop's photographs of the activities of the Greenham Women's Support Group. Source: Reproduced with permission from the Marion Daltrop estate.

favourite Greenham pictures showed nature reclaiming or changing the ugly (hu)man-made barriers and fences (Figure 10.3).

Her colleagues and comrades wryly noted that she was arrested twice – once in Germany for abandoning a military vehicle in a ditch (the implication here was that this occurred through bad driving – Marion was said to 'reverse by ear', while apparently leaving a vehicle is an arrestable offence); the second time she was arrested was at Greenham, and it was said that she 'made a marvellous speech to the judge' ('Sarah', interview).

When I tried to solicit descriptions of Marion's political affiliations, no clear or uniform response would emerge – sometimes socialist, sometimes women-centred, sometimes peace-oriented and green. Interestingly, Marion was not a Zionist, even though she did consider going to work on a kibbutz as a way of working with children, but (as indicated in Decker's interview) she was put off by the nationalism she encountered in some preparatory sessions and only then did she apply for British citizenship. As 'Lily' put it:

> She didn't have much time for political systems, but would express enormous alarm at central government's assault on local government and undermining of local systems, saying what happened in Germany couldn't happen here because of the safeguard of local government which still had some authority; but she talked about how worrying it was politically, saying if only they had the insight of people with her experience, they wouldn't do it [dismantle local systems of governance].

Figure 10.3 Two examples of Marion Daltrop's Greenham pictures. Source: Reproduced with permission from the Marion Daltrop estate.

Childhood

So now, we arrive at the beginning: Marion's childhood, seen backwards through her life. There are, of course, traces in her own accounts of the sense she made of her childhood experiences and their impacts on her. This is even though, or perhaps precisely because of, her own silence: she apparently could not bear to be around any discussion of concentration camps and said little about her own experiences of Nazi persecution to friends and colleagues.[20] I was told that only very late in their lives did she and her brother talk together about this.

While it seems Marion identified in many ways with the oppressed and marginalised, including those who were victims of Nazi genocide, and indeed she did participate in some Jewish and refugee – and even specifically Kindertransport – networks and memorialisation processes (including being interviewed for the British Library on this topic), these were not the obvious or only lines of political-cultural identification with which she aligned herself. She was not particularist in her politics of solidarity and engagement. 'Lily' and 'Naomi' told me that she engaged in some aspects of Jewish practice (such as fasting on Yom Kippur), and I encountered her in Jewish feminist and left local mobilisation around supporting Palestinian rights, but she did not particularly or primarily organise around a Jewish identity. Her politics seemed to be more generally oriented towards anti-militarist and environmentalist concerns – and this is where we can perhaps see a transcultural, even transgenerational, semiotic link via the barbed wire; the gifts of barbed wire brooches that she (and others) made from fencing cut from the Greenham military base (some were apparently turned into toast racks). Certainly, her photos, especially those taken in black and white, are chillingly reminiscent of World War 2 scenes.

In terms of her work with children, and perhaps related to her pedagogies of childhood discussed above, various models of childhood affects and effects can be discerned. For example, in one version of her poem, "Some Reasons Why I Cannot Settle to My Essay" (there are several copies in the file of her writings[21]), she not only used neurophysiological terminology but also annotated this by hand with a more everyday rendering of these neurological functions (as in "My motivation and drive evaporated before it reached the right brain centre", "I am feeling dizzy", "I am hungry", "My memory is going", "I am falling asleep"). The effect of this is not only to offer a 'translation' of the mechanical abstracted descriptions (of brain chemistry) but also thereby to parody the pseudoscientific claims that reduce complex sensations, responses and relations to neurological structures and functions.

What is clear is that Marion had rich funds of technical, specialist, psychological, psychoanalytic and psychiatric knowledge to draw upon. Her colleagues commented that she was Freudian, while 'Adam' noted her incisive dismissal of some specific psychoanalytic currents. She was a theorist of childhood and saw herself as a subject of some of those theories. So, the hints of theoretical commitments she offers in the narration of her own story offer relevant resources reflecting her preferred perspectives as well as available models. A key account is Marion's interview with Decker. Here she describes the fear and anxiety of the time before she left Bielefeld and the distress of being parted from her parents, where she attributes catching a cold on the train journey from Bielefeld to Löhne (first stage of the Kindertransport) to "[...] all the swallowed tears" (120).[22]

She mobilises an account of how children may feel things they do not express, in relation to her unacknowledged affection for her (non-Jewish) foster mother in Britain, Aunt Mabel: "I couldn't show it, I was never able to tell her how fond of her I was" (121). There is an implicit claim here that the lack of showing feelings does not mean they are not present. She indicates the bewilderment of many moves and transitions, including across seven schools; the loneliness of not having friends and the pain of not being believed when she talked. Overwhelmingly, there is a depiction of blocking feelings, including not allowing herself to feel homesick, but especially in the representation of what she called her 'dinosaur defence', or denial/delayed response. So upon receiving a letter from her parents informing her that they were going to be deported ("This is our last letter. We are going to see Gran", 124), she knew what this meant[23] and "didn't know how to deal with it. And so I folded and folded the letter until it was tiny, pushed it into a drawer and pretended I had never received it. I couldn't do anything else" (ibid.). She describes how it was only when she received the letter from the Red Cross informing her that her parents were alive that she talked to other girls at school:

> I had previously never talked about Germany or my parents. And on this evening, as I was thinking that I could possibly find my parents, I started to talk about it to all the other girls. They all climbed up on my bed. And on this evening I was talking like never before – about Bielefeld and about my parents.
>
> (ibid.)

The experience of not allowing herself to feel, or to delay feeling, stayed with her: "I used to apply the 'dinosaur defence' my entire life. The dinosaur only felt the pain two years after putting the tail into the fire" (125).

Marion's account of her childhood escape via the Kindertransport and subsequent early days in Britain overwhelmingly draws on ideas of the importance of continuity of relationships (or what would now be discoursed in terms of attachment theory), the significance and distress of separations and also some indications of how other interventions and relationships can mitigate and support even very severe experiences of anxiety, trauma and disruption.[24] There is also a clear commitment to a representation of the psyche as protecting itself by delaying or denying distress (as in 'the dinosaur defence'). I think it is not over-reaching to see these as interpretative resources she mobilised for her work with children and supporting families.

But just as Seeberg et al. (2013) call for specific empirical research on memory, so we can document how there are always individual responses to shared historical events; it is relevant to finish with one example for which there are accounts of contrasting affects and effects. Before leaving Bielefeld and in the build-up of Nazi persecution, Marion, like the other Jewish children, was excluded from school.[25] My interviewees suggested that John, Marion's brother who later became an international lawyer, "always felt so terribly insulted by having been expelled from school [as a Jew] in Bielefeld", portraying this as fuelling his drive to be "a high achiever and very successful". This response can be contrasted with Marion's account, which emphasises the generosity and perspicacity of the Cantor's wife, Frau Friedemann, in helping to structure this time of great anxiety and uncertainty by convening a makeshift school in her bedroom "[...] which allowed us to be together during those unstructured weeks. I've always been grateful to her for that" (Decker n.d., 119). An account of the same experience of school exclusion was mobilised by Hajo Meyer (one of the last survivors of Auschwitz, who was 2 years older than Marion and died just a week after Marion on 22 August 2014) in asserting solidarity with Palestinian youth in Gaza denied education through Israeli occupation and bombardment.

Marion came to Britain as a child, worked with children and contributed to others' childhoods and adult lives through her work and involvement. Her story highlights the forms and diversities of children and childhoods and shows how migration – even under the most distressing of circumstances – can be used to forge connections across cultures and generations. Recent literature on 'transcultural memory' has called for "an attentiveness to the border-transcending dimensions of remembering and forgetting" (Erll 2011, 18). While this concept has been applied by Michael Rothberg and Yasemin Yildiz (2011) to discuss the ways migrants to Germany engage with the history of the holocaust as an application of Engin F. Isin's (2008) notion of 'acts of citizenship', whereby memory becomes a performance of belonging, as I have tried to show here via discussion of Marion's transnational and intra-national migrations and settlements in Britain, such conclusions may apply more generally.

Indeed, this has implications for how we think about and work with children. Now Marion's ashes lie buried under an unmarked tree in a Manchester meadow. Hers was a situated life that traversed political catastrophe and was nevertheless creative and filled with relationships, a life that, like all lives, bears witness to geography and history, transnational disruption and connection, as well as unique individual responses to these. In Marion's case, as well as the resonances of her trajectory between Bielefeld and Manchester for us now, her particular contributions and participations call for remembrance and appreciation. Her story also provides tangible evidence of the need to resist the ways dominant notions of childhood appear to transcend specific material conditions, even as Marion, as child and adult – and adult looking back at her childhood – did precisely this in refusing some determinations and, in her migrations and recycling of memories as well as materials, creating possibilities for others.

Notes

1 I am grateful to the friends and former colleagues of Marion Daltrop who gave so generously of their time, records and recollections. This chapter can only offer a partial view on and small part of all that I was told. I am especially appreciative of the close attention and positive engagement given to reading earlier drafts of this chapter, offering important factual corrections and helping nuance this account. Yet I should note that not all the people I approached responded to my invitation to be interviewed.

Moreover, although I embarked on this project before she died, Marion's ill health would nevertheless have rendered her unable to participate directly or indeed to give her consent. Further, between first writing this chapter and its publication, interviews with Marion conducted as part of the British Library holocaust survivor archive have become public: http://sounds.bl.uk/Oral-history/Jewish-Holocaust-survivors/021M-C0410X0182XX-0001V0. Since Marion herself placed an embargo on these for six years (which expired in 2006), I have not drawn on them – as my primary concerns lie with the meanings and accounts of others about Marion, rather than delving into material that she considered sensitive during her lifetime.

2 The Kindertransport was organised by the British businessman Nicholas Winter to bring "predominantly Jewish children" (Greschler 2009, xi) out of Nazi-controlled Germany, Austria, Czechoslovakia and Poland between December 1938 (after Kristallnacht) and September 1939. See, for example, Byers 2012; Greschler 2009; Milton 2005 and the highly successful play by Samuels (1998).

3 From "Marion Daltrop's story as told to Brigitte Decker", translated by Peter Schmitt, extracted from Decker (n.d.), copy produced by Jane and David Graham.

4 Names of interviewees are in inverted commas to indicate that some are pseudonyms.

5 Her mother, Lotte Daltrop, survived the war by being put to work in Theresienstadt; she and her husband returned to Bielefeld after the war. Lotte lived until the age of 101.

6 This claim is reiterated by all Marion's former colleagues as well as friends.

7 Of Marion Daltrop's immediate family, 32 died in death camps. Alongside Decker's (n.d.) interview with Marion (see note 3 above) there is a reproduced letter from her father, Albert Daltrop, writing to Marion after being liberated from Theresienstadt in 1945, identifying what had happened to 12 of their close relatives, including Marion's grandmother.

8 On 5 September 1981, the Welsh group Women for Life on Earth arrived on Greenham Common, Berkshire, England. They marched from Cardiff with the intention of challenging, by debate, the decision to site 96 Cruise nuclear missiles there. This started a peace camp outside the RAF base, which lasted 19 years, until 2000. Local women's groups across the UK organised to financially, culturally and physically support the camp. See: www.greenhamwpc.org.uk/.

9 'Sarah' (email, commenting on an earlier draft) commented that her brother in later years told her that she should have been a photographer. Marion used her mother's camera, an Exakta Varex, until she won a Canon with her photo of Greenham women and the police she entitled "You Put Your Left Foot in", see www.fredsakademiet.dk/abase/sange/greenham/song64.htm.

10 In fact, my inquiries to the Open University have indicated that Marion graduated with a BA in 1977 based on courses she studied between 1973 and 1977 that included Biological Bases of Behaviour, Understanding Society, Decision Making in Britain, Social Psychology and – finally – Twentieth Century Poetry.

11 See www.bbc.co.uk/archive/people/53/84.shtml.

12 This was a fundraising event organised by Jane and David Graham to support travel funds for Manchester friends to visit Marion at the care home in the south of England.

13 Said even more directly in the interview: "For me, she was the first person I'd met, suddenly there was a role model - a professional successful woman who had chosen not to marry. [...] and I saw and I saw Marion's way as another option" ('Hilary', interview).

14 "Marion was steadfast in how she preferred to work (no surprises about how steely she could be). She simply made herself available to children and families [...] wherever and whenever, despite organisational pressures to ration her contact time" (Fred Wolstenholme, "Farewell to Marion", funeral address).
15 It should be noted that, according to 'Lily' (post-interview comments on earlier draft), Marion wrote this poem at a time of significant personal turmoil and depression and should not necessarily be interpreted as implying that she always felt this way. Nevertheless, it does offer an alternative perspective on the outwardly maintained conviction.
16 This includes such choice lines as: "Such tight rein on the purse strings I kept/That now I'm Social Work Director Elect" and ending with "I avoid problems that could cause repercussion/And fanciful training or confusing discussion./With such care social work training did I shirk/That now I'm the Director of Social Work" ("The Director Designate's Song by Marion Daltrop (with apologies to W.S. Gilbert)"), extracted from the full text included in the funeral service (on page 11).
17 Fred Wolstenholme, "Farewell to Marion" (delivered at Marion's funeral on 31 July 2014).
18 See www.fredsakademiet.dk/abase/sange/greenham/song64.htm.
19 From post-interview email, commenting on earlier draft.
20 The colleagues included others who had come on the Kindertransport but who say they did not talk much about these experiences.
21 Apparently, Marion did not possess a typewriter so the question of who typed her writing remains open.
22 Page numbers refer to those on the bilingual, dual-language (German and English) version of the text, which is organised to reflect and correspond to the original German version, see note 3 above.
23 "When we were still in Bielefeld there was already talk about concentration camps. This is why we knew what the letter meant. It was clear even before the 9th November [1938] that one wasn't allowed to say anything wrong or else the whole family would end up in a camp" (Decker, 124).
24 She would have trained and practiced at a time when John Bowlby's attachment theory was very much to the fore.
25 Interestingly, this also features in many other Kindertransport stories as a significant turning point. See e.g. Byers (2012).

References

Benjamin, Walter. (1955) 1973. "Theses on the Philosophy of History." In *Illuminations*, translated by Harry Zohn, 253–64. London: Fontana.
Boyden, Jo. 1997. "Childhood and the Policy Makers: A Comparative Perspective on the Globalization of Childhood." In *Constructing and Reconstructing Childhood: Contemporary Issues in the Sociological Study of Childhood*, 2nd ed., edited by Allison James and Alan Prout, 190–229. London: RoutledgeFalmer.
Burman, Erica. 1996. "Local, Global or Globalized? Child Development and International Child Rights Legislation." *Childhood* 3 (1): 45–66.
Byers, Ann. 2012. *Saving Children from the Holocaust: The Kindertransport*. Brainerd, MN: Bang Printing.
Campbell, Duncan. 1983. *War Plan UK: The Secret Truth about Britain's 'Civil Defence'*. London: Paladin.

Chernilo, Daniel. 2008. *A Social Theory of the Nation-State: The Political Forms of Modernity beyond Methodological Nationalism*. London: Routledge.
Decker, Brigitte, ed. n.d. *Heimweh nach Bielefeld. Vertrieben oder deportiert: Kinder aus jüdischen Familien erinnern sich*. Bielefelder Beiträge zur Stadt- und Regionalgeschichte 22. *[Homesick for Bielefeld: Expelled and Deported: Children from Jewish Families Remember]*. Bielefeld Articles Relating to the History of City and Region 22. Bielefeld: Gieselmann.
Erll, Astrid. 2011. "Travelling Memory." *Parallax* 17 (4): 4–18.
Frosh, Stephen. 2003. "Psychosocial Studies and Psychology: Is a Critical Approach Emerging?" *Human Relations* 56 (12): 1545–67.
———. 2010. *Psychoanalysis Outside the Clinic: Interventions in Psychosocial Studies*. London: Palgrave.
Greschler, Lori. 2009. *The 10,000 Children that Hitler Missed: Stories from the Kindertransport*. Charleston, SC: BookSurge. (Copyright held by author).
Harré, Rom. 1994. "Emotion and Memory: The Second Cognitive Revolution." *Royal Institute of Philosophy Supplement* 37: 25–40.
Isin, Engin F. 2008. "Theorizing Acts of Citizenship." In *Acts of Citizenship*, edited by Engin F. Isin and Greg M. Nielsen, 15–43. London: Zed Books.
Lao Tzu. 1944. *The Way of Life According to Lao Tzu*, translated by Witter Bynner. New York: Perigee Books.
Milton, Edith. 2005. *The Tiger in the Attic: Memories of the Kindertransport and Growing Up British*. Chicago and London: University of Chicago Press.
North, Peter. 2007. *Money and Liberation: The Micropolitics of Alternative Currency Movements*. Minneapolis: University of Minnesotta Press.
Parker, Ian. 2002. *Critical Discursive Psychology*. London: Palgrave.
Penn, Helen. 2011. "Travelling Policies and Global Buzzwords: How International Non-Governmental Organizations and Charities Spread the Word about Early Childhood in the Global South." *Childhood* 18 (1), 94–113.
Piper, Heather, and Ian Stronach. 2008. *Don't Touch: The Educational Story of a Panic*. London: Routledge.
Roseneil, Sasha, and Shelley Budgeon. 2004. "Cultures of Intimacy and Care beyond 'The Family': Personal Life and Social Change in the Early 21st Century." *Current Sociology* 52 (2): 135–59.
Rothberg, Michael, and Yasemin Yildiz. 2011. "Memory Citizenship: Migrant Archives of Holocaust Remembrance in Contemporary Germany." *Parallax* 17 (4): 32–48.
Samuels, Diane. 1998. *Kindertransport*. London: Nick Hern Books.
Seeberg, Marie Louise, Irene Levin, and Claudia Lenz, eds. 2013. *The Holocaust as Active Memory: The Past in the Present*. London: Ashgate.
Warner, Sam. 2000. *Understanding Child Sexual Abuse: Making the Tactics Visible*. Gloucester: Handsell.

Section IV
Contemporary British Childhoods between Rights and Regulations

11 The Politics of Child Protection in Contemporary England
Towards the 'Authoritarian Neoliberal State'

Nigel Parton

The purpose of this chapter is to provide a chronological and critical analysis of the changes in child protection policy and practice in contemporary England. In many respects, the growth of concerns about abuse of children has been one of the major developments in relation to childhood in most 'Western' societies over the last 50 years. However, societies conceptualise and respond to this growing challenge in numerous ways so that child protection policies and practices vary and change over time (e.g. Gilbert, Parton and Skivenes 2011). The contemporary problem of child abuse was discovered in England in the late 1960s following developments in the US a few years earlier (Parton 1985). Initially, the policy and practice focus was upon preventing the physical abuse of children by their parents in the family. However, I will argue that from the mid-1990s onwards, the state developed a much broader focus of concern about what caused harm to children and what the role of professionals and official agencies should be in relation to this. The object of official concern was increasingly upon "safeguarding and promoting the welfare of the child". Underlying such developments were new and sometimes competing ideas about risk to children and the best ways of addressing these.

However, the period from late 2008, following the huge social reaction to the tragic death of Baby Peter Connelly, saw policy and practice move in new directions. Such developments were given a major impetus following the election of the Conservative/Liberal Democrat Coalition government in May 2010 so that we can see the emergence of what I call an authoritarian neoliberal approach to child protection and child welfare more generally. This has been reinforced further following the election of the Conservative government in May 2015. There are a number of elements to such an approach: first, in a context of a politics of 'austerity' there are considerable reductions in the range and level of universal welfare benefits and services available to families and children, particularly for those who are the worst off; second, there is an emphasis on all parents taking a greater responsibility for the overall well-being and development of their children but under the close monitoring and surveillance of a wide range of health, welfare and education professionals; third, wherever possible services previously delivered directly by the state are 'privatised' and delivered by a wide variety of voluntary, commercial and third-sector agencies; and fourth, whenever the state does intervene directly this is increasingly with the full weight of the law behind it with the net result that the number of children and families placed on various statutory orders increases. An interesting example of a policy development that draws on a number of these elements is the growing political prominence given to increasing the number of 'in care' children who are being placed for adoption. Such a policy has the effect of both removing 'parental responsibility' from parents who are not deemed adequate for the task and transferring, and thereby (re)privatising, the care and responsibility (including financial responsibility) for the children with a new set of statutorily 'approved' parents.

New Labour and the Move to 'Safeguarding'

Following the public inquiry into the death of Maria Colwell and a series of other high-profile child abuse scandals in the 1970s and 1980s (Parton 1991), the long-established state child welfare services in England came under increasing pressure and came to be dominated by a narrow, forensically orientated focus on child protection. Similar developments were evident in the other nations in the UK. By the early 1990s, the child protection and child welfare systems could be characterised in terms of attempting to identify children who were deemed 'high risk' so that they could be protected from abuse while ensuring that family privacy was not undermined, and thereby scarce resources could be directed to where, in theory, they were most needed (Parton 1991; Parton, Thorpe and Wattam 1997). High risk was conceptualised in terms of 'dangerousness', for the small minority of 'dangerous families' (Parton and Parton 1989) subject to extreme family dysfunctions and violent personalities were seen as the primary cause of child abuse; they therefore needed to be identified so that children could be protected.

However, during the mid-1990s a major debate opened up about the future direction of child protection policy and practice. It was argued that there needed to be a 'refocusing' of the work (Parton 1997). Rather than focus narrowly upon whether "the child concerned is suffering or likely to suffer significant harm" (Children Act 1989 s.31(2)(a)), the work should prioritise the much broader general duty placed on local authorities by Section 17(1) of the Children Act 1989 "to safeguard and promote the welfare of children in their area who are in need". These developments were taken further when the New Labour government launched its *Every Child Matters: Change for Children* (ECM) programme (DfES 2004), where the over-riding vision was to bring about "a shift to prevention whilst strengthening protection" (DfES 2004, 3) and was launched as the government's response to the high-profile child abuse public inquiry into the death of Victoria Climbié (Laming 2003).

However, the aims were much broader than overcoming the problems related to cases of child abuse. The priority was to intervene at a much earlier stage in children's lives in order to prevent a range of problems in childhood and beyond, including poor educational attainment, unemployment, crime and anti-social behaviour. The ambition was to improve the outcomes for all children and to narrow the gap in outcomes between those who did well and those who did not. The outcomes were defined in terms of:

- being healthy
- staying safe
- enjoying and achieving
- making a positive contribution
- achieving economic well-being

Together these were seen as key to improving "well-being in childhood and later life" (Chief Secretary to the Treasury 2003, 14). It was a very ambitious programme and was to include *all children*, as it was felt that any child, at some point in life, could be vulnerable to some form of risk and therefore might require help. The idea was to identify problems before they became chronic. The role of prevention was not only to combat the negatives but also to enhance the positive opportunities for child development via maximising protective factors and processes particularly in the 'early years'. The notion of protection was thus much wider than simply protection from harm or abuse. In trying to maximise childhood 'strengths' and 'resilience', the idea of risk was itself reframed in far more positive ways (Axford and Little 2006). The focus of concern broadened from those children who might suffer 'significant harm' to include all children, particularly those who were at risk of poor outcomes and therefore who may not fulfil their potential. In the process, the systems designed to screen and identify those in need of attention grew in size and complexity, and the challenges and responsibilities placed upon a wider range of agencies and practitioners increased considerably. As a result, it seemed that important changes were taking place in the relationships of children, families and the state, which I characterised at the time as the emergence of the 'preventive-surveillance state' (Parton 2008).

Baby Peter Connelly and the Rediscovery of Child Protection

Because the *Every Child Matters* reforms had been introduced in response to the scandal arising from the death of Victoria Climbié, the government was always likely to come under political attack if and when a similar scandal arose in the future, which would appear to demonstrate that the reforms had failed; this is precisely what happened. On 11 November 2008, two men were convicted of causing or allowing the death of 17-month-old baby Peter Connelly, one of whom was his stepfather. The baby's mother had already pleaded guilty to the charge. During the trial, the court heard that Baby P, as he was referred to at the time, was used as a 'punch bag' and that his mother had deceived and manipulated professionals. There had been over 60 contacts with the family from a variety of health and social care professionals, and he was pronounced dead just 48 hours after a hospital doctor failed to identify that he had a broken spine. He was the subject of a child protection plan with Haringey local authority in London – the local authority that had been at the centre of failures to protect Victoria Climbié back in 2000.

The media response was very critical of the services, particularly the local authority and its Director of Children's Services (Jones 2014; Shoesmith 2016; Warner 2014). The largest selling daily tabloid newspaper, *The Sun*, ran a campaign aimed at getting the professionals involved in the case sacked under the banner of "Beautiful Baby P: Campaign for Justice" (*The Sun*, 15 November 2008). Two weeks later, the newspaper delivered a petition to the Prime Minister, Gordon Brown, containing 1.5 million signatures and claiming it was the largest and most successful campaign of its sort ever. In addition, a large number of *Facebook* groups, comprising over 1.6 million members, were set up in memory of Baby Peter and seeking justice for his killers. This put major pressure on then government Minister, Ed Balls, to be seen to be acting authoritatively in order to take control of the situation. He responded by ordering a number of official investigations including one from the Office for Standards in Education, Children's Services and Skills (Ofsted), the Healthcare Commission and the Police Inspectorate who were to carry out an urgent Joint Area Review (JAR) of safeguarding in Haringey.

On receipt of the JAR on 1 December 2008, which he described as 'devastating', the Minister announced he was using his powers under the Education Act 1996 to direct Haringey to remove the Director of Children's Services, Sharon Shoesmith. Later that month she was sacked by the council without compensation and with immediate effect, and in April 2009 Haringey Council dismissed four other employees connected to the Baby Peter case. In addition, the paediatrician who examined Baby Peter two days before his death but missed the most serious injuries was suspended from the medical register; the family doctor who saw Baby Peter at least 15 times and was the first to raise the alarm about the baby's abuse was also suspended from the medical register.

This was the first time in England that such senior managers had been dismissed because of apparent child protection failures. The death of Baby Peter and the rancorous political and media reaction clearly engendered a sense of very high anxiety amongst government officials, children's service managers and practitioners. Very quickly, reports surfaced that it was becoming very difficult to recruit and retain staff to work in children's social care, particularly social workers, and that morale was at an all-time low (LGA 2009). The case was clearly having wide-scale reverberations. A number of influential commentators, including the House of Commons' Children, Schools and Families Committee (House of Commons 2009) began to argue that the threshold for admitting children into state care was too high. Not only should Baby Peter have been admitted to care some months before his death, but also his situation was not seen as unusual. Similarly, the Children and Family Court Advisory and Support Service (CAFCASS 2009) produced figures which demonstrated that there were nearly 50 per cent more care applications to court in the second half of 2008–2009 compared with the first half of the year; demand for care cases was 39 per cent higher in March 2009 compared with March 2008; and the demand for care continued to remain at an unprecedentedly high level for the first two quarters of 2009–2010 with June 2009 having the highest demand for care ever recorded for a single month. Developments in the wake of the death of Baby Peter had the effect of reinforcing the importance of child protection at the centre of safeguarding policy and practice.

The period after November 2008 was notable for its large increase in referrals to children's social care and growth in the number of children subject to a child protection plan, increase in the numbers of children taken into care and growth in Section 47 Enquiries (Association of Directors of Children's Services 2010). It seemed that early intervention was being interpreted as the need to intervene authoritatively at an earlier stage using the full weight of the law (Hannon, Wood and Bazalgette 2010). What also became evident by the end of the New Labour government was that there was a growing range of criticisms being expressed about the way policy and practice in this area had developed during the previous ten years. No longer were these criticisms only focused on the tragic deaths of young children and the failures of professionals to intervene; many of the changes introduced may have had the unintended consequence of making the situation worse, particularly the introduction of a range of electronic ICT systems. Not only did such systems seem to increase the range and depth of state surveillance of children, young people and parents (Anderson et al. 2009; Parton 2006, 2008; Roche 2008), they also did not seem to work as intended. In particular they seemed to have the effect of deflecting front line practitioners from their core task of working directly with children and parents (Hall et al. 2010); increasing the bureaucratic demands of the work (Broadhurst, Hall et al. 2010; Broadhurst, Wastell et al. 2010; White, Hall and Peckover 2009); and catching practitioners in an 'iron cage of performance management'

(Wastell et al. 2010) unable to exercise their professional judgement in order to safeguard children and promote their welfare (White, Hall and Peckover, 2009; White et al. 2009).

In attempting to widen and deepen attempts at early intervention in order to improve the outcomes for all children, while also trying to strengthen the systems of child protection, there was a real danger that there would be a growth in attempts at 'the risk management of everything' (Power 2004). Rather than overcoming the defensiveness, risk avoidance and blame culture so associated with the child protection system in the 1990s, it seemed that these characteristics were increasingly permeating the whole of the newly integrated and transformed children's services and seemed to prioritise an approach to practice based on 'strict safety' and a 'logic of precaution'. Increasingly, the language of risk was stripped of its association with the calculation of probabilities and was used in terms of not just preventing future harm but also avoiding the 'worst case' scenario (Parton 2011).

Child Protection and the Authoritarian Neoliberal State

Soon after coming to power in May 2010, the Conservative/Liberal Democrat Coalition government announced the establishment of an independent review of child protection in England to be chaired by Eileen Munro, a qualified and experienced social worker and Professor of Social Policy at the London School of Economics. The Review was published in three parts (Munro 2010, 2011a, b; Parton 2012) and clearly aimed to bring about a paradigm shift in child protection policy and practice. The overall aim was to develop a child protection system which valued professional expertise and recommended that the government revise its statutory guidance to "remove unnecessary or unhelpful prescription and focus on essential rules for effective multiagency working and on the principles that underpin good practice" (Munro 2011b, 7). The Review was also clear, along with the other reviews established by the Coalition government (Allen 2011a, b; Field 2010; Tickell 2011), that it wished to emphasise the importance of "early help", for "preventative services can do more to reduce abuse and neglect than reactive services".

However, from the outset it was clear there were several problems with the Review (Parton 2012). First, it never really addressed what it meant by child protection and, in particular, never addressed the fact that the problem of child maltreatment is generally agreed to be around ten times more prevalent than the number of cases that are ever referred to official agencies (Radford et al. 2011). If this were seriously addressed, agencies would be completely submerged. Second, unlike New Labour, which had placed children at the centre of its welfare reforms, the Coalition government made it very clear, following the financial and economic crisis of 2008/2009, that the reduction of public finance debt was its overriding and most urgent political priority. What became increasingly apparent was that the Coalition reform of public services was far more radical than anything that had been seen previously, including the Conservative governments of Margaret Thatcher and John Major (1979–1997).

I have characterised the nature of the Coalition approach to child welfare and protection as the move to an authoritarian neoliberal state, which has a number of key elements (Parton 2014) and for which the *Open Public Services* White Paper (HM Government 2011), the severe cuts to public service expenditure and the introduction of a number of more authoritarian and coercive interventions were key. The *Open Public Services* White Paper made it clear that every public service should be opened up to delivery by a wide range of providers, primarily the private and, to a lesser extent, the voluntary sector. While such policies had been evident under New Labour, the changes under the Coalition were much more wide-ranging, rapid and sweeping in nature.

From the outset, the government introduced major plans for the reduction of public expenditure, including cuts of 28 per cent for local authorities over the course of parliament. It was clear that families with children were no longer considered a priority group in welfare spending (Churchill 2012; Stewart 2011). The *ECM* programme was dropped, and there was a significant shift towards targeting the cuts to both children's benefits and services (HM Treasury 2010). An analysis by the Institute of Fiscal Studies indicated that households with children would lose far more than those without children at all parts of the income distribution because of the government's changes to tax and benefits (Brewer 2010).

A survey by the Directors of Children's Services estimated that the cuts in local authority children's services for the financial year 2010/2011 averaged 13 per cent, ranging from 6 to 25 per cent (Higgs 2011) and Children's Centres and early years' services took a disproportionate cut in the overall reductions to education budgets (Chowdry and Sibieta 2011). The voluntary sector, which relied on central and local government for much of its income, was particularly hard hit (Gill, La Valle and Brady 2011). It became increasingly apparent that the Munro Review's emphasis on the importance of 'early help' was being undermined. Research carried out for the NSPCC (CIPFA, 2011) found that local authority children's social care budgets faced reductions of over 23 per cent and that cuts to early intervention and preventative services were taking the brunt. At the same time, there was clear evidence of the growth in the statutory elements of children's social care, such as the trends evident following the social reaction to the death of Baby Peter Connelly (Table 11.1).

Table 11.1 Growth in Demand for Statutory Children's Social Care: 2007/2008–2014/2015

	2007/2008	2010/2011	2015/2016
Section 47 Child Protection Investigations	76,500	89,300	172,290
Registered Child Protection Plans	34,000	42,900	63,310
Number of Children in Care	59,360	65,520	70,440
Care Applications to Court	6,241	9,203	12,781

(Source: derived from the annual Department for Education annual *Characteristics of Children in Need in England* and *Children Looked After in England;* CAFCASS 2015).

Between 2007/2008 and 2015/2016 there were considerable increases in the number of child protection investigations, child protection plans, care applications to court and children in care. The government's view that more children needed to be taken into care was confirmed in a significant speech by Michael Gove, the Secretary of State, in November 2012. He argued that there had been a failure of leadership in relation to child protection over a number of years and that the interests of adults had been over-riding the needs of children. In addition, and following a major campaign for reform by *The Times* newspaper fronted by Martin Narey (2011), the retired Chief Executive of the national children's charity Barnardo's, the government launched a major initiative to "speed up adoptions and give vulnerable children loving homes" (Department for Education 2012). The plan was to ensure that adoption became a mainstream option for children in care. Local authorities were required to reduce delays in all cases and would not be able to delay adoption in order to find a suitable ethnic match; it would be easier for children to be fostered by approved prospective adopters while the courts considered the case for adoption; if suitable adopters could not be found within three months, the case would be referred to a new National Adoption Register. These various changes were at the centre of the Children and Families Act 2014. As a result, 5,050 children from the care system were adopted during the year ending 31 March 2014, an increase of 58 per cent from 2010 (Department for Education 2014).

Following a key recommendation of the *Munro Review,* the government published revised statutory guidance in March 2013 (HM Government 2013). While it had the same title as the previous guidance (HM Government 2010) and did not change the definition of the key concepts in the 2010 version in other respects, it had a number of important differences. While the focus continued to be "safeguarding and promoting the welfare of children", this was no longer set out in the context of the *ECM: Change for Children* programme. The 2013 guidance adopted "a child-centred and coordinated approach to safeguarding" (para 8) where

> [s]ocial workers, their managers and other professionals should always consider the plan from the child's perspective. *A desire to think the best of adults and to hope they can overcome their difficulties should not trump the need to rescue children from chaotic, neglectful and abusive homes.*
>
> (22, emphasis added)

The theme of "rescuing children from chaotic, neglectful and abusive homes" ran through the guidance and very much reflected the emphasis in other elements of the government's policies of intervening early, admitting more children into care and investing in adoption. Thus, while the language of "safeguarding and promoting the welfare of the child" was retained, we can see a significant shift towards a much more explicit authoritarian child protection orientation. It was not simply that any reference to the *ECM* programme had been dropped but that the idea of 'supporting families', which had been so important ever since the mid/late 1990s, had all but disappeared and that interventions should never be afraid of drawing on the full weight of the law behind them.

It also seemed that 'the politics of outrage', which had characterised much of the public reaction to the case of Baby P in 2008/2009 (Parton 2014, Chapter 5) became normalised in the day-to-day media and political context in which child protection policy and practice operated. There was a series of high-profile scandals, where practitioners and their senior managers were seen to have failed in their primary responsibilities and senior politicians made it very public that they were unhappy not just at the way professionals and statutory agencies had acted but in the way local reviews of the cases had been carried out. For example, the Edlington Case in Doncaster (Carlile 2012), the deaths of Hamzah Khan in Bradford (Bradford Safeguarding Children Board 2013) and Daniel Pelka in Coventry (Wonnacott and Watts 2014) were all subject to considerable media and political outrage. As a result, central government increasingly became much more interventionist where it considered that local authorities were failing in their child protection responsibilities and put outside managers or completely new governance arrangements in place to manage the services.

These issues reached a new level of intensity with the huge political and media anger expressed about the failures in Rotherham following the publication in August 2014 of an inquiry into child sexual exploitation in the borough (Jay 2014). The leader of the Council resigned, and the Chief Executive announced he would stand down at the end of the year. Some weeks later, following considerable media and political pressure, the strategic director for children and young people's services also agreed to leave the council 'by mutual consent'. However, Shaun Wright (Rotherham's deputy leader with lead responsibility for children's services from 2005 until 2010 and South Yorkshire police and crime commissioner in 2012) came under the greatest public opprobrium. Calls for him to resign as police and crime commissioner were voiced by the Prime Minister, the Home Secretary and the chair of the House of Commons Home Affairs Committee; he was suspended by the Labour Party after he refused to resign his post following a call from the shadow home secretary, Yvette Cooper. He eventually resigned nearly four weeks after the publication of the report following a vote of no confidence from the South Yorkshire police and crime commission committee.

The issues in Rotherham became politically explosive partly because of the apparent ethnic, gender and social class elements evident. The United Kingdom Independence Party (UKIP), which had won a number of seats in the Rotherham council elections in May 2014, was preparing to fight two national parliamentary bye-elections in October 2014. The Party pursued a message, which had been evident in the media coverage of the scandal, that it represented a prime example of a local authority failing to protect vulnerable working class white children and young people because those in power were afraid of being deemed racist.

A key findings of the report received considerable publicity: it claimed that approximately 1400 children had been sexually exploited in Rotherham between 1997 and 2013 and that just over a third of the children had previously been known to services because of child protection and neglect; by implication, the local authority had missed clear opportunities to protect these children. In their letter to council leaders Eric Pickles, then Minister for Communities, and Nicky Morgan, then Minister for Education, wrote that

> [w]e cannot undo the permanent harm that these children have suffered. But we can and should take steps to ensure that this never happens again and make sure that *local authorities deliver on their essential duty to protect vulnerable children.*
>
> (2014, emphasis added)

It was clear that not just individual professionals or even the statutory children's services but local authorities themselves were held accountable for the failures. It was also made explicit that local authority responsibilities were to all *vulnerable* children in their borough and not only those on a statutory order or who were deemed 'children in need'. No longer were child protection scandals seen to result from individualised professional failures alone. We were witnessing the media and senior politicians assailing local authorities and increasingly the police with accusations of major institutional failures, so that those who were deemed to carry the major responsibilities for those organisations were

The Politics of Child Protection in Contemporary England

subject to high-profile criticism and anger when they were seen to be failing.

These themes were reinforced further following the election of the Conservative government in May 2015. The first 12 months of the new government were taken up with the political preparations for the referendum about the future of UK membership of the European Union, which took place 23 June 2016. As a result, the government's legislative programme was very limited. However, right at its core were proposals to further reform child protection. In his first major speech following the election, Prime Minister David Cameron said that he wanted to continue much of the work of the Coalition but with a much more explicit focus on opening up opportunity for the most disadvantaged and having "a complete intolerance of government failure" (2015). The example he gave was that of the improvements brought about in adoption, where he said that there had been more than a doubling of the capacity of voluntary adoption agencies to recruit adopters and there was now a much quicker approvals process so that adopters could now be approved in just six months.

> Of course there is much further to go – we need to continue to tackle the obstacles that stand in the way of children being placed with a loving family. But through this work we helped over 5, 000 children find a loving home last year, up 63% since 2011. So when I talk about dealing with state failure, I'm not making an anti-government argument. I'm making an argument about ensuring government works.
>
> (Cameron 2015)

He argued that if Britain wanted to build "the opportunity society", a big focus for government over the next five years would be a major overhaul of child protection, which would include a significant reform of the training of social workers together with an increased emphasis on accountability for all professionals and managers:

> We also need more accountability, to end the tragedies. Victoria Climbié in 2000. Baby Peter in 2007. Daniel Pelka in 2012. Killed by evil, manipulative adults, these were all children who were known to social services but whom no-one ultimately took sufficient responsibility, in a complex landscape of multiple agencies and protocols.
>
> (Cameron 2015)

What was required was not only intervening authoritatively with failing families but also intervening authoritatively with failing practitioners and local authorities. The legislative framework for these changes was to be underpinned by a new Children and Social Work Act. Apart from further prioritising adoption and strengthening the role of voluntary and private adoption agencies, the legislation would considerably strengthen the role of the Secretary of State in controlling the training, education and practice of social workers. The legislation as originally drafted would also allow the Secretary of State to exempt local authorities from requirements imposed by legislation and thereby open the increased possibility that local authority functions could be taken over by the voluntary or commercial sectors. These "power to innovate" clauses proved highly contentious, and they were opposed by a wide range of professional associations and child welfare organisations. They were removed from the draft Bill during its passage through the House of Lords. Although the government sought to reintroduce these powers when the Bill returned to the House of Commons, the final form that this part of the legislation will take is, at the time of writing, unclear.

Then, just a few days before the Government summer recess, the Government launched a consultation exercise (HM Government 2016) that sought views from the public, practitioners and professionals on the possible introduction of one of two new statutory measures:

- a mandatory reporting duty, which would require certain organisations and any person working with children to report child abuse or neglect if they knew or had reasonable cause to suspect it was taking place
- a duty to act, which would require them to take appropriate action in relation to child abuse or neglect if they knew or had reasonable cause to suspect it was taking place

While mandatory reporting systems had been established in all US and Australian states and some European countries for many years (Matthews and Bross 2015), the introduction of a "duty to act" would be unique. It would be broader than mandatory reporting and would include sanctions for breaches by individuals and organisations, possibly including fines or imprisonment. The outcome of this consultation was not known at the time of writing.

These changes to the child protection system were being introduced at the same time the public sector more generally was being subject to further major 'austerity' measures following the budget in July 2015 and the autumn Spending Review in November 2015. It was clear that the cuts in tax/benefits and services, particularly those provided via local authorities, would fall disproportionately upon the poorest sections of society, particularly women and children (De Henau and Reed 2016).

Christina Beatty and Steve Fothergill (2016, 3) have calculated that the post-2015 welfare cuts would take almost £13bn a year from claimants by 2020/2021 – a cumulative loss of £27bn a year since 2010, equivalent to £690/year for every adult of working age. The reforms would impact unevenly across the country, and the older industrial areas, less prosperous seaside towns and some London boroughs would be hit the hardest, while much of southern England and the wealthier London boroughs would escape lightly. As a general rule, the more deprived the local authority the greater the financial loss. Beatty and Fothergill calculated that 83 per cent of the loss from the post-2015 benefit reforms – £10.7bn a year by 2020/2021 – would fall on families with dependent children. On average, couples with two or more children were to lose £1,450 while a lone parent with two or more children would lose £1,750. If we then include the cuts to services, by 2020/2021 the ten per cent poorest households would lose an equivalent of £7,100 a year or 23 per cent of their living standards (Beatty and Fothergill 2016, 3). Female lone parents would have their living standards reduced by 21 per cent (De Henau and Reed 2016). Local authority spending on children's centres and early years' services were particularly subject to major reductions (NCB and The Children's Society 2015).

Conclusion

If we take these various developments together, we can identify a significant shift in government policy in England concerned with child protection and safeguarding from that developed in the mid-1990s onwards, particularly compared to the changes introduced by the ambitious and wide-ranging *ECM* reforms. While changes were evident in the immediate fall-out following the scandal related to Baby Peter Connelly, these have now been taken to a new level, and increasingly it seems that intervention in *both* families *and* local authorities has become more coercive. While the range of universal and secondary prevention benefits and services has been reduced, the role of the state in other areas has become more 'authoritarian' and much more willing to intervene in certain families. It has been made clear that local authorities are required to take the lead responsibility for *vulnerable* children in their areas and not be afraid to take statutory action, including: initiating court proceedings; using section 47 investigations; child protection plans; taking children into care and using adoption as a mainstream option for children in care. This is a context in which the levels of poverty and deprivation have been growing, and the private sector plays an increasingly major role in the organisation and delivery of services. Not only has the state been commercialised and residualised, it has become much more authoritarian for certain sections of the population. All are key elements in what I characterise as the emergence of an authoritarian neoliberal state in services for children and families. This has considerable implications for the role and responsibilities of local authorities and their relationships with children, young people and those who care for them on a day-to-day basis, usually their mothers.

References

Allen, Graham. 2011a. *Early Intervention: The Next Steps – An Independent Report to Her Majesty's Government*. London: HM Government, Cabinet Office.

———. 2011b. *Early Intervention: Smart Investment Massive Savings – The Second Independent Report to Her Majesty's Government*. London: HM Government, Cabinet Office.

Anderson, Ross, Ian Brown, Terri Dowty, Philip Inglesant, William Heath, and Angela Sasse. 2009. *Database State*. York: Joseph Rowntree Reform Trust.

Association of Directors of Children's Services. 2010. *Safeguarding Pressures Project: Results of Data Collection, April 2010*. Manchester: ADCS.

Axford, Nick, and Michael Little. 2006. "Refocusing Children's Services towards Prevention: Lessons from the Literature." *Children & Society* 20 (4): 299–312.

Beatty, Christina, and Steve Fothergill. 2016. *The Uneven Impact of Welfare Reform: The Financial Losses to Places and People*. Sheffield: Centre for Regional Economic and Social Research, Sheffield Hallam University.

Bradford Safeguarding Children Board. 2013. *A Serious Case Review: Hamzah Khan: The Overview Report*. Bradford: Bradford Safeguarding Children Board.

Brewer, Mike. 2010. "The Spending Review and Children." *Presentation to the All Party Parliamentary Group for Children*, November 29; House of Commons.

Broadhurst, Karen, Christopher Hall, David Wastell, Sue White, and Andrew Pithouse. 2010. "Risk, Instrumentalism and the Humane Project in Social Work: Identifying the *Informal* Logics of Risk Management in Children's Statutory Services." *British Journal of Social Work* 40 (4): 1046–65.

Broadhurst, Karen, David Wastell, Sue White, Christopher Hall, Sue Peckover, A. Thompson, Andrew Pithouse, and Dolores Davey. 2010. "Performing 'Initial Assessment': Identifying the Latent Conditions for Error at the Front-Door of Local Authority Children's Services." *British Journal of Social Work* 40 (2): 349–51.

CAFCASS (Children and Family Court Advisory and Support Service). 2009. *CAFCASS Care Demand – Latest Quarterly Figures: 20 October 2009*. London: CAFCASS.

———. 2015. *CAFCASS Care Application Annual Figures: March 2015*. London: CAFCASS.

Cameron, David. 2015. "Prime Minister's Speech on Opportunity." Accessed 30 June 2015. www.gov.uk/government/speeches/pm-speech-on-opportunity.

Carlile, Lord. 2012. *The Edlington Case: A Review by Lord Carlile of Berriew CBE QC*. London: Department for Education.

Chartered Institute of Public Finance and Accountancy (CIPFA). 2011. *Smart Cuts? Public Spending on Children's Social Care*. London: NSPCC.

Chief Secretary to the Treasury. 2003. *Every Child Matters* (Cm 5860). London: Stationery Office.

Chowdry, Haroon, and Luke Sibieta. 2011. *Trends in Education and School Spending. IFS Briefing Note*. London: Institute for Fiscal Studies.

Churchill, Harriet. 2012. "Family Support and the Coalition: Retrenchment, Refocusing and Restructuring." In *Social Policy Review 24: Analysis and Debate in Social Policy 2012*, edited by Majella Kilkey, Gaby Ramia and Kevin Farnsworth, 35–54. Bristol: Policy Press.

De Henau, Jerome, and Howard Reed. 2016. "10 Years of Austerity: The Impact on Low-Income Households and Women." *Poverty* 154: 6–9.

Department for Education. 2012. *An Action Plan on Adoption: Finding More Loving Homes*. London: Department for Education.

———. 2014. *Children Looked After in England (Including Adoption and Care Leavers) Year Ending 31 March 2014: Statistical First Release*. London: Department for Education.

———. 2015. *Children Looked After in England (Including Adoption) Year Ending 31 March*. Annual Statistics. London: Department for Education.

———. 2015. *Characteristics of Children in Need: Annual Statistics*. London: Department for Education.

Department for Education and Skills. 2004. *Every Child Matters: Change for Children*. London: DfES.

Department of Health. *Children Act 1989*. London: HMSO.

Field, Frank. 2010. *The Foundation Years: Preventing Poor Children Becoming Poor Adults – Report of the Independent Review on Poverty and Life Chances*. London: HM Government, Cabinet Office.

Gilbert, Neil, Nigel Parton, and Marit Skivenes, eds. 2011. *Child Protection Systems: International Trends and Orientations*. New York: Oxford University Press.

Gill, Chloe, Ivana La Valle, and Louca-Mai Brady. 2011. *The Ripple Effect: The Nature and Impact of the Cuts on the Children and Young People's Voluntary Sector*. London: National Children's Bureau.

Gove, Michael. 2012. "The Failure of Child Protection and the Need for a Fresh Start." Speech presented at the Institute for Public Policy Research, London. November 16.

Hall, Christopher, Nigel Parton, Sue Peckover, and Sue White. 2010. "Child-Centric Information and Communication Technology (ICT) and the Fragmentation of Child Welfare Practice in England." *Journal of Social Policy* 39 (3): 393–413.

Hannon, Celia, Claudia Wood, and Louise Bazalgette. 2010. *In Loco Parentis*. London: Demos.

Higgs, Lauren. 2011. "Exclusive Survey: Youth Services and Children's Services Worst Hit as Cuts Average 13 Per Cent." *Children and Young People Now*, January 24, www.cypnow.co.uk/cyp/news/1044853/exclusive-survey-youth-services-and-childrens-centres-worst-hit-as-cuts-average-13-per-cent-in-one-year.

HM Government. 2010. *Working Together to Safeguard Children Consultation Document: A Guide to Inter-Agency Working to Safeguard and Promote the Welfare of Children*. Nottingham: DCSF.

———. 2011. *Open Public Services White Paper*. (Cm 8145). London: The Stationery Office.

———. 2013. *Working Together to Safeguard Children: A Guide to Inter-Agency-Working to Safeguard and Promote the Welfare of Children.* London: Department for Education Office.

———. 2016. *Reporting and Acting on Child Abuse and Neglect: Government Consultation.* London: The Stationary Office.

HM Treasury. 2010. *Spending Review 2010.* London: The Stationery Office.

House of Commons Children, Schools and Families Committee. 2009. *Looked After Children.* Accessed 6 August 2009. www.publications.parliament.uk/pa/cm200809/cmselect/cmchilsh/111/11106.htm.

Jay, Alexis. 2014. *Independent Inquiry into Sexual Exploitation in Rotherham 1997–2013.* Rotherham: Rotherham MBC.

Jones, Ray. 2014. *The Story of Baby P: Setting the Record Straight.* Bristol: Policy Press.

Laming Report. 2003. *The Victoria Climbié Inquiry: Report of the Inquiry by Lord Laming* (Cm 5730). London: Stationery Office.

LGA (Local Government Association). 2009. *Councils Struggling to Recruit Social Workers in Wake of Baby P.* London: LGA.

Matthews, Ben, and Donald C. Bross, eds. 2015. *Mandatory Reporting Laws and the Identification of Severe Child Abuse and Neglect.* New York: Springer.

Munro, Eileen. 2010. *The Munro Review of Child Protection, Part One: A System's Analysis.* London: Department for Education.

———. 2011a. *The Munro Review of Child Protection: Interim Report. The Child's Journey.* London: Department for Education.

———. 2011b. *The Munro Review of Child Protection: Final Report. A Child-Centred System.* (Cm 8062). London: Department for Education.

Narey, Martin. 2011. *Narey Report on Adoption.* Special Supplement of *The Times*, July 5.

National Children's Bureau and The Children's Society. 2015. *Cuts that Cost: Trends in Funding for Early Intervention Services.* London: NCB and the Children's Society

Parton, Nigel. 1985. *The Politics of Child Abuse.* Basingstoke: Palgrave.

———. 1991. *Governing the Family: Child Care, Child Protection and the State.* Basingstoke: Macmillan.

———. ed. 1997. *Child Protection and Family Support: Tensions, Contradictions and Possibilities.* London: Routledge.

———. 2006. *Safeguarding Childhood: Early Intervention and Surveillance in a Late Modern State.* Basingstoke: Palgrave.

———. 2008. "The Change for Children Programme in England: Towards the 'Preventive-Surveillance State'." *Journal of Law and Society* 35 (1): 166–87.

———. 2011. "Child Protection and Safeguarding in England: Changing and Competing Conceptions of Risk and their Implications for Social Work." *British Journal of Social Work* 41 (5): 854–75.

———. 2012. "The Munro Review of Child Protection: An Appraisal." *Children & Society* 26 (2): 150–62.

———. 2014. *The Politics of Child Protection: Contemporary Developments and Future Directions.* Basingstoke: Palgrave.

Parton, Christine, and Nigel Parton. 1989. "Child Protection, the Law and Dangerousness." In *Child Abuse: Public Policy and Professional Practice*, edited by Olive Stevenson, 54–73. Hemel Hempstead: Harvester-Wheatsheaf.

Parton, Nigel, David Thorpe, and Corrine Wattam. 1997. *Child Protection: Risk and the Moral Order.* Basingstoke: Macmillan.
Pickles, Eric Rt. Hon., and Rt. Hon. Nicky Morgan. 2014. *Safeguarding Vulnerable Children: Letter to Leaders of Councils in England, 24 September.* London: Department for Communities and Local Government and Department for Education.
Power, Michael. 2004. *The Risk Management of Everything: Rethinking the Politics of Uncertainty.* London: Demos.
Radford, Lorraine, Susana Corral, Christine Bradley, Helen Fisher, Claire Bassett, Nick Howat, and Stephan Collishaw. 2011. *Child Abuse and Neglect in the UK Today.* London: NSPCC.
Roche, Jeremy. 2008. "Children's Rights, Confidentiality and the Policing of Children." *International Journal of Children's Rights* 16 (4): 431–56.
Shoesmith, Sharon. 2016. *Learning from Baby P.* London: Jessica Kingsley.
Stewart, Kitty. 2011. "A Treble Blow? Child Poverty in 2010 and Beyond." In *Social Policy Review 23: Analysis and Debate in Social Policy 2011*, edited by Chris Holden, Majella Kilkey and Gaby Ramia, 165–84. Bristol: Policy Press.
Tickell, Dame Clare. 2011. *The Early Years: Foundations for Life, Health and Learning – An Independent Report on the Early Years Foundation Stage to Her Majesty's Government.* London: Department for Education.
Warner, Joanne. 2014. "'Heads Must Roll'? Emotional Politics, the Press and the Death of Baby P." *British Journal of Social Work* 44 (6): 1637–53.
Wastell, David, Sue White, Karen Broadhurst, Sue Peckover, and Andrew Pithouse. 2010. "Children's Services in the Iron Cage of Performance Management: Street-Level Bureaucracy and the Spectre of Svejkism." *International Journal of Social Welfare* 19 (3): 310–20.
White, Sue, Karen Broadhurst, David Wastell, Sue Peckover, Christopher Hall, and Andrew Pithouse. 2009. "Whither Practice – Near Research in the Modernization Programme? Policy Blunders in Children's Services." *Journal of Social Work Practice* 23(4): 401–11.
White, Sue, Christopher Hall, and Sue Peckover. 2009. "The Descriptive Tyranny of the Common Assessment Framework: Technologies of Categorization and Professional Practice in Child Welfare." *British Journal of Social Work* 39 (7): 1–21.
Wonnacott, Jane, and David Watts. 2014. *Daniel Pelka Review: Retrospective Deeper Analysis and Progress Report on Implementation of Recommendations.* Coventry: Coventry Safeguarding Children Board.

12 Dressing up for School
Beyond Rights and Welfare

Daniel Monk

Taking dress seriously is not new in childhood studies. Indeed, one could argue that Ariès's seminal thesis about the invention of childhood, based on representations in Western art, relied too extensively on dress. Yet at the same time, dress, particularly when coupled with the ambivalent term 'fashion', can still sometimes be perceived as trivial, especially in the context of ever-increasing inequality. Moreover, within mainstream legal studies, a discipline that privileges the text, there exists a marked reluctance to acknowledge the significance of the visual (Moran 2012). This is paradoxical, for the legal profession attaches more importance to costume than most and law itself has played, and continues to play, a critical role in the regulation of dress, from the sumptuary laws of the past to present-day disputes based on human rights (Robson 2013). In contemporary Britain, conflicts between children and schools dominate these disputes.

> 20 girls sent home in row over skimpy skirts.
> (*Metro*, 5 January 2017)

> Schoolboy in skirt protest wins right to wear shorts.
> (*Daily Telegraph*, 26 May 2012)

> Boy, 12, fights 'racist' school ban on his cornrow hair.
> (*Daily Telegraph*, 12 May 2011)

> Teenager isolated over cancer charity haircut.
> (BBC News, 3 February 2015)

> Muslim boys told their beards breach school rules.
> (*The Guardian*, 7 November 2013)

> School sends girl, 14, home for wearing a Sikh bracelet.
> (*Daily Mail*, 7 November 2007)

> More pupils sent home in uniform row.
> (BBC News, 7 September 2016)

The above are just a few examples of headlines that appear on a regular basis in the British media. Legislation provides the framework for establishing and enforcing school dress codes and conflicts in the courts are resolved by judges through the creative arts of statutory interpretation and the application of human rights' doctrines. The aim here is not to suggest a correct way of resolving these conflicts. Rather, the key argument is that school dress, located at the point where education policies intersect with broader cultural and political concerns about religion, sexuality, gender and class, provides a rich site for thinking about childhood in contemporary Britain.

A key premise is that taking school dress seriously requires thinking critically about the existing frameworks within which contemporary debates are located. This chapter begins by highlighting the limitations of thinking about school dress through the framework of the uniform/ no uniform binary and suggests reasons for the contemporary move towards uniforms. It then looks at how law frames the issue as a disciplinary matter and examines the implications of this for contemporary debates about gender, bullying and school governance. It concludes by looking at two cases where children – unusually – were successful in challenging a dress code; and in doing so highlights the contingency of contemporary understandings and applications of children's rights.

Framing Dress Codes as School Uniforms

Conversations about school dress codes are often reduced to a debate about school uniforms in which opponents tread a familiar path. On one side are arguments against uniforms premised on autonomy, freedom of expression and a liberal, individualistic understanding of child development. These are arguments that can easily lay claim to being supportive of 'children's rights'. They are countered, on the other side, by claims about the individual and collective benefits of uniforms (such as improved school behaviour, self-respect/discipline, economic savings and social cohesion). These arguments can lay claim to representing the 'best interests' of children and, consequently, advocates of school uniforms can also claim to be supportive of 'children's rights'. Consequently, the debate provides a classic example of how 'rights' – and children's rights in particular – are open to conflicting definitions and applications and function as rhetorical legal tools (Eekelaar 1994).

While opposing school uniforms is often perceived as a more 'progressive' position, the stance too easily elides with a tendency within liberal rights accounts generally (and certainly with children) to juxtapose juridical commands – such as dress codes – against a notion of freedom and the enhancing of individualism. In this formulation, repealing a uniform code 'liberates a child' enabling a 'real' authentic child to be made visible. In other words, a school uniform functions discursively, and not just materially, "as a layer on top of an underlying subject" (Lesnik-Oberstein 2011, 4). This restrictive narrative is not unusual, even in accounts that adopt an explicitly constructivist approach to childhood, despite the fact, as Karín Lesnik-Oberstein (2011) has highlighted, that to reach this position constructivism is not necessary and is to a certain extent misunderstood.

Yet while the representation of the un-uniformed child as a more autonomous subject overlooks the complexities of power and governance, it is not that arguments in favour of school uniforms are in any way more compelling. Rather, a more critical reading of the pro-school uniform discourse questions not the claimed effects of uniforms, but the underlying aspirations attributed to them. In other words, the opposing desires – to liberate children *from* uniforms and to empower children *by* uniforms – are both investments in the mastery of childhood and rather than questioning the category, they both demonstrate the enduring resilience of childhood as a category within adult imagination.

One way to mark the closeness of these investments is to note how the uniform/no uniform binary masks the often very detailed regulation of dress in schools that do *not* have uniforms. While these rules are framed in the negative, unlike uniform policies that dictate what *must* be worn, they too represent dress codes and are legitimised and enforced by the same laws. Moreover, these dress codes are particularly revealing as a site for thinking about contemporary childhood, for they are premised not on what is appropriate for a particular school but assumptions about what is appropriate for children *per se*. At stake here is the relationship between idealised 'pupil-hood' and legitimate 'childhood'.

One could, justifiably, ask: what debate about uniforms? For arguably, one of the most notable contemporary aspects about the uniform question is the very absence of it. Those who argue in favour of uniforms have – to put it crudely – won. Silences are revealing here. From the Children's Commission of England, there is not a word against uniforms or dress codes. When they are mentioned, it is only in the context of their cost, the appropriate penalties for non-compliance and their impact on ethnic minorities (OCC 2012, 2013). This is a notable shift and reflects the extent to which moves to relax or do without uniforms in the 1970s have been halted or reversed. Putting aside the validity of the arguments for or against uniforms, which raise complex empirical questions of causality, what is clear is that the aspirations for childhood, which uniforms are currently imbued with, cohere with broader political shifts and ideologies. That this is the case is all the more evident by the very British nature of the concern about school dress. That uniforms and dress codes are extremely rare in most other European countries reinforces the conclusion that the importance attached to them in Britain is far more than a concern about child welfare. Comparative perspectives here reveal national and political histories (Dussel 2001), but while schools in Scotland and Wales are markedly less likely to adopt uniforms than those in England or Northern Ireland (OFT 2012), the reasons for this have yet to be explored.

The traditional conservative school uniform – blazers and ties – has a long tradition in the independent school sector and it was adopted by most grammar schools (Davidson 1990). Apart from the small number of progressive private schools, relaxation of dress codes and abolition of uniforms was far more common among comprehensive schools. In this way, upper- and middle-class childhood was visibly distinguished: the more traditional and strict the uniform, the 'posher' the children; the elaborate uniforms of Eton – the grandest of all public schools – exemplifies this visual material hierarchy. But with the increasing 'privatisation' of maintained schools, in particular with the introduction of 'independent' academies and a steady weakening of the role of local authorities (Harris 2012), the traditional model of uniforms has increasingly been applied to non-selective maintained schools (Mintel 2010). The resulting rendering of class inequalities less visible has occurred at a time when social mobility, in practice, has been significantly reduced (Dorling 2015). Uniforms achieve two ends here; first, they serve to mask inequality, reinforcing the myth of classlessness; second, they communicate a subtle solution to inequality, in which 'private' is best. In his diary, New Labour's media advisor Alastair Campbell records the following conversation with Tony Blair in 2000: "He said the problem with schools was *uniformity* of teaching. I said the problem was the background of poorer kids and he just rolled his eyes at me" (quoted in Wagg 2014, 179, emphasis added). This exchange indicates how the adoption of uniforms – a very visual way of communicating pedagogical uniformity and the centrality of a focus on 'standards' – has all the right connotations in what Stephen Wagg has described as a culture war; an explicit rejection of permissive education policies of the past and a "disinclination to see a child's educational performance as being utilized by social factors" (2014, 179).

This contemporary symbolic use of uniforms is evident in the image from the Bede Academy School in Northumberland (Figure 12.1).

Established in 2009 by the Emmanuel Foundation, the traditional uniform, which is typical, indeed almost de rigueur, for academies, albeit unremarked on, asserts its commitment to a nostalgic image of childhood and at the same time aspirations informed by the traditions of the private sector. Strict traditional uniforms visibly communicate their distinctiveness and superiority. Whether or not the uniforms achieve their stated aims is a complex empirical question. The point here is the extent to which concerns about contemporary childhood draw on the uniform as a signifier.

It is well documented that the structural changes to state education since 1979 have recast parents as consumers; albeit that the reality of parental choice and power is questionable and, without any doubt, deeply

Figure 12.1 Pupils at Bede Academy, Blyth (Part of the Emmanuel Schools Foundation).

classed (Ball 2008; Harris 2007). In an increasingly market-based education system, the image of the pupils from the Bede Academy is targeted at parents who, less than children, are largely in favour of uniforms (Mintel 2010). In this way, emphasising tradition and discipline, they mirror broader political shifts in education where the emphasis is on playing "to the aspirations (and fears) of a particular demographic – the upwardly mobile and/or lower-middle class voter" (Wagg 2014, 180).

The market for uniforms and clothes that conform to dress codes is highly competitive, with supermarkets such as Tesco and Aldi challenging the monopoly of traditional school outfitters by providing 'uniforms' at significantly lower prices. Yet despite the lower prices, the increase in secondary schools adopting uniforms has meant that the school wear market – worth £450M per annum – is still forecast to increase (Mintel 2010). The availability of cheaper uniforms to a certain extent rebuts arguments against uniforms based on expense (Hawkes 2009), and while individual schools have discretion about uniforms, the government, eager to support uniforms, has issued specific guidance about cost to facilitate them (DfE 2015).

The annual 'back to school' campaigns by supermarkets to advertise their school wear present representations similar to that of the Bede Academy. The children are imbued with nostalgia for a past where childhood is perceived to have been safer and more innocent. Yet, at the same time, the images are not traditional in the sense of the children being 'seen but not heard'; rather, they are portrayed laughing, smiling and relaxed and, perhaps most importantly, seemingly happy. The dominant contemporary construction of childhood requires children to be good, studious, hardworking pupils, but, now, also happy. The relative *un*happiness of children in contemporary Britain has been widely reported, albeit that the basis of these claims has been effectively critiqued (Morrow and Mayell 2009). The images skilfully reconcile the contemporary injunction for children, as well as everyone else, to be happy, with the critique of the progressiveness of permissive education policies.

The images of happy children in traditional uniforms also bare a remarkable resemblance to the preeminent fictional contemporary child: Harry Potter. David Rudd (2014) has commented on the tendency to comment on contemporary children's literature as either 'infantalising' or 'adultifying' children. One can read the images here through the same lens. The uniforms draw on adult-like suits and imbue the children with the ideal adult-like qualities of hard work and self-discipline. At the same time, the evident nostalgia locates them in a space free from adult-like concerns and dangers and contemporary uncertainties. For Rudd, the "entrenched notions of 'essence' of either child or adult persisted precisely because these categories were no longer so secure: there was a slippage" (2014, 124). Heightened concern with school dress demonstrates both the commitment to childhood as a category and its fragility.

Framing Dress Codes as 'School Discipline'

Within education law and policy, dress codes are categorised as a discipline issue. The current government guidance to schools, under the heading 'Discipline', states that: "The head teacher can discipline your child for not wearing the school uniform. Your child can be suspended or excluded if they repeatedly ignore the uniform rules" (GOV.UK 2016; see also DfE 2013). The statutory basis for this is in Chapter 1, 'School Discipline', of the Education and Inspections Act 2006, which places the responsibility for discipline and behaviour on Governors (Section 88) and Head Teachers (Section 89). Framing the issue of dress as a discipline issue is not a 'neutral' categorisation. Law does not simply stipulate rules and procedures but legitimises particular narratives. Critically in this context, it frames challenges and resistance to dress codes as a behavioural problem of individual pupils and restricts the formal debate to questions about the appropriate methods of enforcement. A key concern has been the use of exclusions. In 1999, the New Labour government, as part of a broader attempt to reduce school exclusions, issued Guidance that advised that breaches of dress codes would be an inappropriate ground for exclusion (DfEE 1999). Under pressure from head teachers and teachers' unions, this was revised to enable more flexibility (DfEE 2000), and contrary to the recommendations of the Children's Commissioner (2012), there is now no question that breaches of dress codes can give rise to exclusion (DfE 2013).

The centrality of law in the regulation of school dress is not inevitable. This 'juridification' is marked across many areas of society and especially education. Indeed, in many countries the category or practice of Education Law is looked on with astonishment. "But what has law got to do with special educational needs, admissions or school discipline?" is a question

216 Daniel Monk

English lawyers are asked by continental colleagues. Noting the contingency of law is critical to reading law as narrative rather than as doctrine or simply as rules, as it enables law to be understood as "artefacts that reveal a culture, not just policies that shape that culture" (Gewirtz 1996, 3).

Gender and Bullying

One consequence resulting from the framing of dress-as-discipline is the extent to which dress is absent from mainstream concerns about bullying. For example, empirical research about homophobic bullying has repeatedly found that non-conformity with gender stereotypes, rather than sexual identity *per se*, is a critical causal factor of bullying behaviour (Monk 2011). Framed as a discipline issue, the problematic behaviour is the physical and verbal behaviour of other pupils. The role of dress codes in policing gender performance is not the object of concern. Pupils who fail to comply with gendered dress codes are not perceived as victims of bullying; they are themselves often legitimately 'disciplined'. The individualisation of the bullying discourse consequently silences the institutional policing of gender roles. Campaigns against homophobic bullying are sometimes complicit with this and demonstrate the contingency of mainstream concerns. An example of this is a poster produced by a national campaign in Ireland in 2006, which was praised as "Good Practice" in 2009 by a Committee of the Council of Europe (Figure 12.2).

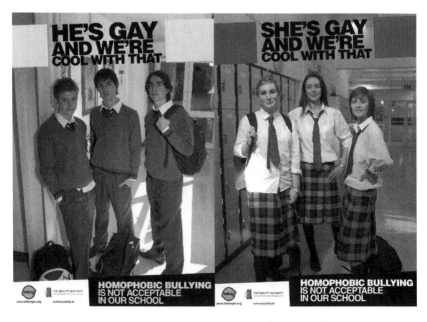

Figure 12.2 BeLonG campaign in partnership with the Equality Authority.

Posing under the headlines, "He's Gay and We're Cool with That" and "She's Gay and We're Cool with That", uniformed school pupils send out the message that gay and lesbian pupils are just the same as everybody else, an important, and hard won, achievement. But in equating 'equal treatment' with 'sameness', the image fails to address the evidence that pupils who present and behave in ways that are *not* the same are most likely to be victims of bullying. In doing so, the image coheres with concerns by numerous commentators about the conditionality of inclusion (Brown 1995). Moreover, in this context compliance with the gendered uniforms – the boys in trousers and the girls in skirts – inscribes uniforms as a form of protection from harm. In other words, it suggests that uniforms, by rendering sexuality invisible, can aid cohesion and a sense of belonging, an argument that is used generally as a defence for school uniforms, in relation to socio-economic distinctions between pupils.

Decisions about the gendered aspects of school dress codes have wider significance. Recently, albeit exceptionally, some head teachers, exercising their discretion, have relaxed rules and demonstrated an awareness of the existence of trans children (Griffiths 2016). 'Progressiveness' can work in other directions, too. For example, promoting equality between men and women has been upheld as a legitimate basis for banning the jilbab (Carney and Sinclair 2006). Cases about Islamic clothing have been highly politicised by legal challenges. Law is complicit with this emphasis by providing no possibility of redress for gendered dress codes. Discrimination law – while emerging in both the UK and the US – is of limited use in this context (Murray 2013; Wintemute 1997). An example of this is the case of *McMillen (Chairman of the Board of Governors of Ballyclare High School), Re Judicial Review* [2008] NIQB 21, where a pupil attempted to challenge rules about the hair length of boys. The decision made clear that it was a discipline issue and not a school management issue and that while questions about procedural fairness can legitimately be challenged, the rules themselves cannot. In upholding the sanctions against the boy, the court held that "its legality is the issue rather than its wisdom" (at para [45]).

Further gendered dimensions of dress codes are evident in the policy of Fortismere School, a co-educational comprehensive in north London. Proudly distinguishing itself from the growing trend of schools to adopt uniforms, the school's dress code policy opens with the following statement: "Clothing can be a powerful means of expression. We are proud of our students and respect their individuality". However, it then lists the following various prohibitions:

> However, some clothing is inappropriate for school. So absolutely no [...] see-through clothing or strapless tops [...] inappropriately ripped or torn garments [...] sheer leggings [...] T shirts or other clothing with offensive slogans or images [...] drug or alcohol logos.
> (Fortismere 2017)

Cartoon images of the prohibited items are included and drawn in a playful humorous fashion. While the clothing illustrated is deemed inappropriate, there is at the same time a 'knowingness', a Carry On film/seaside postcard humour about them, which acknowledges that children will be able to understand the humour. The vehicle of the cartoon itself provides a licence that is perhaps not available for photographic images. The form in this way conveys an ambivalent message: pupils may 'know' about drugs and sex but cannot dress in a way that *performs* their knowingness. This approach to dress codes coheres closely with the development of policies about Sex and Relation Education introduced by the New Labour government. In marked contrast to the approach of the previous Conservative administrations, statutory reform supported by new guidance to schools demonstrated a willingness to more openly acknowledge the reality of sexual activity amongst young people. However, it did so explicitly in order to reduce teenage pregnancy and to advocate the benefits of delaying sexual activity (Monk 2001).

Jane Pilcher has noted how the contemporary focus on sexualised clothing marks a shift of concern away from 'teenagers' toward fashions of children more generally and that while the explicit focus is gender neutral, the concern is primarily about girls (2014). Rebecca Raby similarly notes that, "boys' (hetero)sexuality was only relevant" to the extent that boys might be "distracted by girls' provocative clothing, a position holding girls responsible for boys' sexual desires" (2010, 350). In research with girls about how they experience these rules, it is clear that they sometimes desired the problematised clothing but "gave meaning to these terms in ways that are different from adults" (Pilcher 2014, 264) and negotiated them in complex and often contradictory ways (Bragg 2012; Raby 2010). For example, Raby quotes girls in a focus group commenting on the rules in the following way:

CATHERINE: That's like, the spaghetti strap rule is like kind of unfortunate because it's like, for boys it's not a problem, and it's just like, 'Sorry I'm a female like and it's hot and I would like to wear a spaghetti strap tank top', but it's like 'No, no you must not expose skin', which is kind of ridiculous 'cause
JANICE: You are not even showing anything, just your arm [laughs]
CATHERINE: Yeah, you're really not; it's just your body; it's like 'Oh no the human body!'

(2010, 340)

The wide-scale application of these largely unquestioned and un-researched dress codes reflects deep-seated fears about child sexuality. Childhood innocence is one of the most consistent constructions of modern and contemporary childhood, and its dominance is clear from the title of the DfE's policy paper, which addresses some of these concerns: "Letting Children be Children" (2011). The school is a particularly critical space for upholding the norm of the, ideally, non-sexual child. Practical advice for children who are sexually active is now more readily available, but it is more frequently located outside of the school in health settings; advocating 'good health' for children is more palatable than 'good sex' (Monk 2001). Taking the long view, Christine Piper notes that "there is a sense in which the benefits of welfarism have always gone hand in hand with desexualising children" (2000, 40).

Concerns about sexualisation are linked to more recent concerns about the commercialisation of childhood. The Labour Party manifesto in 2010 stated that it would provide support for parents who wished to challenge "aggressive or sexualized commercial marketing" and would "ask Consumer Focus to develop a website for parents to register their concerns about sexualized products aimed at children" (2010, para 6.3). Pilcher discusses the varied ways in which this focus has continued to dominate government agendas, with the British Retail Consortium encouraging "responsible retailing guidelines to preserve the innocence of our children" (2014, 262). This is the wider context to the adoption of restrictive dress codes and the perception of them as seemingly uncontroversial common sense, even by avowedly progressive schools that reject uniforms. It can best be explained by a curious concatenation of contemporary discourses: traditional and welfarist desires to 'protect childhood/treasure innocence', feminist concerns about the sexual objectification of young women's bodies and a progressive/left critique of the tentacles of neo-liberalism.

Reconstructing Head Teachers and Parents

While ideals of childhood are explicit in school dress codes, contemporary conflicts about dress also highlight the shifting roles of head teachers and parents, which similarly reflect broader social and educational developments.

The power of head teachers, in matters of school discipline in particular, has become a highly politicised issue with political parties competing to emphasise their support for enhancing their powers (Monk 2005). The attempts by New Labour to limit school exclusions, noted above, were met with fierce and effective resistance. School Exclusion Panels no longer have the power to order a reinstatement, and persistent breaches of dress codes are a lawful basis for temporary and permanent exclusions (Revell 2001). One of the underlying rationales for exclusions being perceived as proportionate responses to breaches of dress codes is that it is disobedience *per se*, and in particular a refusal to acknowledge the authority of the head teacher, which justifies the ultimate punishment, and not the consequences of the unacceptable article of clothing or hairstyle.

Head teachers now have more power than ever before. This reconstruction of the head teacher has been represented as a return to the past, where head teachers are imbued with a common sense natural authority – not dissimilar to the image of matrons in hospitals. Like uniforms, this nostalgic vision of head teachers owes much to the valorisation of the traditions of public schools. Alongside this is a more recent managerialism discourse (Ball 1994). Ken Jones has argued that the emphasis on leadership and 'superheads' demonstrates how schools are defined more strongly than at any time since 1944 "as places where management authority, rather than collegial culture, establishes the ethos and culture of the school" (2003, 161). A heightened emphasis on uniforms and stricter dress codes supports the nostalgic discourse and heightened resistance to any challenges to the breaches of them supports the new model of managerial authority.

The authority of the head teacher has implications not only for pupils but also for parents. For legal scholars, the shifting meaning of parental responsibility is a key contemporary issue. Debates about whether the concept emphasises parental authority and enhances privacy rights, or whether it defines appropriate parenting and legitimises increased surveillance of parents, are longstanding, and the shift to the latter identified and variously praised or critiqued (Eekelaar 1991; Reece 2009). Compliance with dress codes is one contemporary indicator of 'responsible' parenting, alongside others such as obesity and school homework and attendance more generally. The shifting regulation of dress codes in this way is part of a broader move towards heightened surveillance of parents. Legitimised through concerns premised on child welfare, the legal framework emphasises the overarching individualistic focus. Law consequently plays a role in formally masking the extent to which the increasing emphasis on the 'responsibilisation' of parents has marked classed and raced effects (Gillies and Edwards 2011; Parton 2014). Middle-class parenting is offered as the solution to cycles of poverty for working-class parents and childhoods; as Val Gillies notes, "the concept of 'the personal is political' is increasingly articulated as 'the personal is the only political'" (2011, 207).

Children's Rights

For some, it might appear paradoxical that the contemporary presence of dress codes has been sustained, indeed re-energised, in an age when children's rights have become increasingly embedded in law and more widely accepted. This can most easily be explained by the fact that 'children's rights', like all rights, are open to conflicting interpretations, and in this context welfare-based concerns have simply trumped claims based on autonomy. Where pupils do attempt to challenge dress codes through the courts, they are invariably unsuccessful, as the judges have demonstrated a marked reluctance to interfere with the discretion of schools and head teachers. The rare cases where the courts uphold a pupil's challenge are often hailed as 'children's rights' victories; the accuracy of these claims is questionable, and two of these cases are explored below. Whether successful or not, the cases as a whole, which often receive wide coverage in the media, reflect not just individual challenges but texts about moments of rupture and tension in contemporary childhood.

Many of the high-profile cases about school dress codes frequently concern religion. Without any doubt, the issue that has received the most attention is 'the veil', the wearing of either the hijab or jilbab by Moslem girls. The key case in the UK is *R (on the Application of Begum) v Headteacher and Governors of Denbigh High School* [2006] UKHL 15, which upheld a school's ban on the wearing of the jilbab. A huge amount has been written about this case and the issue more widely, both in the UK and in other jurisdictions. Indeed 'the veil' has become one of the flashpoint issues in Western societies, a symbol that brings to the fore tensions and contradictions within liberal democracy and feminism (Lyon and Spini 2004; Marshall 2008; McGoldrick 2006; Smith 2007). Moreover, to the extent that these issues are informed by and intersect with debates about global politics – 'the war against terror' and 'islamophobia' – in relation to concerns about children, they can be connected to the recent and highly controversial government 'Prevent' agenda and concerns about 'radicalisation' (Coppock and McGovern 2014; McDonald 2011; Stanley and Guru 2015). The degree to which 'the veil' is a focal point for concerns is also demonstrated by the relatively little attention that school dress codes more generally attract. Its very exceptionality – its otherness – is reinforced by the attention. Other issues, uniforms more generally and hair length, shoulder straps, visible underwear, attract very little attention, but the seeming mundanity of these issues, the 'common sense' acceptance of them, and the relatively little scholarly attention to they receive, are significant in understanding contemporary childhood. Law is critical here, for 'religion' as a protected category is to a certain extent privileged in challenges; these are not always successful – as the *Begum* case attests – but what is accepted is that religion creates the space for the most legitimate exception to school dress codes. The uniform policy of Hampstead School, a large London co-educational comprehensive, highlights these distinctions in practice. Exercising its lawful discretion in this area, and demonstrating a commitment to diversity and inclusion, the policy permits the wearing of the jilbab – the full body covering that led to the exclusion of Begum – but at the same time does *not* permit: "Hair dye which is not a natural colour" or "[p]atterns shaved or cut into hair" (Hampstead School 2016).

Such a policy is without any doubt lawful, and the aim here is not to question its wisdom. But it highlights a particular form of public – albeit local – negotiation around children's bodies, in particular the contingent symbolism of hair (Lesnik-Oberstein 2006). While the policy may appear to be contradictory from a children's rights perspective that emphasises autonomy, the analysis of the following successful challenges indicates the underlying rationality of such a contradiction.

In *R (on the Application of Watkins-Singh) v Aberdare Girls School Governors* [2008] EWHC 1865 (Admin), Sarika Angel Watkins-Singh, a 14-year-old Sikh girl, challenged her school's refusal to allow her to wear the Kara – a religious steel bangle. The wearing of the Kara contravened the school's policy relating to jewellery, which permitted only one pair of plain stud earrings and a wristwatch. In *G v St Gregory's Catholic Science College* [2011] EWHC 1452, an 11-year-old boy challenged his school's refusal to allow him to wear his hair in cornrows, a form of braiding. This hairstyle contravened the policy of the school, which stated that:

> Hair must be clean, neat and of a moderate style (boys must not wear braids). Peculiar and bizarre styles are quite unacceptable. These styles include, for example, hair that falls below the collar (for boy's), wearing of hair extensions, bleached, dyed, tinted or highlighted hair, closely cropped or shaved hair, and patterns and lines cut into the hair. Furthermore pupils must be clean-shaven at all times and the shaving of eyebrows is not acceptable. Pupils whose hairstyles are unacceptable will not be admitted to school and risk disciplinary action.
>
> (para 19)

In both cases, it was accepted that the rules *per se* were lawful. As the court stated in the *Gregory* case, the school was "entitled to adopt a uniform policy, including what haircuts are permissible, which is or may seem to be very restrictive or conservative" (para 8). The legal question in both cases was whether the pupils could legitimately be exempt from the rules. In other words, from the outset, the cases rest on 'exceptionality', requiring the pupils to establish that they are outside of the norm. The challenges in both cases succeeded by establishing that the school policies were a form of indirect indiscrimination under the Race Relations Act 1976 and the Equality Act 2010, in the first case against Sikhs and in the second against boys from an African-Caribbean background. What in this context is interesting is noting how the courts distinguish these claims from the far more prevalent unsuccessful claims. In particular, why the wearing of a Sikh kara was acceptable but not the jilbab or a Christian 'purity' ring. And why cornrow braided hair was acceptable for boys from one background but not for others. The different doctrinal rules provided a formal means of distinguishing the cases, in particular the differences between Human Rights claims based on religious freedom of expression and indirect discrimination claims based on equality legislation (Howard 2011). Another distinction often drawn refers to practical or 'health and safety' issues relating to particular articles of clothing or long hair. But underlying these arguments, reading between the lines of the judgements – or in the words of the critical legal theorist Alan Norrie, "not taking law's word for it" (2005, 8) – it is possible to explain the exceptionality of these claims as judicial and social constructions of contemporary 'good' childhood.

The first key point emphasised in both cases is that the decisions to wear the Kara and adopt the cornrow style, while individual choices, are expressions of collective religious and ethnic identity, respectively; in other words, they are explicitly *not* expressions of individuality. The wearing of the Kara here was contrasted with the wearing of a purity ring in an earlier case of *R (on the Application of Lydia Playfoot (A Child) v Millais School Governing Body* [2007] EWHC 1698 (Admin). The girl in that case failed in her challenge largely because it was held that she was not 'obliged' by her religion to wear the ring, as it was not considered to be 'intimately linked' to her Christian beliefs. Similarly, a factor that went against Begum was the suggestion that large numbers of Muslim girls at the school, supported by religious authorities, complied with Islamic religious requirements by wearing the hijab as opposed to the full jilbab. In the context of these religious symbol cases, a binary is constructed between individual choice and obligation to a higher authority; the former, while recognised, is at the same time problematised. As Bruno Latour writes in the context of iconoclasm, there is "an impossible double bind": "If you say it is man-made you nullify the transcendence of the divinities [...] The more the human hand can be seen as having worked on an image, the weaker is the image's claim to offer truth" (2002, 18).

A similar ambivalence about 'choice' is evident in distinguishing the cases about hairstyles. In the *Gregory* case, the boy obviously had no choice over his ethnicity that legitimised his claim. As the judge made clear: "more than choice is needed to constitute a particular disadvantage" (para 38). It was, consequently, essential for the cornrows to be distinguished from 'fashion'. As the judge noted: "[C]hoice or a desire to adopt a particular fashion is no good reason to be permitted not to abide by the policy" (para 8). There is an acknowledgement here that, for some, the cornrow hairstyle is 'merely' a question of 'fashion'. Indeed, the boy himself is quoted in the case as saying:

> Every race has differences, in religion and culture, the plaiting is ours, and I would like to keep it, it's the one thing I really like, and the best part was when I saw my idol, David Beckham, cornrow his hair, it showed me that he appreciated African hair styling, and that we are all the same underneath it all.
>
> (para 33)

While the boy in this statement appears to read Beckham's hairstyle as a form of cultural appreciation, the clear implication of the ruling, however, is that white boys in the school are forbidden from adopting the cornrow hairstyle. For them to do so would be a pure choice, whether informed by a desire to be 'fashionable' or to express, implicitly or otherwise, an expression of solidarity or celebration of multi-culturalism. Legal discourse's requirement of 'exceptionality', while informed by respect for difference and inclusion, ironically, fosters ethnic demarcation. The law here also implicitly coheres with an emerging contemporary trend that would crudely judge Beckham's adoption of the cornrow style to be a problematic form of 'cultural appropriation' (Patterson 2015).

Both cases indicate that forbidding expressions of anything that might be termed 'political' – broadly defined – is one of the justifications for the dress codes and a means to demarcate *legitimate* religious or cultural 'choices'. In the *Gregory* case the school's banning of skinheads was justified on the basis of its association with far right political groups; arguments made to suggest that it is a style 'common in some eastern European cultures' (para 47), and in this way akin to cornrows, were firmly rejected. As the judge made clear: "There is […] not a shred of evidence to suggest that anything but choice could lead to a skin head cut" (para 48). That *pure* choices, those not required by religion or motivated by belonging to an ethnic group, can be perceived as 'political' and the claimants as potential or real troublemakers is clear from earlier cases. In the *Begum* case, the claimant's behaviour was described as "unnecessarily confrontational" (Lord Scott at para [80]). Concerns were raised that she was under the influence of her brother, that she was effectively, in contemporary political parlance, "at risk of radicalization" (Coppock and McGovern 2014). Conversely, in the *Gregory* case, it was emphasised that the boy "was not coached in any way" (para 34). He had also moved to another school where he was able to keep his cornrow hairstyle. Begum was criticised for not making such attempts, allegedly, because she was "intent upon enforcing her 'rights'" (Lord Hoffmann, para 52). In the *Playfoot* case, the pupil was described as having adopted a "moral stance" (para 8), and the ring was described as "ostentatious". In *Watkins-Singh*, the judge explicitly rejected the "possibility that she is insisting on wearing the Kara in order to be rebellious or just to defy authority" (para 62). The legal discourse is avowedly secular, but one can read these distinctions as expressing a particular and traditional liberal Anglican suspicion of fundamentalism, a commitment to religious and ethnic diversity, alongside a rejection of any form of proselytising.

Reading the successful challenges alongside the others reveals a policing of the adult/child boundary and once again concerns about the sexualisation of young girls. On the surface, the wearing of the jilbab and the purity ring appear distinct from concerns about sexualisation, as both express commitments to traditional sexual morality and a desexualising of the school space. But the refusal to allow them arguably coheres with the codes that refuse to allow girls to reveal too much of their bodies, as the jilbab in *Begum* was perceived by some as unnecessary for girls and as a form of adult women's clothing, and the chastity ring in *Playfoot* made visible the reality that school-girls do indeed make sexual choices.

Gender was also critical in the cases about boys' hairstyles. For in both the *Gregory* case and the *Ballyclare* case, the pupils argued that the school dress codes amounted to unlawful sex discrimination: neither prevented long hair for girls and African Caribbean girls were permitted to wear cornrows. Drawing on earlier cases in the employment field, the judge in *Gregory* stated that "Rules concerning appearances will not be discriminatory because their content is different for men and women if they enforce a common principle of smartness or conventionality" (para 54). Applying that rule, the judge held that:

> A rigid appearance policy at a school is clearly entirely reasonable provided it complies with equality law. Permitting long hair for girls and not for boys may be regarded as discriminatory since boys nowadays not unusually wear their hair longer. But I have no doubt that 'not unusual' does not equate to conventional and an appearance policy such as the one operated by the defendants is not discriminatory albeit it applies different rules to girls than for boys.
>
> (para 60)

Putting aside the circularity of this argument – the judge overlooks the impact of dress codes on what is considered conventional – what is clear here is the extent to which enforcing conventionality in effect becomes an additional legitimate aim of dress codes.

Children's rights – as an autonomy right – are almost totally absent from the cases. In the *Ballyclare* case, the fact that the school council had been consulted was held to be significant (para 4, 8, 9, 27). The judge referred to both the requirements in Article 12 of the United Nations Convention on the Rights of the Child, which emphasise listening to children, and the importance of school councils as vehicles or mechanisms whereby a policy can be changed: "[I]t is necessary to establish that there is capacity for review of the [dress] code and there is capacity for the voice of the child to be heard [...]" (para 30). Despite noting the Children's Commissioner's criticisms of the procedures in that school, it had no effect on the decision (para 31). While a particular case, it reflects an increasing tendency whereby formal acceptance of the rhetoric about the importance of listening to children is translated into law in a way that becomes procedural and formalistic and easily marginalised (Fortin 2009). In the specific context of schools, this demonstrates a tension between the potential accountability provided by school councils and their functioning as a form of soft governance whereby they become a vehicle for legitimising 'conventionality' (Gillies 2011). Injunctions to hear children and empower them through participatory processes and, at the same time, to effectively restrict their choices can be seen as contradictory. To do so overlooks the inclusion of contemporary childhood in the shift toward self-governance. Through this lens, it is possible to make sense of the fact that girls can access contraception under the age of 16 while being prevented from adopting a particular hairstyle. While starkly contradictory in terms of respecting bodily autonomy, to the extent that contraception precludes the presence of a pregnant girl in the classroom and coheres with government aims to reduce teenage pregnancy, accessing contraception and adhering to school 'hairstyle' codes both represent 'responsible' decisions (Monk 2002). Children in contemporary Britain, consequently, have an active role to play in ensuring that childhood remains in place.

Conclusion

'Children's rights' may have come of age in contemporary Britain, and there may be much to celebrate as a result, but it is important to recognise the inherent contradictions. These come to the fore in the context of contests about school dress, for what is evident are deep-seated tensions between autonomy rights, emphasising individual freedom and welfare rights, premised on perceived benefits and risks of codes and certain clothing. There is a degree of triviality; it, perhaps, does not actually matter too much what children wear in school. However, the aim here has been to demonstrate why and how it matters if one is interested in understanding contemporary British childhood. Underlying the welfare- and autonomy-based arguments about what real children should wear and what rules about clothing can achieve are a complex array of deeper assumptions and calculations. In education, the contestation is a window into and visual representation of political debates about the perceived benefits of privatised education and a pedagogic shift from perceived permissiveness to uniformed standards. More widely, the trends and contests highlight the shifts in long-established and new concerns and fears, such as sexualisation, radicalisation and 'irresponsible' parenting. Taking school dress seriously does not reveal contemporary childhood, but it is a method for unmasking some of the conditions of the terms of its contestation, persistence and resilience as a site of political imaginations.

References

Ball, Stephen. 1994. *Education Reform: A Critical and Post-Structural Approach*. Philadelphia, PA: Open University Press.
———. 2008. *The Education Debate*. Bristol: Policy Press.

Bragg, Sara. 2012. "Dockside Tarts and Modesty Boards: A Review of Recent Policy on Sexualisation." *Children and Society* 26 (5): 406–14.

Brown, Wendy. 1995. *States of Injury*. Princeton, NJ: Princeton University Press.

Carney, Damien, and Adele Sinclair. 2006. "School Uniform Revisited: Procedure, Pressure and Equality." *Education and the Law* 18 (2–3): 131–48.

Coppock, Vicki, and Mark McGovern. 2014. "'Dangerous Minds'? Deconstructing Counter-Terrorism Discourse, Radicalisation and the 'Psychological Vulnerability' of Muslim Children and Young People in Britain." *Children & Society* 28: 242–56.

Davidson, Alexander. 1990. *Blazers, Badges and Boaters: Pictorial History of School Uniform*. Hants: Scope International.

DfEE. 1999. Social Inclusion: Pupil Support (DfEE Circular 10/99).

———. 2000. *Exclusion from School: Changes to the Guidance*. (4 August 2000) HMSO.

DfE. 2011. *Letting Children be Children*. London: Department for Education.

———. 2013. *School Uniform. Guidance for Governing Bodies, School Leaders, School Staff and Local Authorities*. London: Department for Education.

———. 2015. *Cost of School Uniform*. London: Department for Education.

Dorling, Danny. 2015. *Injustice: Why Social Inequality Still Persists*. Bristol: Policy Press.

Dussel, Inés. 2001. "School Uniforms and the Disciplining of Appearances: Towards a Comparative History of the Regulation of Bodies in Early Modern France, Argentina, and the United States." PhD diss., University of Wisconsin-Madison.

Eekelaar, John. 1991. "Parental Responsibility: State of Nature or Nature of the State?" *Journal of Social Welfare and Family Law* 3 (1): 37–50.

———. 1994. "The Interests of the Child and the Child's Wishes." *International Journal of Law Policy and the Family* 8 (1): 42–61.

Fortin, Jane. 2009. *Children's Rights and the Developing Law*. 3rd ed. Cambridge: Cambridge University Press.

Fortismere School. 2017. "Dress Code Policy." Accessed 13 February 2017. www.fortismere.haringey.sch.uk/_files/documents/Our%20school/5D828D-B4EC8C28F8817B280BED8AA25E.pdf.

Gewirtz, Paul. 1996. "Narrative and Rhetoric in the Law." In *Law's Stories*, edited by Peter Brooks and Paul Gewirtz, 2–13. London: Yale University Press.

Gillies, Val. 2011. "Social and Emotional Pedagogies: Critiquing the New Orthodoxy of Emotion in Classroom Behaviour Management." *British Journal of Sociology of Education* 32 (2): 185–202.

Gillies, Val, and Rosalind Edwards. 2011. "Clients or Consumers, Commonplace or Pioneers? Navigating the Contemporary Class Politics of Family, Parenting Skills and Education." *Ethics and Education* 6 (2): 141–54.

GOV.UK. 2016. "School Uniform." Accessed 12 February 2017. www.gov.uk/school-uniform.

Griffiths, Sian. 2016. "Let Boys Wear Dresses, Head Teacher Tells Parents." *The Sunday Times*, February 21. Accessed 12 February 2017. www.thesundaytimes.co.uk/sto/news/uk_news/Education/article1670412.ece.

Hampstead School. 2016. "Policies." Accessed 12 February 2017. www.hampsteadschool.org.uk.

Harris, Neville. 2007. *Education, Law and Diversity*. Oxford: Hart.
———. 2012. "Local Authorities and the Accountability Gap in a Fragmenting Schools System." *Modern Law Review* 75 (4): 511–46.
Hawkes, Steve. 2009. "Tesco Tops Class with £3.75 Uniform." *The Sun*, June 12, 2009. Accessed 12 February 2017. www.thesun.co.uk/sol/homepage/news/money/2476817/Tesco-tops-class-with-375-uniform.html.
Howard, Erica. 2011. "Bans on the Wearing of Religious Symbols in British Schools: A Violation of the Right to Non-Discrimination." *Religion and Human Rights* 6 (2): 127–49.
Jones, Ken. 2003. *Education in Britain: 1944 to the Present*. Cambridge: Polity Press.
The Labour Party. 2010. *The Labour Party Manifesto: A Future Fair for All*. London: Labour Party.
Latour, Bruno. 2002. "What Is Iconoclash?" In *Iconoclash, Beyond the Image-Wars in Science, Religion and Art*, edited by Peter Weibel and Bruno Latour, 14–37. Cambridge, MA: MIT Press.
Lesnik-Oberstein, Karín, ed. 2006. *The Last Taboo: Women and Body Hair*. Manchester: Manchester University Press.
2011. "Introduction: Voice, Agency and the Child." In *Children in Culture, Revisited: Further Approaches to Childhood*, edited by Karín Lesnik-Oberstein, 1–17. Basingstoke: Palgrave.
Lyon, Dawn, and Debora Spini. 2004. "Unveiling the Headscarf Debate." *Feminist Legal Studies* 12 (3): 333–45.
Marshall, Jill. 2008. "Conditions for Freedom? European Human Rights Law and the Islamic Headscarf Debate." *Human Rights Quarterly* 30: 631–54.
McDonald, Laura Zahra. 2011. "Securing Identities, Resisting Terror: Muslim Youth Work in the UK and Its Implications for Security." *Religion, State and Society* 39 (2–3): 177–89.
McGoldrick, Dominic. 2006. *Human Rights and Religion: The Islamic Headscarf Debate in Europe*. Oxford: Hart.
MINTEL. 2010. "Schoolwear – UK." Accessed Feburary 13 2017. http://academic.mintel.com/display/479952/#.
Monk, Daniel. 2001. "New Guidance/Old Problems: Recent Developments in Sex Education." *Journal of Social Welfare and Family Law* 23 (3): 271–91.
———. 2002. "Children's Rights in Education: Making Sense of Contradictions". *Child and Family Law Quarterly* 14 (1): 45–56.
———. 2005. "(Re)constructing the Head Teacher: Legal Narratives and the Politics of School Exclusions." *Journal of Law and Society* 32 (3): 399–423.
———. 2011. "Challenging Homophobic Bullying in Schools: The Politics of Progress." *International Journal of Law in Context* 7 (2): 181–207.
Moran, Leslie. 2012. "Legal Studies after the Cultural Turn: A Case Study of Judicial Research." In *Social Research after the Cultural Turn*, edited by Sasha Roseneil and Stephen Frosh, 124–33. Basingstoke: Palgrave.
Morrow, Virgina, and Mayell Berry. 2009. "What Is Wrong with Children's Wellbeing in the UK? Questions of Meaning and Measurement." *Journal of Social Welfare and Family Law* 31 (3): 213–25.
Murray, Patrick Eoghan. 2013. "Constitutional Challenges to Gender-Restrictive School Dress Codes in the Ninth Circuit." *The Modern American* 8: 18–28.
Norrie, Alan. 2005. *Law and the Beautiful Soul*. Abingdon: Routledge.

Office of the Children's Commissioner. 2012. *They Never Give up on You: School Exclusions Inquiry*. London: Office of the Children's Commissioner.
———. 2013. *Always Someone Else's Problem: Report on Illegal Exclusions*. London: Office of the Children's Commissioner.
Office of Fair Trading. 2012. *Supply of School Uniforms*. OFT.
Parton, Nigel. 2014. *The Politics of Child Protection: Contemporary Developments and Future Directions*. Houndsmills: Palgrave.
Patterson, Steve. 2015. "Why Progressives Are Wrong to Argue Against Cultural Appropriation." Accessed February 12 2017. http://observer.com/2015/11/why-progressives-are-wrong-to-argue-against-cultural-appropriation/.
Pilcher, Jane. 2014. "The Politics of Children's Clothing." In *Thatcher's Grandchildren?*, edited by Stephen Wagg and Jane Pilcher, 258–74. Basingstoke: Palgrave.
Piper, Christine. 2000. "Historical Constructions of Childhood Innocence: Removing Sexuality." In *Of Innocence and Autonomy: Children, Sex and Human Rights*, edited by Eric Heinze and Katherine O'Donovan, 26–45. Aldershot: Ashgate.
Raby, Rebecca. 2010. "'Tank Tops Are Ok but I Don't Want to See Her Thong' Girls' Engagements with Secondary School Dress Codes." *Youth Society* 41 (3): 333–56.
Reece, Helen. 2009. "The Degradation of Parental Responsibility." In *Responsible Parents and Parental Responsibility*, edited by Rebecca Probert, Stephen Gilmore and Jonathan Herring, 85–102. Oxford: Hart.
Revell, Phil. 2001. "Hair Today". *The Guardian*, November 6.
Robson, Ruthann. 2013. *Dressing Constitutionally*. Cambridge: Cambridge University Press.
Rudd, David. 2014. "A Coming or Going of Age? Children's Literature at the Turn of the Twenty-First Century." In *Thatcher's Grandchildren?*, edited by Stephen Wagg and Jane Pilcher, 118–39. Basingstoke: Palgrave.
Smith, Rhona. 2007. "Unveiling a Role for the EU? The Headscarf Controversy in European Schools." *Education and the Law* 19 (2) 111–30.
Stanley, Tony, and Surinder Guru. 2015. "Childhood Radicalisation Risk: An Emerging Practice Issue." *Practice: Social Work in Action* 27 (5): 353–66.
Wagg, Stephen. 2014. "Whiteboard Jungle: Schooling, Culture War and the Market at the Turn of the Twenty-First Century." In *Thatcher's Grandchildren?*, edited by Stephen Wagg and Jane Pilcher, 179–203, Basingstoke: Palgrave.
Wintemute, Robert. 1997. "Recognising New Kinds of Direct Sex Discrimination: Transsexualism, Sexual Orientation and Dress Codes." *The Modern Law Review* 60: 334–59.

13 The Recognition and Distribution of Children's Agency in the UK

Michael Wyness

Introduction

Since the 1990s, there has been an important shift within sociology from viewing children as having a dependent and subordinate social status to recasting them as social agents with the capacity to make a difference. Current theoretical debate over the nature of children's agency within the sociology of childhood in some respects confirms the status of the concept as part of research orthodoxy, a taken-for-granted feature and starting point for researching children and childhood (Valentine 2011; White and Choudhury 2007). Agency emphasises that "children are not simply beings, they are significant doings. They are actors, authors, authorities and agents. They make a difference to the world we live in" (Oswell 2013, 3). In research terms, children's agency has achieved a level of recognition; we can borrow the 'idiom of recognition' and assert the legitimacy of children as social agents (Fraser 2000). In this chapter, I want to explore this recognition of children's agency in a broader political context within contemporary Britain. To what extent is this theoretical notion of children's agency an integral feature of the roles and expectations of children and childhood within the public realm? In the first part of the chapter, I locate agency within the shift from a modern to a more contemporary twenty-first century conception of childhood and explore this conception of childhood in terms of UK social policy relating to children.

In the second half of the chapter, I examine a potential challenge to the recognition of children's agency within this broader context. If agency becomes a critical feature of a contemporary British childhood, then we would expect it to make considerable material and social differences to all children's lives. However, research has tended to focus on children's agency as an end rather than a means to an end. As Alan Prout (2000, 16) points out "the observation that children can exercise agency should be a point of analytical embarkation rather than a terminus". An emphasis on ontology and children's identities would seem to obscure questions around the distribution of agency, in particular, the extent to which the distribution of agency gives some children advantages over other children.

The issue of distribution generates questions on the groups of children that are likely to benefit from the public recognition of agency. Moreover, if we explore the relationship between different groups of children and the deployment of agency, we can identify different conceptions of agency. I focus on differences between children in the UK rather than the idea of children as a social minority group in search of recognition. In doing so, I switch attention to the distribution of agency. I take up Nancy Fraser's (2000) call to focus on socio-economic differences and explore this distribution in social class terms. I discuss the different ways that middle-class and working-class children deploy their agency that reinforces their class positions. A particular dominant institutional form of agency unwittingly puts more affluent children at an advantage and can further alienate working-class children and their families from the social and cultural mainstream. However, this is not the last word on the distribution of agency. In the final section, I touch on recent work within the sociology of childhood that identifies an alternative model of agency, a more embedded version that has limited public recognition. Nevertheless, this form of agency is likely to emerge within more complex family networks, arguably typifying a range of material and emotional roles that children take on, particularly, within contexts of socio-economic poverty.

Changing Conceptions of Childhood and the Recognition of Agency

Throughout most of the twentieth century, a modernist conception of childhood dominated. Harry Hendrick (1997) in his historical analysis of British childhoods talks about this in terms of the 'welfare' and 'schooled' child. Welfare structures developed in many Western countries throughout the first half of the twentieth century providinged legal and social frameworks within which children and their nuclear families were entitled to material support and protection. Mass compulsory schooling was introduced in Britain in the 1870s, much later than in other Western countries, with working-class children not fully incorporated into the education system until the 1902 Education Act. The education system produced sophisticated forms of moral, social and educational regulation for children. Along with the rising popularity of the bourgeois nuclear family, children were repositioned as incompetents and dependents. That is, children's social and economic learning and activities located within the home, the street and the work place were eschewed in favour of mass compulsory schooling where children were incrementally introduced to a moral, spiritual and technical curriculum. Moreover, the individual child was impelled along moral and social pathways before exposure to the public world of politics and economics.

As children gradually become more social within the world, they were carefully incorporated into decision-making processes over their welfare and development. This became a powerful Western and latterly global standpoint within which children and families were regulated (Prout 2000).

A later twenty-first century model of childhood offers a nuanced version of the modernist form. One crucial difference between the two models is the heightened role that children's agency plays with respect to the later version. The earlier modernist period constructed the child as a dependent, with parents, educators and policymakers defining what was in child's 'best interests'. In the later version, the rights and participation political agendas underpin the view that children have a capacity to play a formative role within their own lives and the lives of those around them. There is now more recognition that children participate within a wider range of fields, including local politics (Cockburn and Cleaver 2009), health care provision (Alderson 2008), schools (Fielding 2007) and in social care settings (Kirby and Gibbs 2006).

If we turn to the policy and institutional realm where children and families encounter the state, there is a shift in children's status. At the same time, there is some ambiguity as to whether this shift presages more recognition for children's agency. The modernist conception of childhood incorporates the child as a legal dependent subsumed within the private realm of family (Wyness 2014). Parents had proprietorial interests in their child's welfare; parents would speak on their behalf when they were exposed to agencies of the state (Dingwall, Eekelaar and Murray 1995). Agency here was attributed to either the parents or the professionals with children's capacities hidden and their voices muted. In the latter decade of the twentieth century, children's legal status changed with the 'welfare of the child' rather than proprietorial interests of parents taking precedence. Children were to become the main focus for practitioners and their welfare defined as paramount. The 1989 Children Act in England and Wales and the 1995 Scottish Children Act made 'paramountcy' a dominant principle repositioning children outside of the family in legal and institutional terms as independent entities. This was reinforced globally when the UK signed up for the United Nations Convention on the Rights of the Child (CRC) in 1990 where children were redefined as rights holding individuals (UN 1989).

While this shifted the emphasis away from the family towards the child, in one sense this did little to strengthen children's agency. In focusing on the concept of children's welfare at international and national levels, the emphasis has been on adults and institutions taking responsibility for this. One recurring refrain within the policy realm in the UK over the past two decades has been the concept of 'parental responsibility'. Children's 'separate' status means that parents are less likely to be recognised as having proprietorial relations with their children.

Nevertheless, children's dependence is emphasised in the way that social policy focuses on the parent as the responsible agent ensuring that children follow appropriate moral and social trajectories. The state in effect delegates the welfare of children to parents: parents are held morally and socially responsible for their children. The concept of responsibility has been invoked within a number of different realms including child protection and care, education and criminal justice (Hollingworth 2007). For example, the issue of truancy is periodically covered by the media in the UK with parents being targeted for their inability to ensure their children attend school (Curtis 2009). The legal position here goes back to the 1944 Education Act, where parents rather than children are held legally responsible for children's school attendance.

While the concept of parental responsibility appears to be at odds with children's agency, policy relating to children in the UK has also promoted the idea that children have the capacity to take part in consultations that hitherto involved only parents and professionals. In returning to the 1989 Children Act, professionals working with children have to "ascertain their wishes and feelings", and the more recent 2004 Act reinforces the importance of consulting with children (England and Wales). Similarly, in Scotland children's hearing panels emphasise the importance of adult members of panels consulting children (Vis and Thomas 2009). The CRC offers a similar space for children. Articles 12 and 13 of the convention introduce a more discursive dimension to children's wellbeing, children have 'voice' based rights that in theory give them opportunities to articulate their interests in a number of different ways. It is generally accepted that CRC provides the moral and political impetus to governments in promoting ways in which children can have a voice in arrangements that affect them. Research has questioned the range and efficacy of this consultation (Parton 2006; Vis and Thomas 2009). Nevertheless, policy at global and national levels has created a framework within which children's agency has become more visible.

Importantly, social policy challenges the assumed bipartite relationship between parents and the state in matters concerning children. The latter are now in a position to assume a third-party status that compromises and complicates assumed relations within the family. While the family was opened up to more public scrutiny in the 1970s due to the influence of feminism, the recognition of children's demands and those working on behalf of children have generated considerable debate about the role that children now play. Research has explored the different ways in which child protection experts work with children in raising their voices (Holland et al. 2005). One major issue confronting professionals is how to respect children's agency within the family where there is an increased risk of abuse and where children's voices are likely to be muted. Despite children's legal status as rights holders, professionals and researchers continue to identify difficulties 'separating' children within their families. In tackling this issue, one approach used by professionals has been to try to increase the dialogue between children and their parents through family group conferences (Dalrymple 2002; Holland et al. 2005). The work of Sally Holland et al. (2005) is important here as children were physically present at these conferences. Formerly, children were usually absent from negotiations between parents and professionals over their welfare. Holland and her colleagues observed a more common practice within social work: family group conferences were open forums within which children, as well as parents and social workers, were involved in discussions on a range of issues and problems. While the agenda-setting powers of the state and the social worker as 'expert' perspective were both evident, the authors note the attempts of the social workers to promote children's participation within these forums, particularly children whom hitherto had little sense of voice within their families. Children were in a position to exercise some agency in the way that they talked about their feelings and requested more input into domestic decision-making processes.

Within an educational context, there are other possibilities for children to play a third party role. While schools have been slow to pick up on children's agency and voice, there is now a surfeit of initiatives promoting student or pupil voice (Fielding 2007). The expectation is still that parents speak on behalf of children when families come into contact with schools. Nevertheless, there are some examples of children's involvement extending communication networks across families and schools. For example, the notion of a partnership or a more contractual relationship between home and school has created space for children to participate. Research on home–school relations picks up on the complexity of this tripartite relationship (Beveridge 2004). There is now an expectation that children as well as parents are involved with written communication between home and school in relation to activities that take place in the classroom and more formal reports. It is now fairly routine in UK schools for children as well as parents and teachers to 'contract into' schooling at the beginning of every school year. Children are expected to sign declarations drafted by the school around the commitments that all three parties make toward their schooling. There is little consensus between school staff and parents over the presence of children at meetings involving parents and staff. However, where children are involved in meetings with parents and teachers, they are sometimes in a position to strengthen their points of view and provide balance in any possible disagreements that parents and teachers might have (Beveridge 2004).

The Social Distribution of Agency

The current paradigm in researching children and childhood is rooted in the view that children are assumed to have agency (James and Prout 1997). Children are now viewed as research subjects and collaborators.

They are able to reflect on their lives and participate at various levels in the research process (Christensen and James 2008). Moreover, I have argued that there are trends within the political and institutional realm that alongside the academic field promote the recognition of children as a social minority group with human rights and social capacities to make a difference. Fraser (2000) discusses the role of social and political movements globally from the latter part of the twentieth century in terms of the 'reification of identity politics' – various minority groups have contested their right to be recognised as legitimate cultural forces with members asserting their individual rights to self-expression. Recognition according to Fraser (2000) has become the dominant focus for political struggle rather than issues relating to economic distribution. Issues of cultural identity have overshadowed movements that focus on addressing socio-economic inequalities. In applying this approach to the status of children, we could argue that research and policy have tended to assert the social positions of children, with agency an assumed positive collective good.

In turning to the distribution of agency, on the other hand, I am drawing on Fraser's (2000) distinction between recognition and distribution. The emphasis on establishing children *per se* as an integral force and group within society has tended to overshadow the differences within the child population, how this newfound status affects different groups of children and whether more conventional socio-economic differences are reinforced, albeit unwittingly through the promotion of agency. In the following section, I want to explore this with reference to two different conceptual forms of agency, *institutional* and *embedded* forms. The institutional form refers to a highly regulated discursive form of agency, recognised as a legitimate form in social and political terms. The political emphasis here is on the way that policy and practice recognise the agency of all children. Nevertheless, my analysis identifies the way that the institutional form reinforces socio-economic differences between different 'classes' of children favouring middle-class children at the expense of their working-class counterparts.[1] At the same time, research within the sociology of childhood identifies embedded forms of agency, relatively hidden practices found within working-class families that highlight children's capacities.

The Institutionalisation of Agency

The institutionalisation of agency arises out of political and policy arrangements discussed earlier that generate powerful expectations among child professionals as to the meaning of children's agency. The emphasis here is on the idea of children having a voice. Children have some involvement in decision-making processes, the precise nature of this involvement is determined by the demands of the contexts within which children are located. With reference to the third-party role of children, voice is also apparent through the disaggregation of children from families as rights holders. What might the implications be for children and families from different socio-economic backgrounds of an emphasis on voice and consultation? In referring back to the work of Holland et al. (2005) on family group conferences, there was a commitment among the professionals to hear children's voices along with those of their parents. Children reported being able to articulate their interests at these conferences. Holland et al. (2005) claim that family group conferences had beneficial effects on family relations. Follow-up interviews with participants six months later found that they felt more confident of having a voice in family affairs. At the same time, the conferences were heavily institutionalised, with professionals structuring the agendas and the discussions. While the professionals took account of the level of resources in each family, the demands made by professionals to continue the 'democratic' dialogue of the conference sometimes felt heavy handed. For example, in the conferences the social workers made lists of agreed areas and topics with the families, and these were to be taken away by the families to be acted upon in their own private time. There is also the suggestion that on occasion the promotion of children's agency by professionals may be at the cost of parents, which could potentially lead to more conflict within the families. For some voice is part of a zero-sum struggle with the creation of spaces for children's voices interpreted by parents as a challenge to their sense of authority. We can only speculate here: the move towards more democratic relations where children have stronger voices is more difficult to develop in poorer families.

The work of earlier Marxist theorists may be useful in identifying class differences in the distribution of children's agency. Basil Bernstein's (1971) work on communication structures in families is useful here. Where parents are struggling with institutionalised versions of agency, there may be evidence of communication structures found within *position-oriented* families. The generational order is more hierarchical with positions and roles relatively fixed; parents have more overt power and authority. There is limited discursive space to reason and negotiate between the generations: parents tend to assert their power and authority over their children through imperative commands and language that offers fewer opportunities for dialogue with children. This is contrasted with a more middle-class discursive model, *the person-oriented* family, with more fluidity between the generations, personalities being as important as generational positions. Middle-class parents are more likely to reason with their children and less likely to insist that their generational status is sufficient to engender compliance from their children. Within the context of the former, the distribution of agency across generations is probably limited; parents are more likely to view the promotion of children's voices as a form of intrusion.

Annette Lareau (2011) expands on this work by distinguishing among the dynamics, language and atmosphere found in 'lower-' and middle-class families. Children from the latter are viewed as the projects of parents through forms of *concerted cultivation*. Children grow up within a much more rational and verbal context. Here, there is a much stronger sense of their entitlements among children to a voice and an opinion. Agency here is discursive and fluid with the home environment much more open to reflection and debate. Lower- or working-class families, on the other hand, are typified by the *accomplishment of natural growth*. Parents' childcare strategies here revolve around stressing children's emotional and social wellbeing with their intellectual growth being left more to fate or more concretely seen as the responsibility of the school teacher. Lareau's (2011) conceptualisation of class differences comes close to Gillian Evans's (2006) ethnographic study of working-class life in South London. Here the comparison is between the author's 'concerted cultivation' approach to her own children's lives and the working-class mothers in her study. In the latter case, parenting revolved around children's physical and emotional care. The emphasis on 'natural growth' was important here with parents having little commitment to intervening in their children's lives in order to improve their life chances. A combination of material disadvantages and a belief that their children's intellectual growth was genetically pre-ordained rendered attempts at parental intervention both challenging and futile. There is much less dialogue and reasoning here and therefore fewer opportunities for children to display more legitimate institutionalised forms of agency.

There are two sets of implications. First, the distribution of agency exacerbates tensions that already exist within families. Children's agency as a form of consultation is less likely to be practiced within the home or potentially aggravates fairly well-established positions within the family. Second, and more generally, there is a culture clash between middle-class professional values and the more traditional working-class values with the former disrupting the latter. Parents already known to and working with the state are likely to view children's agency in more negative terms as another set of criteria against which they can be judged.

An institutionalised version of agency also operates within a school context. The form of agency that is developed and encouraged within the middle-class home allows children to slot into school life without too many problems. Schools thus become an important means of social reproduction with middle-class parents ensuring their children's class positions are maintained, if not enhanced, through the connections they make with the schools and the teachers (Bourdieu 1984). There is, as it were, a more general expectation in schools in both state and private sectors that parents are involved in the concerted cultivation of their children (Ball 2003). Working-class children and their parents have more difficulties adjusting to these expectations of the discursive child.

In Pierre Bourdieu's terms, working-class children lack the ability to generate cultural capital to connect with the dominant middle-class culture found within state schools (Bourdieu and Wacquant 1992). If we address agency and social class in terms of schooling and participatory initiatives directed at children rather than families, then we potentially have similar issues facing working-class children as opposed to middle-class children.

In focusing on school structures, children from poorer backgrounds are less likely to connect with participatory initiatives in school than their more affluent counterparts. My recent research on the development of agency through participatory work in English secondary schools and in local communities suggests that schools tended to focus on confident articulate and high-achieving children who are already likely to be involved in a range of initiatives in school, referred to by one child participant as the "usual school child" (Wyness 2009, 546).

These children were familiar with the school norms and structures and immersed in the culture of the school. Moreover, particular forms of participation in school, for example, membership of a school council, was seen by one respondent as an opportunity for more affluent children to display their agency. This in turn had a negative effect on the ability of less educationally able children to participate. As one adult involved in the setting up of a municipal council for children stated, "it's just another opportunity for young people's involvement has gone. It's being taken up by somebody who's already got an avenue to make their voice heard" (547). In these terms, voice and, by implication, agency are class based. The claim here is that middle-class and academically oriented students tend to gravitate toward school councils, arguably those children least likely to need political representation (Giroux 1989, 199). Children who were struggling with their schooling, in terms of learning or behaviour, and those children intermittently outside of the school system, those excluded from schools, were likely to see attempts at introducing greater pupil voice in school as further alienating them from school. For these children, the processes that precede the setting up of school councils and the election or selection of school councillors were likely to be viewed as obstacles to their involvement. This further reduced their capacity to participate and develop the cultural capital required to succeed within the school system (Bourdieu 1984).

Embedded Agency

The distribution of agency here is about a particular institutional form connecting with the lifeworlds of middle-class children, at the same time reinforcing pre-existing advantages in terms of their educational life chances. Working-class children, on the other hand, struggle to connect with these more discursive forms. These are forms of agency that have been shaped through policy and professional practice and in some cases have limited purchase within families where the involvement of children is material, emotional and embodied. Research suggests that families in general have become more discursive, more democratic (Williams and Williams 2005). At the same time, work within childhood studies has also identified different forms of agency where children have become increasingly more assertive through the responsibilities that they have had to assume (Mayall 2002). Agency here emerges from routine ongoing commitments and relations with others where emotional investments are made. Children's agency here is embedded in these routine practices.

While the family has long been viewed as a relatively closed social institution with the concept of family privacy obscuring the agency that children deploy, in recent years there has been a move towards greater understanding of children's multiple roles within families both in social and sociological terms. Two factors are crucial: the opening up to institutional and public scrutiny of families referred to earlier, particularly working-class families, and major restructuring of families. If we focus on the latter, the restructuring of family in the UK since the 1970s has opened up possibilities for viewing children in more agentic terms. A longstanding increase in the number of children having to routinely negotiate different households as their parents separate and divorce would suggest a more active involvement in family routines and the deployment of a range of forms of embedded agency. Just under a quarter of UK children have experience with parental separation and divorce (ONS 2014). There is here a move toward breaking the link between biological and social parenting, with lone-parent families, stepfamilies and gay families emerging out of adults and children making multiple transitions in the life course. Family structure has become more diverse and complicated, generating familial networks within which children are immersed.

The research on the effects of divorce on children in recent years has focused more on concepts such as resilience that take a more positive view on the outcomes for children. Children are depicted as having the capacity to manage divorce by taking on family responsibilities when a father moves out of the family home (Hetherington 2003). Children also adjust to new family forms as they move from a relatively stable lone-parent family situation to a stepfamily. Stepfamilies have become a more common feature of children's social landscape in the UK with 11 per cent of all children now living in stepfamilies (ONS 2014). Many of these children are likely to experience further disruptions as these new family formations break down (Flowerdew and Neale 2003). Nevertheless, the consistent rise over the past generation or so in the numbers of children having to move from a biological nuclear family to a lone-parent family and then into a stepfamily certainly exercises children's capacities to manage new family situations, sometimes with great rapidity. There is no necessary relationship between social class and family here. However, poverty is one consequence of fragmented families. Lone mothers in particular are likely to experience a substantial drop in income due to the separation of the family from the male breadwinner, exacerbating what some have referred to as the feminisation of poverty (Chant 2007). Where children are having to negotiate multiple family transitions, working-class families have fewer resources and are more likely to rely on children to help out within families. In the absence of paid professional childcare, parents are more likely to rely on older children to take on caring responsibilities for younger siblings.

Berry Mayall's (2002) research on working-class children's family life offers an illustration of this trend in highlighting the work that they routinely carry out within multi-family settings. Interviews with groups of girls aged between 9 and 14 living in London revealed that they had to negotiate a number of factors, the birth of younger siblings whose fathers are different from theirs, mothers struggling with ill health and poverty and households where their separated fathers live. Children's agency here is embedded and stretched across a range of family and household settings. The girls are able to reflect on the different ways that they relate to their parents, siblings and friends in negotiating a range of quite diverse circumstances. One 12-year-old interviewee, Sandra, had a close relationship with her mother. In the absence of her father within the household, she spent a lot of time helping her mother by looking after her younger siblings. Sandra reports on the birth of her youngest sibling and the difficulties that her mother experienced during the labour. Sandra was both knowledgeable about the process of giving birth and her mother's condition (having an emergency Caesarean due to pre-eclampsia). She was also able to think through the implications of her new sibling for her relationship with her mother and able to reflect more broadly on the implications of having another child within her family (Mayall 2002, 90–4).

If we focus more specifically on the issue of poverty, it is evident that children are able to play prominent roles within their families. This is particularly pertinent within a country that has one of the highest levels of child poverty within Europe, with just over a quarter of all children defined as being in poverty (Barnardo's 2016). Poverty has a major impact on excluding children in school and more broadly within society. Tess Ridge (2006) refers to the ways that children talk about being excluded from 'normal' things including school trips, membership of clubs, access to leisure facilities and participation as consumers. Poverty also makes it difficult for children to participate with their peers in a range of leisure activities due to the prohibitive cost of these activities. Thus, poverty can have an isolating experience with children in school being bullied by their peers and made to feel different and inferior. In one sense, then, we can say that this has implications for children's agency, if we associate agency with children's ability to participate and voice their concerns. The general lack of resources and opportunities both to participate and to challenge obstacles to their participation restricts children's agency (Ridge 2006).

However, a more embedded conception of agency is about children's capacity to make a difference to their circumstances and those around them. At another level, children in poverty draw on their agency in mitigating a lack of social and political participation, which directly confronts more discursive forms of agency. Thus, agency can operate in the absence of participation. Children are able to mediate the effects of poverty on themselves and their families in a number of ways. First, there are the demands made on families by schools; these can lead to what Ridge (2006, 31) calls children's "self-denial of need". Children conceal the need to replace school uniforms by carefully hiding their old and worn uniforms from their parent. They are less likely to pass on requests to parents for resources needed from school. They are also less likely to tell parents that they are being bullied because of the way they look or quite simply due to their poverty. In effect, children are trying to protect parents from the guilt and embarrassment of being poor. Second, children take on part-time work in order to offer their parents some financial respite from the demands of consumerism (Leonard 2004). Thus, the conventional view of children's part-time work, providing them with non-essential money and having socialising functions, is challenged in the way that children contribute to the domestic economy and taking the pressure off parents to provide them with consumer goods that keep them in line with their peers.

In some respects, we have generated two distinctive forms of agency: first, an institutionalised form that emphasises children's voices and their capacity to be consulted. The child is addressed as an individual project with some degree of autonomy and space within which he or she is able to participate at various levels of decision-making. A second model of agency in some respects eschews issues of autonomy with voice a more embedded feature of routine material activities. There is an important relational dimension. As Peter Moss and Pat Petrie argue (2002, 143), "the child is not regarded as an autonomous and detached subject, but as living in networks of relationships, involving both children and adults". Research has identified this more relational work in professional contexts with younger children (Moss and Petrie 2002). We can find examples of this in the Reggio Emilio schools in Northern Italy, where the emphasis is on democratic engagement rather than child empowerment (Ghirotto and Mazzoni 2013). However, relational forms of agency are more likely to emerge in and through families where children have to negotiate increasingly complicated networks of relationships.

I have argued that the institutional form typifies attempts by the state and various professionals to engage with children in highly regulated ways. These are practices that incorporate children into the norms and culture of professional settings. These forms of discursive agency are more likely to incorporate middle-class children. Arguably, institutional forms of agency have the opposite effect on working-class children and their families, reinforcing cultural and social differences between working-class children and state structures.

As I have argued, more material and embedded forms of agency are practiced in relatively private and hidden contexts. These are usually family- and peer-based networks of relations where there are expectations that children take on tasks and responsibilities that help to alleviate challenging social and economic circumstances. Recent research within the sociology of childhood has uncovered the various ways in which these forms of agency are immersed in daily family routines. These practices are often hidden from public purview. Interestingly, where they come to public attention, the issue is potentially one of misrecognition. Children's caring responsibilities are sometimes viewed in more negative terms as safeguarding issues for policymakers and professionals (Becker 2007). While voluntary agencies have taken a more sympathetic approach to 'young carers' or 'child carers', there is still a sense that children here are overburdened with material responsibilities, with various state agencies converging on the child carer as a social problem. In some respects, despite the resilience and capacity demonstrated by working-class children through their work within the family, the state still tends to categorise the child with material responsibilities as a problem. Children's embedded agency in the UK still has an ambiguous social and political status.

Conclusion

In this chapter, I have focused on the policy domain and the partial recognition of children's agency. Within the practices of the child-related professional, there has been a much stronger emphasis on the independent voices of children. At a political level, there has been the recasting of links between state and family as a more complex network of relations among parents, child professionals and children. The shift to a more tripartite arrangement offers the potential for children to play more formative roles in mediating between family and state. In the second part of the chapter, the focus switched from more general claims about children's agency to an analysis of how agency is distributed across the child population. While there is a degree of recognition of children's agency at a general political level, the diversity of childhood, the distinctive economic, social and political contexts within which children live, generate distinctive modes of agency. A number of social dimensions differentiate the child population, and in the chapter I have focused on social class. In very crude terms, social inequality as defined by socio-economic criteria helps to shape the quantity and quality of agency with which children are able to deploy. Agency is thus unevenly distributed across the child population in contemporary Britain. Two points are critical here. First, there are legitimate and socially sanctioned forms of children's agency, particularly within UK schools and child protection contexts. The framing of agency this way can lead to the misrecognition of children's activities outside of this dominant discursive frame. Children who struggle with the rules and norms of schools are not only likely to be socially excluded from the school system, they may openly reject the social and moral structures that underpin schools and thus initiatives that promote the idea of children's agency. These activities are less likely to be recognised in terms of children's agency. Moreover, the work that children do within the home similarly lacks recognition, particularly where domestic and care responsibilities are said to compromise their legitimate school 'responsibilities'. Second, despite the difficulties that children might face due to their class position, they are still capable of exercising their agency in the interests of themselves, their families and peers. By reframing agency in embedded and relational terms, we are in a stronger position to recognise different kinds of children's agency.

Note

1 The distribution of agency also has global implications. See Wyness 2013.

References

Alderson, Priscilla. 2008. *Young Children's Rights, Exploring Beliefs, Principles and Practice*, 2nd ed. London: Jessica Kingsley.
Ball, Stephen. 2003. *Class Strategies and the Education Market: The Middle Classes and Social Advantage*. London: RoutledgeFalmer.
Barnardo's. 2016. "Child Poverty: Statistics and Facts." Accessed 19 February 2016. www.barnardos.org.uk/what_we_do/our_work/child_poverty/child_poverty_what_is_poverty/child_poverty_statistics_facts.htm.
Becker, Saul. 2007. "Global Perspectives on Children's Unpaid Caregiving in the Family: Research and Policy on 'Young Carers' in the UK, Australia, the USA and Sub-Saharan Africa." *Global Social Policy* 7 (1): 5–22.
Bernstein, Basil. 1971. *Class Codes and Control*, vol. 1. London: Paladin.
Beveridge, Sally. 2004. "Pupil Participation and the Home-School Relationship." *European Journal of Special Needs Education* 19 (1): 3–16.
Bourdieu, Pierre. 1984. *Distinction: A Social Critique of the Judgement of Taste*. London: Routledge and Kegan Paul.
Bourdieu, Pierre, and Loic J. D. Wacquant. 1992. *An Invitation to Reflexive Sociology*. Chicago: Chicago University Press.
Chant, Sylvia. 2007. *Gender, Generation and Poverty*. London: Edward Elgar.
Christensen, Pia, and Allison James, eds. 2008. *Research with Children: Perspectives and Practices*, 2nd ed. London: Falmer.
Cockburn, Tom, and Frances Cleaver. 2009. *How Children and Young People Win Trust and Influence Others*, London: Carnegie Trust.

Curtis, Polly. 2009. "More Parents Jailed as Truancy Rates Soar." *The Guardian*, February 12.
Dalrymple, Jane. 2002. "Family Group Conferences and Youth Advocacy: The Participation of Children and Young People in Family Decision Making." *European Journal of Social Work* 5 (3): 287–99.
Dingwall Robert, John Eekelaar, and Topsy Murray. 1995. *The Protection of Children: State Intervention and Family Life*, 2nd ed. Oxford: Blackwell.
Evans, Gillian. 2006. *Educational Failure and Working Class White Children in Britain*. Basingstoke: Palgrave.
Fielding, Michael. 2007. "Beyond 'Voice': New Roles, Relations and Contexts in Researching with Young People." *Discourse: Studies in Cultural Politics of Education* 28 (3): 301–10.
Flowerdew, Jill, and Ben Neale. 2003. "Trying to Stay Apace: Children with Multiple Challenges in Their Post-Divorce Family Lives." *Childhood* 10 (2): 147–62.
Fraser, Nancy. 2000. "Rethinking Recognition." *New Left Review* 3: 107–20.
Ghirotto, Luca, and Valentina Mazzoni. 2013. "Being Part, Being Involved: The Adult's Role and Child Participation in an Early Childhood Learning Context." *International Journal of Early Years Education* 21 (4): 300–8.
Giroux, Henry. 1989. *Schooling for Democracy: Critical Pedagogy in the Modern Age*. Routledge: London.
Hendrick, Harry. 1997. "Constructions and Re-Constructions of British Childhood: An Interpretive Survey, 1800 to the Present." In *Constructing and Reconstructing Childhood: Contemporary Issues in the Sociological Study of Childhood*, 2nd ed., edited by Allison James and Alan Prout, 34–62. London: Falmer.
Hetherington, Mavis. 2003. "Social Support and the Adjustment of Children in Divorced and Remarried Families." *Childhood* 10 (2): 217–36.
Holland, Sally, Jonathan Scourfield, Sean O'Neill, and Andrew Pithouse. 2005. "Democratising the Family and the State? The Case of Family Group Conferences in Child Welfare." *Journal of Social Policy* 34 (1): 59–77.
Hollingworth, Kate. 2007. "Responsibility and Rights: Children and Their Parents in the Youth Justice System." *International Journal of Law, Policy and the Family* 21 (2): 190–219.
James, Allison, and Alan Prout, eds. 1997. *Constructing and Reconstructing Childhood*, 2nd ed. London: Falmer.
Kirby, Perpetua, and Sarah Gibbs. 2006. "Facilitating Participation: Adults' Caring Support Roles within Child-to-Child Projects in Schools and After-School Settings." *Children and Society* 20 (3), 209–20.
Lareau, Annette. 2011. *Unequal Childhoods: Class, Race and Family Life*, 2nd ed. Berkeley: University of California Press.
Leonard, Madeline. 2004. "Children's Views on Children's Right to Work." *Childhood* 11 (1): 45–61.
Mayall, Berry. 2002. *Towards a Sociology of Childhood: Thinking from Children's Lives*. Buckingham: Open University.
Moss, Peter, and Pat Petrie. 2002. *From Children's Services to Children's Spaces*. London: RoutledgeFalmer.

Office for National Statistics (ONS). 2014. "Step-families in 2011." Accessed 19 February 2017. www.ons.gov.uk/ons/rel/family-demography/stepfamilies/2011/stepfamilies-rpt.html.

Oswell, David. 2013. *The Agency of Children: From Family to Global Human Rights*. Cambridge: Cambridge University Press.

Parton, Nigel. 2006. *Safeguarding Childhood*. Basingstoke: Palgrave.

Prout, Alan. 2000. "Childhood Bodies: Construction, Agency and Hybridity." In: *The Body, Childhood and Society*, edited by Alan Prout, 1–17. Basingstoke: Macmillan.

Ridge, Tess. 2006. "Childhood Poverty: A Barrier to Social Participation." In *Children, Young People and Social Participation: Participation for What?*, edited by E. Kay Tisdall, John Davis, Malcolm Hill, and Alan Prout, 23–8. Bristol: The Policy Press.

United Nations 1989. *Convention on the Rights of the Child*, Geneva: United Nations.

Valentine, Kylie. 2011. "Accounting for Agency." *Children and Society* 25 (5): 347–58.

Vis, Svein Arild, and Thomas Nigel. 2009. "Beyond Talking: Children's Participation in Norwegian Care and Protection Cases." *European Journal of Social Work* 12 (2): 155–68.

White, Sarah, and Shyamol Choudhury. 2007. "The Politics of Child Participation in International Development: The Dilemma of Agency." *The European Journal of Development Research* 19 (4): 529–50.

Williams, Stephen, and Lynda Williams. 2005. "Space Invaders: The Negotiation of Teenage Boundaries through the Mobile Phone." *Sociological Review* 53 (2): 314–31.

Wyness, Michael. 2009. "Children Representing Children: Participation and the Problem of Diversity in UK Youth Councils." *Childhood* 16 (4): 535–52.

———. 2013. "Global Standards and Deficit Childhoods: The Contested Meaning of Children's Participation." *Children's Geographies* 11 (3): 340–53.

———. 2014. "Children, Family and the State: Revisiting Public and Private Realms." *Sociology* 48 (1): 59–74.

Index

9/11 139
1989 Children Act 4, 161, 194, 232, 233
2004 Children Act 4, 233

adult/adulthood 1, 3, 6, 21, 24, 27, 29–30, 34–48, 50, 52– 4, 56–7, 61, 63, 69, 72–3, 77, 87–8, 92, 94–101, 104, 107–12, 116–7, 120–2, 124–7, 129, 131, 133–4, 137, 139, 141–3, 145–8, 154–5, 160, 166–7, 171, 178, 186, 200–1, 203, 205, 212, 215, 218, 224–5, 232–3, 238–9, 241
age 6, 20, 21, 24, 27, 98, 103–5, 116–7, 156–7, 159–60, 164, 171–2, 205, 220, 226
animation 92–3, 112–3, 117
Ariès, Philippe 7, 137

Bildungsroman 28, 34–7, 39–40, 43–8
Blair, Tony 213
book cover 120–34, 145, 173
Bourdieu, Pierre 237–8
Bowlby, John 157
Brexit see EU referendum
British Broadcasting Company (BBC) 88–93, 96, 101, 104, 108–9, 176, 210
Brown, Gordon 196
Buckingham, David 1, 19–20, 96–7
Bulger, James 5
bullying 1, 11, 211, 216–7
Burman, Erica 5–6, 103, 124–5, 130

Cameron, David 5, 203
capitalism 81, 181
Carnegie Medal 19–21, 23–4, 26, 29–30
child: abuse 4, 26, 30, 39, 41, 43, 45–6, 59, 63, 124, 176–7, 193–6, 198, 204, 233; actor 1, 104–8, 111; development 95–6, 103, 162, 166, 195, 211; murder 4, 51, 57; narrators 10, 50, 52–4, 62–3; obesity 1, 98, 220; readers 22–3, 25–6, 143, 146, 149
childcare 2, 11, 153–6, 158, 160–1, 165–6, 175, 237, 240
child-centred approaches 162, 177
child's body 103–6, 113–5, 117, 120, 222
child's sexuality 11, 73–5, 123–4, 130, 134, 144, 171, 211, 217–8
childhood: agency of 6, 28, 103, 143, 198, 230–43; concepts of 21, 23, 27, 30, 34, 56, 61, 93, 101, 143–4, 230–2; constructs of 6–7, 19, 34, 36–8, 47–8, 60, 72, 87, 95, 123, 141, 155, 214, 218, 223, 232; contemporary 2, 5, 7–9, 19, 31, 37, 60, 97, 138, 141, 155, 211–5, 218, 221, 223, 226, 230; disappearance of 1, 61, 138; films about 2–3, 92–3, 104–6, 110–3, 115–7, 124, 133; history of 154–5, 166; innocence of 5, 21, 35–6, 40–1, 47, 51, 54, 56–7, 59, 60–1, 63, 68, 95, 127, 129, 131, 141, 144, 155, 214, 218–19; literary criticism of 50, 52, 77, 129; neo-liberal politics of 3, 219; novels of 2–3, 20, 25–30, 34–9, 41–3, 45, 47–8, 50–2, 54–7, 59, 61–3, 120–5; plurality of 20, 24–5, 28–31; protection of 23, 27, 61–2, 97, 113, 138, 180, 193–205, 217, 231, 233, 243; Romantic construct of 5–7, 22, 28, 54, 59–62, 99, 129; study of 5, 7, 11–2, 50, 54, 88, 137, 170; sociology of 6,

248 Index

230–1, 235, 242; temporality of 40, 104, 117
Childhood Studies 5–7, 9, 37, 149, 210, 239
children at risk 5, 34, 51, 56, 58, 60–2, 104, 157, 193–5, 198, 224, 226, 233
Children's Commissioner of England 4, 215
children's literature 3, 7, 19–24, 27, 29–31, 35, 60, 67–73, 76, 78, 80, 101, 123, 129, 133, 215
children's rights 4, 211, 220–2, 225–6
children's voice 6, 25, 29, 50–5, 57, 225, 233–8, 240–1
children's wellbeing 9, 156–7, 233, 237
class: differences in 236–7; middle class 25, 51, 54–5, 108, 175, 213–14, 220, 231, 235–8, 242; social class 94, 202, 231, 238–9, 242; working class 59, 176, 202, 220, 231, 235, 237–40, 242
Climbié, Victoria 4, 59, 195–6, 203
Colwell, Maria 4, 194
Connelly, Peter 4, 193–9
Conservative/Liberal Democrat coalition government 193, 198
Constructivism 6–7, 50, 54, 63, 120, 129, 212
consumerism 92, 241
contemporary Britain 1–2, 5, 19, 59, 67, 75–6, 81, 87, 170–1, 210–1, 214, 226, 230, 243

Dahl, Roald, *Charlie and the Chocolate Factory* 120–3, 125–9, 132–3
digital revolution 1
diversity 7, 94–5, 103, 148, 221, 224, 242
divorce 1, 239
dress codes 211–21, 224–5

early intervention 5, 75, 154, 197–9
education 2, 4, 23, 36, 67, 89, 95, 97, 100, 103, 153, 156–65, 172, 174, 186, 194–6, 199–200, 202, 204, 211, 213–5, 217–9, 221, 226, 231, 233–4, 238
ethnicity 53, 223
Every Child Matters 5, 194–5

evolutionary psychology 68, 74–5, 77–80
EU referendum 2, 81, 203

family practices 1, 138, 239
father/fatherhood 38–9, 41–7, 59, 108–9, 112, 114–16, 138–9, 147, 149, 157, 164, 196, 239–40
feminism: 69, 130, 173, 184, 219, 221, 233

gang crime 63
gaze 115, 120, 123, 129, 131–2, 134, 146
gender 8, 90, 144–6, 148–9, 154, 171, 202, 211, 216–18, 225
globalisation 87, 171
growth 35, 100, 103–4, 106–18, 156, 161, 193, 197–9, 237

hair 108, 111, 116, 129, 132, 146, 159, 179, 210, 217–9, 221–6
Harry Potter series 3, 106, 120–6, 215
homophobia 216
Hunt, Peter 21, 129

inappropriateness 72–3, 105, 107, 123–4, 126–7, 129, 131, 133, 215, 217–8
interdisciplinarity 5, 7, 9, 11
islamophobia 221

James, Henry, *The Turn of the Screw* 35, 70–2, 74
juvenile delinquency 1, 5

Kelman, Stephen, *Pigeon English* 3, 50–2, 54–8, 60–3

late modernity 8–9, 35
Latour, Bruno 223
Lesnik-Oberstein, Karín 6–7, 53–4, 129–30, 133, 212
liminality 6, 21, 117
Litt, Toby, *deadkidsongs* 34, 36–41, 43–5, 47, 50
lone parent family see single parent families

Major government 161
Major, John 161, 199
masculinity 41, 144, 147–9
media literacy 97

Index

memory 20, 69, 109–10, 114, 155, 158, 172, 174–5, 180, 184–6, 196
mirror neurons 77–8
mother/motherhood 25, 29, 41–2, 59, 63, 88, 90, 108–10, 114, 116, 120, 130–2, 134, 156–8, 163–6, 172, 176–8, 180, 184, 196, 206, 237, 240
Munro Review 199–200

Nabokov, Vladimir, *Lolita* 123–4, 133
neoliberalism 4, 138, 171, 193, 198–9, 205
neuroscience 67, 74–5
New Labour 4, 8, 57, 194, 197–9, 213, 215, 218–19
New Right 9
nursery 145, 153–4, 156–65, 171

Outnumbered 104, 110, 114, 117

parental choice 213
parental responsibility 194, 220, 232–3
play 40, 43, 57, 59–60, 95, 97, 100, 116, 138, 140–1, 149, 153, 159–65
picture books 137, 141, 143
politics of austerity 4, 193, 204
pornography 1, 57
Postman, Neil, *The Disappearance of Childhood* 1, 61, 97
poverty 4, 26, 55, 63, 181, 205, 220, 231, 240–1
psychoanalysis 69–70, 75, 174

race 55, 144–5, 147–8, 176, 220, 222–3

racism 29, 107, 202, 210
religion 171, 211, 221–4
Rose, Jacqueline, *The Case of Peter Pan: The Impossibility of Children's Fiction* 68–9, 74–5, 78
Rudd, David 69, 215

schooling: compulsory 156, 213, 231; private 159, 163, 213, 220, 237; state 97, 213, 237–8
school uniform 111, 211–3, 215, 217, 241
Second World War 24–5, 88, 94, 138, 140, 155
single parent families 116, 205, 239
social media 123, 134
social work 172, 175–6, 180, 204, 234
socialisation 6, 21, 162, 165
surveillance 4, 15, 51, 194–5, 197, 220

Taylor, Damilola 4, 51
teachers 41, 160, 162–5, 215, 219–20, 237
television 1, 87–93, 95–100, 103–5, 108, 110, 117
Thatcher, Margaret 3–4, 34, 161, 199
Thatcherism 8, 181
transdisciplinarity see interdisciplinarity

United Nations Convention on the Rights of the Child 3–4, 225, 232

visual art 1, 140–50

Winterbottom, Michael 111, 114–5
World War II see Second World War